Mobilizing human resources in the Arab world

Mobilizing human resources in the Arab world

R. Paul Shaw

KPI
London, Boston, Melbourne and Henley

First published in 1983 by KPI Limited
14 Leicester Square, London WC2H 7PH, England
Published in paperback 1985

Distributed by
Routledge & Kegan Paul plc
14 Leicester Square, London WC2H 7PH, England

Routledge & Kegan Paul Inc
9 Park Street, Boston, Mass. 02108, USA

Routledge & Kegan Paul
464 St. Kilda Road, Melbourne,
Victoria 3004, Australia and

Routledge & Kegan Paul plc
Broadway House, Newtown Road,
Henley-on-Thames, Oxon RG9 1EN, England

Set in Press Roman
by Cambrian Typesetters, Farnborough
and printed in Great Britain
by The Thetford Press Ltd
Thetford, Norfolk

Library of Congress Cataloging in Publication Data

Shaw, R. Paul.
Mobilizing human resources in the Arab world.
(Arab world studies)
Bibliography: p.
Includes index.
1. Manpower policy – Arab countries.
I. Title.   II. Series.
HD5836.A6S5 1983   331.11'0917'4927   82-21671
ISBN 0-7103-0137-5

For Buff and the Arab people
May the richness of their culture survive the onslaught of modern
technology

Contents

Contents

Contents

Contents

Tables

Appendix Tables

Tables

Figures

Preface

This book is an outgrowth of my experience as the Population and Labour Policies Adviser to the Arab Countries for the International Labour Organization. When I first took up residence in the Arab world, I learned four things very quickly. I found that much of my training in development theory was inappropriate for the newly emergent capital-rich/labor-short Arab economies. I found that the use of sophisticated econometric techniques — which tend to dominate the development literature in Western journals — was virtually ruled out by data of limited quantity and quality. I recognized that the only meaningful way to size up the rapid pace of economic events in the region was to experience many of the countries first hand. And finally, I came to appreciate and admire the extent to which the Arab people are intent on attaining self-sufficiency and self-reliance in their pursuit of growth and development.

In view of the above, work on this book began by piecing together an overview of major problems and issues in countries of the Middle East and North Africa. My visits with domestic and regional planners produced two dominant impressions which were to have an important effect on the direction I have taken. On the one hand, planners seemed genuinely excited and well informed about growth-related investments in the major oil exporting countries. They were also a rich source of information concerning growth-related problems in their own countries as well as the irrelevance or failure of many 'standard' approaches to their problems. On the other hand, they seemed far less enthusiastic, informed or attentive on the subject of development-related problems. This was particularly evident when rather broad human resource issues pertaining to, say, poverty in agriculture, population distribution, or manpower planning were treated superficially or were passed off as being unique or limited to a particular country or countries. This led me to believe that a synthesis or overview of human resource problems and prospects in the region was much needed.

This book consolidates empirical information with a view to shifting the balance from a preoccupation with growth-related investments to a concentration on development-related population, manpower and employment issues. It aims to identify population or manpower problems that are likely to become more fully entrenched if neglected at this early stage of Arab development. By focusing on five broad problem areas which are directly or indirectly related to mobilizing human resources, the book should be of interest to students of population, migration, employment, inequality, the emancipation of women, construction and agriculture. By proposing policy directives which are sensitive to the problems as perceived by the Arab governments themselves, the book should also offer something of pragmatic worth to Arab planners and policy-makers. Finally, the book should be useful as a reference source. It consolidates a vast amount of empirical information in one volume and contains recent data, in varying depth, on some twenty Arab countries.

On the whole, I am optimistic that the new found wealth and motivation of Arab governments will be brought swiftly to bear on human resource problems which are dehabilitating development progress in the region. At the same time, however, I am apprehensive about a most important ingredient of successful development in the region, namely regional economic cooperation and integration. My concern over this issue stems from the reality that hostilities and friction exist among so many countries in the region. To my mind, governments must take more positive steps toward promoting more stable forms of economic cooperation and integration among oil-rich and oil-poor countries alike. Otherwise, it is my opinion that the Arab dream of economic self-sufficiency and collective self-reliance will remain rhetoric for a long time to come.

R. Paul Shaw
Vancouver,
Canada

Acknowledgments

One of the most rewarding aspects of working on this book concerns the support and encouragement that I have received during its preparation. Foremost, I am grateful to Canada's International Development Research Centre, its 1979—80 Research Associate Award, and the kind logistical help of Louise Rohonczy and Reginald MacIntyre. These alone have enabled me to pursue my work uninterrupted.

Thanks are also due to my friends at the International Labour Office (Geneva). Kailas Doctor, Ghazi Farooq, Richard Anker, Roger Bohning and Henry Azzam have all come to my rescue at one time or another. To Ann Mortifee and Henry Azzam, I am especially grateful. During our residence in war-torn Beirut and our field work in at least a dozen Arab countries, they have been indispensable friends during times of elation, frustration and outright disillusionment.

I also wish to acknowledge, with much gratitude, the many individuals and organizations which helped me in the collection, preparation and write-up of my empirical material: Khalid Ali of the Arab Fund for Economic and Social Development (Kuwait), Riad Tabbarah and Joseph Chamie of the United Nations Economic Commission for Western Asia (Beirut), Ronald Fagan and staff of the Economic Statistical Library of the United Nations (New York), Robert Sandoval of the Food and Agricultural Organization (Rome), William Sands, Richard Parker and the library staff of the Middle East Institute (Washington DC), the World Bank joint library staff of the International Monetary Fund (Washington DC), and Elia Zureik, editor of the Arab World Studies series of Routledge & Kegan Paul Ltd. Facilities at the

University of British Columbia (Vancouver) have also been generously extended by James MacMillan, Carol Clark and Kenneth Burridge.

Finally, I am grateful to the many Arab officials and planners who took the time to discuss the development problems which bear on the well-being of their families and their culture.

Chapter 1

Policy concerns, or why this study matters

Introduction

Since 1973, the Arab world has been host to a growth frenzy. Upheavals in virtually every sector of the political economy have relegated social scientists to the spectator gallery. Political scientists have sought refuge in daily newspapers merely to keep abreast of the continuous drama of power plays and interregional tension. Sociologists have been consumed by speculation about the psychological dangers of transforming desert outposts into industrial states virtually overnight. Development economists, saddled with analytic tools largely inappropriate to capital-rich, labor-short situations, have offered little more than a culture-bound brand of Western modernization and industrialization. Indeed, those who are in touch with the frenetic pace of events in the Arab Middle East and North Africa recognize that they are students of a region truly unique in modern economic history.

Needless to say, the catalyst to this unfolding was the unprecedented hike in crude oil prices from $2.71 a barrel in 1973 to $12.41 in 1974. The continued upward spiral topped $34 a barrel by late 1981. With over 65 per cent of the world's proven oil reserves, eight resource-poor, less developed countries changed status in one fell swoop.[1] By 1976, governmental and private purchasing power had become so massive that staggering amounts of investment capital were acting like a huge magnet on human and material resources throughout the entire Arab world. What a refreshing exception to the intransigent rigidities in the distribution of wealth between rich and poor countries and the impassioned platitudes for a 'new international economic order'.

Consolidation of oil interests by the Organization of Arab Petroleum

1

Exporting Countries (OAPEC) has done much to bring an Arab dream to the edge of fruition. That dream is to attain economic self-sufficiency. And in this context the importance of regional economic cooperation and integration can hardly be overstated.[2] Hopes for a common market in the production of food, free flows of human capital between labor-surplus and labor-short countries, and massive transfers of aid from oil-rich to oil-poor countries now hinge on the premise of Arab solidarity, cemented by bonds of Arab brotherhood and Islam.

Of course, such frenzied growth has also encountered many constraints. In a political economy wracked by domestic upheavals and international power games, progress in regional economic integration has often been held at a standstill.[3] This factor alone has worked to undermine Arab dreams of economic self-sufficiency and collective self-reliance by jeopardizing worthy development goals in several countries.[4] Scores of projects have been delayed, shelved or simply destroyed as a result. But development planners are marching on, as indeed they must, in the expectation that consolidative efforts will succeed in reducing the toll of such conflict in the future.

For the development economist, the myriad problems and possibilities confronting the Arab growth machine are documented in the national development plans. Development plans have now been drawn up for all twenty Arab countries. Some are clearly overambitious. Others carry the earmark of Western consultants or Western educated Arabs to the extent that they are out of alignment with the needs and ideals of Arabic culture. Still others have been implemented so rapidly that questions of direct or indirect impacts of projects in one country on another have been relegated to afterthought. Differences and weaknesses aside, however, all have one thing in common. *Deficiencies in the quantity, quality and distribution of human resources are perceived to be the single most important bottleneck in the region.*

Problems of human resource development are hardly limited to disequilibriums in the demand and supply of labor, or wage and price inflation. They include the quality of manpower that will be needed as economies develop over time, the relationship between the growth of population and employment, and the geographic distribution of human resources in relation to non-human resources. They also pertain to problems and prospects of integrating Arab women more fully into employment and modernization.

From a theoretical standpoint, the emphasis on human resources in the national development plans is certainly justified. There can be little doubt that the contribution of labour to productivity or gross national product parallels that of fixed capital in the process of economic development. This has been ascertained by a growing number of studies which have utilized the Cobb-Douglas production function to estimate labor's performance in both industrialized and agricultural settings.[5] Moreover, there is no end of quantitative evidence to show that investments in the quality of human resources (e.g. education) are a prerequisite to augmenting worker productivity, to adopting new technology, and to redefining beliefs in ways that are conducive to modern economic growth.[6] It is precisely this type of evidence that has given rise to the new theory of human capital.[7]

In addition to the above, development theorists have become increasingly concerned with the fact that governments consistently channel disproportionate shares of national and international funds into the growth of modern enclaves where social overhead capital, employment opportunities, exports and imports, are geared to the incomes and consumption of the relatively wealthy. Quite aside from rhetoric concerning the human capital needs of the poor, such policies typically exclude large segments of the population from equal participation in the benefits of modernization. The favoring of populations in modern enclaves is not unrelated to oft-cited problems of 'urban bias' in development expenditures (Lipton: 1977), the failure of the 'trickle down' theory to redistribute growth benefits to the rural poor (Griffen and Ghose: 1979), the negative effect of multinationals on rural/urban income equality (Evans and Timberlake: 1980), and criticisms that the 'green revolution' has disproportionately benefited larger, well-to-do farmers on the perimeter of urban areas (Stryker: 1979).

From a policy standpoint, Arab governments are equally justified in expressing urgent concern over deficiencies in human resources. Growth-related investment has invaded their horizon with such speed and intensity that a large majority of the Arab population has been caught in a whirlwind of confusion. The push for rapid development has one predominant characteristic. It is being guided by twentieth-century technology with highly skilled foreign labor in the driver's seat. In contrast, the majority of Arab onlookers are largely illiterate. Upgrading the capacity of the population to the point where they could take control implies a huge challenge. Since the gap between indigenous ability and that required is simply immense, the continued importation of and reliance on foreign skills are holding Arab goals of self-sufficiency at bay.[8]

A second problem is that literature dealing with employment and human resource potential in the Arab world is replete with misconceptions concerning population problems, the potential of agriculture as an employer of labor, the impact of Arab culture on worker motivation, etc. It follows that many prescriptions for Arab development, especially those by Westerners involved in library studies, have been ill-informed, misdirected or largely speculative. Indeed, the absence of explicitly formulated population and employment strategies has meant that efforts to develop human resources have been no less than haphazard, with confused priorities and poorly marked approaches at every turn.

Finally, analysis of manpower issues has been virtually paralyzed by severe data limitations. As Sayigh (1978a, p. 5), a leading Arab development economist, puts it: 'Only recently have development plans begun to reflect awareness of manpower. . . . But this creditable improvement is yet to be supplemented by far-reaching, satisfactory information and reporting on population and manpower.' Indeed, before 1970, empirical cornerstones of Arab development plans or scholarly inquiries were seldom more than informed guesses. This alone has worked to keep social scientists in the dark.

How does all this add up? Quite simply. Policy measures to broaden employment and human resource potential are in great demand. This implies a need to (i) consolidate empirical information with a view to tipping the balance from a preoccupation with growth-related to a concentration on development-related population, manpower and employment issues; (ii) identify population or manpower related problems that are likely to become more fully entrenched if neglected at this early stage of Arab development, and (iii) propose remedies or policy directives which are sensitive to the problems as perceived by Arab governments themselves.

Problem areas

If we are meaningfully to tackle deficiencies in the quantity, quality and distribution of human resources we must first appreciate what the deficiencies are, how they have arisen, and how they are being perpetuated. Accordingly, this study identifies five broad problem areas which are having an important bearing, either directly or indirectly, on Arab human resources. These include problems associated with the construction boom, the poor performance of agriculture, swelling population, sluggish integration of women into the development process, and deficiencies in manpower and educational planning.

Before undertaking a brief review of the problems involved, it will be useful to dichotomize the Arab countries into an 'oil-rich' versus an 'oil-poor' group. The aim of such a dichotomy will be to convey broad differentials in the access to liquid, disposable assets that can be invested in capital stock.[9] According to proven oil reserves, as of 1979, as well as the value of projected oil exports between 1980 and 1985, eight member states of the OAPEC countries have been included in the oil-rich group.[10] These countries are Bahrain, Iraq, Kuwait, Libya, Oman, Qatar, Saudi Arabia and the United Arab Emirates. On a per capita basis, proven oil reserves in these countries range from about 21,000 barrels for every man, woman and child in Saudi Arabia to about 1,000 in Bahrain.

Algeria has not been included in the oil-rich group because its oil revenues have not been a major factor in government expenditures until very recently. Accordingly, for purposes of this study, Algeria has been classified along with eleven other Arab countries in the oil-poor group. These include Egypt, Jordan, Lebanon, Mauritania, Morocco, Somalia, Sudan, Syria, Tunisia, North Yemen (Yemen Arab Republic) and South Yemen (People's Democratic Republic of Yemen).[11]

The construction boom

Construction occupies center stage in my inquiry because it has been the leading economic sector in the oil-rich OAPEC countries since 1973. A tidal wave of residential and non-residential building and a vast array of infrastructural projects have redistributed population, swollen employment and inflated incomes in record time. By 1975, expenditures of approximately US $9,000 million per year had attracted over 1.7 million foreign workers. This influx accounted for approximately 25 per cent of the total labor force of the oil-rich OAPEC countries. In world perspective, this share exceeded expatriate labor in Western and South Africa, North and South America and the European and OECD countries.[12] No less than 41 per cent, or some 704,000, of the expatriates in the Arab region were employed in construction alone.

Offshoots of this incredible migration are that (i) remittances to the oil-poor Arab countries tripled between 1973 and 1980 to over US $3,500 million per year, (ii) emigration of sorely needed skills from the oil-poor countries has created shortages, and (iii) migration-fed congestion and inadequate housing facilities have plagued several of the OAPEC countries. These developments have caught policy-makers totally off guard. They have been inept at channelling the massive remittances into productive investments, and they have failed to plan for the mushrooming growth of their largest cities. On the latter point, at least eight of twelve governments in the Middle East and six of the eight Arab governments in North Africa have made it clear that problems of spatial distribution are out of control. Not only are huge capital investments in individual urban areas bringing an influx of international migrants, but high salaries and consumer expenditures by migrants are enhancing the magnetic pull of the cities on indigenous workers from rural areas and small towns.

Without intervention, the huge disparities in development expenditures between the oil-rich and the oil-poor Arab countries can only exacerbate these problems. According to the 1976 to 1981 round of national development plans, the oil-rich countries planned to spend approximately US $35.7 billion per year versus only US $14.5 billion for the oil-poor countries (see Appendix 1.1). In per capita terms, this represents a twelve-fold differential between the two groups of countries (Table 1.1, column 1).

Table 1.1 *Comparison of planned expenditures in the national development plans, 1976–81 versus 1981–6*

	National development plan periods	
Country groupings	*1976–81*[a] *(1)*	*1981–86*[b] *(2)*
	Average *yearly* expenditures per capita in US $	
Oil-rich	$1,361	$3,115
Oil-poor	$ 115	$ 531
Oil-poor – excludes Algeria	$ 117	$ 396
Algeria[c]	$ 100	$1,005

Source: National development plans of each country; Lebanon excluded throughout due to devastating effects of the civil war.
Notes: a Population data used for the per capita calculations pertain to 1975.
b Population data used for this calculation pertain to estimates for 1980.
c Previous to 1981, it is appropriate to include Algeria among the oil-poor countries as oil revenues had not yet taken off.

While the relative differential between oil-rich and oil-poor countries may drop to about six-fold or eight-fold during the 1981 to 1986 round of national development plans, differentials in *absolute* per capita expenditures between the two groups of countries are likely to be in the order of $2,600. This compares with about $1,200 for the 1976 to 1981 plan period.[13]

Such differentials in developing expenditures are hardly a sleeping giant. They have been bulldozing a great rift in the rates of growth of employment and wages between the two groups of countries. While the Arabian peninsula may have waned as the Eldorado of the world construction industry, this will hardly deflate the continuing importance of the building boom. Faced with expected growth in the construction industry of 38 per cent in Iraq, 46 per cent in Egypt, and over 46 per cent in Syria, Jordan and Lebanon between 1978 and 1982, and forecasts for renewed booms in Abu Dhabi, Bahrain, Oman and Saudi Arabia between 1981 and 1986, we are witnessing a market that is just coming of age.[14]

Traditional agriculture

Just as construction is the leading sector, agriculture is the lagging sector. At least five of the oil-poor countries registered declining agricultural output per capita between 1965 and 1980. At best, improvements in productivity per capita have been lethargic among the balance. For the region as a whole, the average yield per hectare for cereals has been less than one half of the international average of 1.8 tons. Only one Arab country (Libya), has achieved growth of agricultural output per capita in excess of 2 per cent per year over the last decade.

In some countries, population growth has outstripped production, whereas failure to introduce fertilizer and high-yielding varieties into traditional agriculture has been the culprit in others. The range of problems confounding traditional farmers and landless workers has been so vast and seemingly persistent that standard references to high underemployment, landlessness, rural exodus and wide disparities in income have begun to fall on deaf ears.

At the same time, many governments have been expressing great alarm over their increasing reliance on food imports from non-Arab countries. Since the jump in oil prices, the ratio of food imports to exports doubled from 3.1 in 1968 to 6.0 by 1978. Dollar values of vegetable and animal imports increased four-fold and six-fold, respectively, between 1967 and 1978. In view of the large share of household expenditures going to food (see Table 1.2), governments of the OAPEC countries view mushrooming food imports as a constant and real threat to their goal of self-sufficiency. This threat is heightened by fears that non-Arab countries may initiate an international food embargo in protest against high oil prices.

While agricultural workers have been assured that the national development plans are coming to the rescue, an analysis of governmental budget allocations for agriculture reveals quite a different story. For the

Table 1.2   *Shares of household expenditures allocated to food, selected countries, 1958–78*

Country	Time	Type or place of household	% household expenditures on food
Kuwait	1977/8	Urban Kuwaiti	37.8
		Urban non-Kuwaiti	35.7
Oman	1974	Hhlds in salary range of US $1,800–3,600 per year	56.0
Iraq	1972	Urban	48.8
		Rural	65.9
Egypt	1958/9	Urban	48.2
	1964/5	Urban	49.6
	1974/5	Urban	50.1
	1958/9	Rural	64.3
	1964/5	Rural	62.3
	1974/5	Rural	61.6
Libya	1977	Tripoli Town	37.2
Morocco	1973	Rural	61.7

Sources: National statistical abstracts, Central Bank annual reports and special surveys.

Arab world as a whole, only 8.8 per cent of total development funds were allocated to this sector between 1976 and 1981, though it employed no less than 50 per cent of the total Arab labor force (see Table 1.3). In contrast, urban-based manufacturing with 9.0 per cent of the labor force was allocated approximately 20.3 per cent of the development budget. On a per worker basis, this amounted to approximately US $219 in agriculture versus US $2,534 in manufacturing. Such differentials in allocations to agriculture versus manufacturing are equally evident in the 1981 to 1986 round of national development plans (see Chapter 3).

The meagre development expenditures per agricultural worker are particularly alarming in the poorest of the oil-poor countries. Five of these countries, Mauritania, Somalia, Sudan and the two Yemens, are not only predominantly rural with large shares of impoverished subsistence farmers, but each qualifies as a member of the world's '25 hardcore least developed countries'.[15] Though these countries represent a sizable share of the Arab brotherhood (population about 29 million), preoccupation with exciting developments in the OAPEC block has clearly obscured their particular dilemma.

Table 1.3 Distribution of labor force and development plan expenditures by economic sector, 1976–81

Country grouping	Total 1975 labor force (000's) (1)	% of total 1975 labor force in: Agriculture (2)	Manufacturing (3)	% share of 1976–81 development expenditures going to: Agriculture (4)	Manufacturing (5)	Average yearly development expenditures in US $, 1976–81; per economically active worker in: Agriculture (6)	Manufacturing (7)
All Arab countries	38,640	53.4	9.0	8.7	20.3	219	2,534[a]
Oil-rich	6,307	45.1	6.1	6.1	19.0[b]	712	11,987[b]
Oil-poor	32,333	55.4	9.6	15.5	23.0[c]	129	1,032[c]

Source: All data have been obtained from national development plans.
Notes:
  a This average is based on data for fifteen countries only.
  b This average is based on data for five countries and should be construed as very crude.
  c This average is based on data for ten countries and should be construed as crude.

Policy concerns, or why this study matters

Swelling population

Population growth is important to the study of Arab manpower because it is an acknowledged driving force behind the demand for jobs and services which are considered to be in short supply in many countries. Population growth rates of, say, 3 per cent per year or more in the region imply (i) a doubling of the population within twenty years, (ii) a need to double employment and social overhead capital to keep abreast, and (iii) a need to increase national production by at least 3 per cent per year just to make headway. More alarming still is the caveat that even if rates of natural increase were drastically reduced today, population growth over the next two decades would hardly change because tomorrow's parents have already been born.

On the whole, Arab governments have paid little heed to the Malthusian threat posed above. They rightly contend that the demand for family planning services has been minimal in most Arab countries in the past. Egypt, Jordan, Morocco and Tunisia are the only countries which perceive their rates of fertility or natural increase to be 'excessive'. The remaining countries have not encouraged national family planning as an instrument of intervention to lower their rates of natural increase, and in cases where modern methods of contraception have been made available, it is known that rates of usage have been very low.

In one respect, I am sympathetic to the Arab stance on population planning, especially where it concerns the philosophy, or rather biases, of population control advocates. At the same time, however, the likely effect of two important agents of change on the future demand for children should not be overlooked. To a large extent, both are post-oil developments. The first is tied to the fact that health authorities have been waging war or female sub-fecundity, foetal deaths and infant mortality to the extent that losses have been dropping by 5 to 10 per cent per year in most countries. The implication for Arab families is that ten live births will no longer be needed to guarantee a desired family size of five or six *surviving* children. In addition, there are good grounds for arguing that massive investments in education will precipitate a drop in family size desires, and that the demand for family planning will be stimulated as a result. Unless Arab governments anticipate the effects of socio-economic improvements that they are undertaking now, the welfare of Arab couples may be compromised in the future.

Integrating women

Closely related to the subject of population is the status of women.

Careful assessment of how Arab women are or should be integrated more fully into the process of development is rare. Understanding of the cultural context tends to be shallow, empirical impressions are usually fragmentary or biased, and assumptions concerning the desire of women to participate in the labor force are often unfounded. As a result, the development literature is replete with platitudes, and misconceptions about the Arabic culture have prompted implausible or insensitive policy recommendations.

What is needed is a more realistic consideration both of barriers and of possibilities open to boosting the quantity and quality of female skills that exist or are in demand. On the one hand, any attempt to 'upgrade the other half' must begin by dispelling some of the myths about women's opportunities and participation in the Arab economy. These myths concern (i) barriers to women's emancipation in the Moslem culture and the Holy Qur'an, (ii) assumptions that Arab women make almost no contribution to the economy, or that their participation in the formal labor force is insignificant, and (iii) that dictates of Islamic custom are largely responsible for the concentration of females in service occupations.

On the other hand, it is important to acknowledge that some barriers are simply not amenable to change overnight. In such cases, proposals for dramatic intervention would probably fall on deaf ears. Invariably, these would have failed to appreciate the overwhelming importance of the family and traditional sources of women's power gained through devotion to the family.

Manpower and education

Few topics are more central to the question of human resource development than educational planning. As oil reserves begin to dry up, the new generations will be carving their future out of the land with new business and industry. Foundations of future self-sufficiency will require a vastly improved network of academic and technical training. The challenge to provide such training is immense as educational planners are being driven by a technological revolution that 'demands to be understood', and by their desire to shun their international image as the world's illiterate.

To date, the onslaught against ignorance has followed one of two general paths. First, some governments perceive high rates of illiteracy as an unbearable thorn in the backside of their national ideology. All-out efforts have been undertaken to provide functional literacy to the masses in the interests of ensuring 'a most basic human right'. In

11

some countries, this has meant bombarding the countryside with intensified learning by the relatively learned. In other countries, it has meant side-stepping the thrust for universal literacy because of acute needs for semi-skilled and skilled manpower. Thus, compared with Somalia which dispatched some 125,000 students to their home region for seven months to educate some 1.25 million of their illiterate brothers and sisters, the government of the Sudan has been more concerned with the war against illiteracy among its work force. This concern has been based on such down-to-earth pragmatics as workers endangering themselves with new tools, machines and products because they can not read simple operating instructions.

The second approach is long-term in nature in its emphasis on investments in the system of formal schooling. According to Table 1.4, cols 1 and 2, the oil-rich countries spent approximately 13 per cent of their current government budget on education between 1977 and 1978. Among the oil-poor countries, where a much greater infrastructure exists, the figure was about 22 per cent. At the same time, the share of development expenditures for education among the oil-rich countries amounted to 16 per cent compared with 10 per cent for the oil-poor countries. For the region as a whole, current plus development expenditures on education for the fiscal year 1979 to 1980 exceeded US $18 billion.

While the attention to formal schooling is certainly positive, it is also blemished with problems galore. First, expenditures per capita in the oil-poor countries are a shadow of those in the oil-rich countries (Table 1.4, col. 6). Implications for long-run planning are that the quantity and quality of demand/supply disequilibriums in human capital will greatly differ within and between the two groups of countries. Second, the system of education in most of the oil-rich countries is simply incapable of producing applied skills needed to implement the current round of national development plans. Moreover, the imperative thrust to increase vocational or higher training institutes cannot be implemented quickly. All this is to say that neither petro-dollars, enthusiasm nor impatience can displace the fact that the development of modern facilities and quality instruction will remain an extremely demanding and time consuming task. In the meantime, reliance on foreign skills will continue to undermine hopes for self-sufficiency.

Methodological approach

Subsequent chapters in this book document each of the aforementioned

Table 1.4 *Government expenditures on education, 1977–8*

Countries	Percentage share on education		Yearly avg.		Total government expenditures (approximate value, 1977–8)	
	In the current government budget, 1977–8 (1)	In the national development plan, 1976–81 (2)	In the current government budget, 1977–8 (US $ million) (3)	In the national development plan, 1976–81 (US $ million) (4)	(US $ million) (5)	Per capita (US $) (6)
All Arab countries	15.4	15.2	8,844	7,723	16,567	109
Oil-rich	13.0	15.9[a]	5,508	5,776	11,284	436
Oil-poor	22.3	9.9[b]	3,336	1,947	5,283	42

Sources: National statistical yearbooks and national development plans.
Notes: a Figures based on data for six of eight countries only (Oman and Qatar excluded).
b Relatively crude figures; based on six of twelve countries only.

problem areas by drawing on a wide variety of empirical studies and data sources. This will accommodate three ends. It will seek to familiarize the reader with the breadth and complexity of the issues involved. It will attempt to consolidate a vast amount of empirical information, relevant to the study of human resources in the region, in one volume. And, it will strive to lay the foundation for appropriate policy action by indicating gaps that must be filled.

No pretense is made that the five problem areas reviewed above subsume the entire gamut of human resource issues confronting Arab development. Nor are the policy directives that I have in mind intended to serve as a panacea or 'blueprint for action'. Rather, each problem area has been selected in view of its relevance to long-term development goals, and in the light of my personal knowledge and experience of the situation. My aim is to sketch out preliminary frameworks for policy action which are intended to make students of development, planners and policy-makers take a second look at the possibilities open to them of achieving, at a stroke as it were, a range of desirable population, employment and human resource aims.

In view of the diversity of the problems being considered, the analyses and policy directives in each chapter tend to differ in scope, methodology and timing. However, they have also been formulated with several common guidelines in mind. First, they are concerned with increasing labour force participation rates and reducing problems of structural and demand deficient unemployment (see Appendix 1.2 for elaboration). This is important as it is an anomaly that in an aggregate population of some 150 million Arabs, only 27 per cent are in the active labor force.[16]

Second, they are concerned with augmenting the quality of human capital, as well as the supply price or return to a given unit of labor. On the one hand, this may involve improved health, nutrition, housing or a variety of related social services which are known to bear on worker productivity. It may also involve augmenting skills through on-the-job training and formal schooling. On the other hand, it may involve intervention in the labor market toward removing barriers to the full utilization or productivity of existing skills.

Third, they aim to correct inequalities in the distribution of human resources in relation to non-human resources. In some cases, this involves criticism of biases in the allocation of government revenues for development of heavy industry to the neglect of agriculture. Such inequalities in distribution threaten to perpetuate the *status quo* and the development of modern enclaves to the extent that large factions of the population and labor force have been excluded from benefits of modernization.[17]

Fourth, they strive to complement UN policies advocating 'basic needs' or 'integrated rural development' by emphasizing the plight of poor peoples in both urban and rural areas. The 'basic needs' policy, as promoted by the International Labour Organization and others, favors a 'consumption-oriented approach' which is concerned with providing the necessary conditions for survival through greater participation in the economy (i.e. sufficient food, water, housing and training). The 'rural development' policy, as pursued by the World Bank and others, favors a 'production-oriented approach' which endeavors to provide the necessary and sufficient conditions for achieving productivity increases and real income growth among self-employed farm families and landless workers.

Fifth, they attempt to improve on human resource potential by drawing attention to resources or 'building blocks' that are in the policy-makers' domain. The concern here is to minimize additional development costs and to maximize self-reliance by resisting the use of additional resources from outside the Arab region. Accordingly, when formulating rather general policy recommendations, I have attempted to draw on potentially successful policy interventions that the Arab governments have initiated themselves.

Sixth, they attempt to heed the fact that countries in the region are extremely diverse in terms of resources and structure of production. As noted in the introduction to this chapter, the predominant means of dealing with this problem has been to split the Arab countries into an oil-rich versus an oil-poor group. The eight OAPEC countries in the oil-rich group can be said to differ from the twelve countries in the oil-poor group not only in terms of their relatively high per capita incomes and abundant government revenues. The oil-rich countries are also similar in terms of their status as major labor importers, and in terms of their relatively limited agricultural potential (excluding Iraq).

In the process of analyzing problems or marshalling evidence in support of particular policy recommendations, I have avoided the explication of elaborate economic or statistical models. On the one hand, deficiencies in the quantity and quality of data would likely rule out the utility of such an approach. On the other hand, it is my view that an understanding of human resource deficiencies in the region can be better served at this time by a broad survey of the problems involved in conjunction with a review of potentially promising policy directives. In a few cases, however, I have employed a standard statistical technique called multiple regression analysis. This technique is becoming increasingly popular in studies of Arab development as a means of shedding light on multiple determinants of economic characteristics such as differentials in rates of employment, migration or fertility. Where applicable, I have presented the results of such techniques in a non-technical language in the body of the text. This approach has been adopted toward ensuring accessibility to the layman. In contrast, to accommodate the specialist interested in greater detail, results of regression analyses or material of a more theoretical or technical nature have been relegated to appendices.

Finally, in view of political realities in the region, I have avoided placing undue emphasis on prospects for regional economic integration and cooperation. It would have been most convenient to assume that Arab solidarity and regional economic integration would be viable inputs in Arab development over the next decade. But, alas, a look at realities in the region confirms that such assumptions have also led to fruitless research.[18] To ignore these realities would mean that I would surely be building my inquiry on a neo-populist pipe-dream. At the same time, however, as improvements in regional harmony would clearly add to the potential success of the policy directives that I have in mind, the issue of self-reliance in the region as a whole is discussed in the concluding chapter.

A caveat concerning data sources

Over the last decade, domestic and international agencies have made a laudable effort to collect and distribute survey and census data on a wide array of socio-economic indicators for most Arab countries. While access to such data represents an exciting development in itself, it is also true that most sources of empirical information should be approached with caution. Good data are not born overnight. They require a long process of refining and testing questionnaires, refining census and survey field methodology, refining tabulation procedures, and performing endless checks and rechecks on accuracy. Most Arab governments are only beginning to subject their data sources to such refinements.

With the above disclaimer in mind, it would be unwise to place too much faith on the reliability of individual census or survey figures that have been reported in this book. This means that the comparison of absolute levels of, say, unemployment between individual countries should be minimized. Accordingly, the approach adopted in the following chapters has been to utilize the data in, say, clusters in the search for broad patterns or structural differences between countries, or groups of countries. The fact is that we are only beginning to construct a preliminary 'road map' of empirically measured economic events and characteristics in the region.

For the most part, empirical data presented in tables or in figures in the text have been derived by amalgamating, checking and rechecking statistics from a great many domestic and international sources. Indeed, most tables draw on so many sources that space limitations prevent elaborate documentation or footnoting at the base of each table. Rather, a list of official domestic sources, specific to each country, has been provided in a separate bibliography entitled 'Government Statistical References'. This bibliography is useful in so far as it gives an idea of the agencies that are now providing data on the Arab countries.

As for the frequency, consistency and timeliness of data, the following should be kept in mind. First, many publications such as statistical abstracts or yearly serials appear irregularly (say, every two or three years). This means that the evaluation of an economic characteristic for all Arab countries at the same point in time (e.g. 1975 or 1980) is well nigh impossible. Second, national censuses or surveys usually differ in their coverage of different economic sectors, in their time frame of enumeration, and in their definition or inclusion of terms to be measured (e.g. women in the labor force). Such differences tend to undermine rigorous comparison between countries. They also tend to rule out time-series comparisons in any one country. Third, the administration of a census between, say, 1975 and 1980 requires many years in which to compile, tabulate and publish results. It takes even longer for international yearbooks to amalgamate and publish such results. Accordingly, it is likely to take some time before statistics on Arab human resources which pertain to the mid- or late-1970s will be effectively updated with information pertaining to the 1980s.

Appendix 1.1   National development plan expenditures

(See Tables on pages 18–19)

Table A.1.1 *Development plan expenditures per capita, Arab countries, 1976–81*

Groups	No. countries (1)	Total population (millions)[a] (2)	Average GNP per capita (US $)[a] (3)	Average yearly public investment in the development plans	
				Total (US $) million) (4)	per capita (US $) (5)
Oil-rich	8	26.7	5,663	35,672	1,361
Middle-income	5	54.4	881	7,908	145
Poorest	6	68.5	270	6,616	97
COUNTRIES					
I. Oil-rich					
Bahrain		0.3	2,410	374	1,247
Iraq		12.2	2,000	4,407	361
Kuwait		1.1	15,480	3,021	2,746
Libya		2.8	6,310	6,166	2,202
Oman		1.5	2,680	580	387
Qatar		0.2	11,400	724	3,620
Saudi Arabia		7.8	4,480	17,500	2,244
UAE		0.8	13,990	2,900	3,625

II. Middle-income

Algeria	18.4	990	1,835	100
Jordan	2.9	610	515	177
Morocco	18.9	540	1,262	67
Syria	8.2	780	2,296	280
Tunisia	6.0	840	2,000	333

III. Poorest

Egypt	39.6	280	5,218	132
Mauritania	1.5	100	80	53
Somalia	3.4	110	124	36
Sudan	17.1	290	750	44
Yemen AR	5.0	280	400	80
Yemen PDR	1.9	250	44	23

Source: National development plans of each country; Lebanon excluded due to devastating effects of the civil war.
Note: a Data pertain to estimates for 1978.

Appendix 1.2 Disaggregating the labor force participation rate

The labor force participation rate (LFPR) can be disaggregated as follows:

(1) $LFPR = LF / (LF + NLF) = (E + U) / (E + U + NLF)$,
where;
(2) $U = U_D + U_S + U_F$,
and where;

LF = No. in the labor force	U_D = deficient demand un-
NLF = No. not in the labor force	employment
E = No. employed	U_S = structural unemployment
U = No. unemployed	U_F = frictional unemployment

To increase LFPR, we might first attempt to raise employment to the extent that U in equation (1) would decline. Such action would require expansionary measures to reduce U_D in equation (2), which represents unemployment due to deficiencies in the aggregative effective demand for labor. On the other hand, we might attempt to reduce structural unemployment (U_S) which arises when the unemployed are mismatched with job vacancies because they do not possess the right skills, live in the right places, or are hampered by nepotistic barriers. Such problems can often be corrected by the geographic mobility of labor or by on-the-job training.

To increase LFPR, we might also attempt to reduce frictional unemployment (U_F) which arises when market imperfections allow unemployment and unfilled vacancies to exist side by side. Such problems can often be corrected by improving information on vacancies or smoothing channels for, say, qualified women to gain easier access to jobs. Finally, we might attempt to increase LFPR either by bidding more members of the non-labor force (NLF) into the actual labor force (e.g. wives), or by reducing the size of NLF. Over the long run, reductions in NLF would require reductions in rates of population growth or policies promoting emigration.

Chapter 2

Harnessing construction and labor migration

Overview

During the mid-1970s, the oil-rich members of the OAPEC countries were one huge construction site.[1] Spurred by burgeoning oil revenues and ambitious development plans, they were willing to buy virtually anything at any price on one condition; they wanted it quickly. For Western contractors, this amounted to a gold-rush. Inflated bids were readily accepted, ports were jammed by fleets of imported materials and equipment, and controls and regulations were unable to keep pace with the erection of new buildings. Between 1974 and 1977, government expenditures on projects were growing at an average rate of US $34 million per day. Expenditures on hard construction alone jumped from US $7,000 million in 1973 to US $42,000 million in 1977.

The rush of residential and non-residential building boosted employment, inflated incomes and redistributed population in record time. By 1975, the OAPEC countries had attracted over 1.7 million foreign workers, representing an incredible 23 per cent of their total labor force. No less than 41 per cent of these expatriates, or 704,000, were employed in construction alone.

Policy-makers were caught totally off guard by this massive migration. The concentration of investments and expatriate workers in the largest cities led to urban congestion, housing shortages and wild real estate speculation. As internal migrants responded to the lure of urban bright lights as well, aspirations for more balanced rural/urban and small town development were reduced to rhetoric. Easy money in the public sector promoted consumption of a wide range of imported luxury goods and fuelled huge increases in the cost of living. Importation of skilled and semi-skilled labor saw a concentration of OAPEC nationals in the service sector versus expatriates in the key production sectors, while scarce skills were being siphoned off from the oil-poor countries. The promise of an escape valve for unemployment was being realized only partially in the oil-poor countries because OAPEC was turning to cheaper labor from East Asia. For the most part, the sizable benefits to labor emigration in the form of remittances were not being channelled into productive investments in the oil-poor countries. Finally, existing national policies for correcting the above were not only few, but were largely ineffective. Interregional policies simply did not exist.

By mid-1977, the first shock had hit. Projected expenditures in the Gulf, Iraq and Saudi Arabia were to be drastically cut back. The United Arab Emirates and Oman were short of funds and the Gulf states and Saudi Arabia were suffering from acute economic indigestion caused by trying to implement too much money too quickly. Rumors were widely touted that the gold-rush was over. Between 1977 and 1978, however, it had become apparent that the growth rate of the construction industry had merely steadied and that it was undergoing an important reevaluation and clean-up. Inflated Western contracts were being dumped in favor of more reasonable Third World companies (particularly in Saudi Arabia and Bahrain), port capacity was being put in order, building materials industries were being developed, and quality control was being taken more seriously in project design.

By 1980, construction and contracts for social overhead capital (e.g. public schools, hospitals, communications networks) had again recorded healthy advances. OAPEC countries were shifting from the construction of high-rise blocks of luxury flats to government projects, including buildings for ministries and institutions, planned towns, housing and industrial plant. In the oil-poor countries, hopes for bilaterial aid were promoting far-reaching construction plans for schools, hospitals, irrigation schemes and much needed housing.

In short, projected long-term expenditures in Saudi Arabia, Oman, Iraq and Libya, and projected growth rates for building in Egypt, Syria, Jordan, Lebanon and the Sudan, imply that construction is really a market that is just coming of age.[2] According to national development plan estimates, 923,000 more expatriates were required to realize OAPEC development expenditures during the 1976 to 1981 period.[3] Projections to 1985 foresee a foreign labor requirement of approximately 3.6 million compared with 1.7 million in 1975 (Serageldin and

Socknat: 1980).[4] At the same time, however, the migration-related problems noted above are just as evident today as they were during the mid-1970s. Virtually no progress has been made toward solving them. Moreover, the huge disparities in planned expenditures between the oil-rich and oil-poor countries cannot help but exacerbate these problems throughout the 1980s.

My concern is with alleviating population and employment problems which have arisen out of the investment frenzy in the construction of social overhead capital. I am particularly interested in evaluating the extent to which construction might be harnessed to manipulate or redirect flows of both international and internal migrants. I focus on labour migration because it is largely through the *laissez-faire* interaction of migration and the construction boom that problems such as wage disparities, inflation, income inequalities, loss of skills, and imbalances in population distribution have become increasingly serious. As a special case, I intend to discuss the possibility that policy-makers might alleviate migration-related problems by increasing or decreasing the rate of housing and related construction in different sized urban areas. My aim in this respect is to promote a more balanced distribution of human resources in relation to non-human resources.

To set the stage for a discussion of appropriate policy directives, the first half of this chapter conveys the overwhelming magnitude of interregional labor flows which have responded to the massive investments in the construction of social overhead capital. This makes use of a one-of-a-kind database which was virtually non-existent prior to the International Labour Office's International Migration Project.[5] It includes a brief review of six problems which have been aggrevated by the massive migrations for employment. The latter half of this chapter discusses empirical relationships between migration and construction to explain why I believe that intervention in the construction sector could do much to alleviate the aforementioned problems.

Quantifying labor migration

Throughout the 1970s, the geographic mobility of labor was the most dynamic feature of human resources in the Arab world. By 1975, expatriate labor had contributed anywhere from 29 per cent to 84 per cent of the labor force in most OAPEC countries (Table 2.1). For the most part, expatriate labor originated from the oil-poor Arab countries (71.2 per cent of all expatriates). Some 19.9 per cent originated from Asian countries (largely India and Pakistan), whereas only 2.1 per cent

Table 2.1 Immigrant labor in the major labor importing Arab countries, 1975

Major labor importing countries	Total labor force (000's)	Number (000's)	As % of total labor	Non-national labor force				
				Ethnic composition			Skill composition	
				% Arab	% Asian	% European or North American	% professional or technical	% unskilled or manual
	(1)	*(2)*	*(3)*	*(4)*	*(5)*	*(6)*	*(7)*	*(8)*
Bahrain[a]	83	36	43.4	21.2	56.7	15.2	11.6	83[c]
Iraq	2,941	16	0.5	66.6	15.2	0.8	—	—
Jordan[b]	652	33	5.1	84.7	9.8	5.0	—	70
Kuwait	305	213	69.9	69.4	15.9	0.9	15.2	64
Libya	677	223	32.9	93.4	1.7	2.1	16.1	38
Oman	222	65[e]	29.3	12.4	83.0	4.0	4.4	75
Qatar	66	54	81.2	27.9	63.3	1.6	5.0	75[d]
Saudi Arabia	1,800	773	42.9	90.4	4.9	1.9	—	60
UAE	298	252	84.4	24.6	63.7	1.9	—	60
TOTAL	7,044	1,665	23.6	71.2	19.9	2.1	—	59

Sources: ILO Migration for Employment Project (Geneva), ILO funded International Migration Project (Durham University, England), World Bank, national statistical yearbooks, national censuses.

Notes:
a 1976 data.
b East Bank only.
c 1971 data.
d 1976 data.
e 1970 data.

originated from Europe and North America. In at least four countries, however (Bahrain, Oman, Qatar and United Arab Emirates), Asian migrants outnumbered Arab expatriates. This has not gone unnoticed. Fears that Arab identity is being undermined have led Iraq, Libya and Saudi Arabia to urge that priority be given to Arab migrants so that homogeneity of their culture will be retained. Moreover, the Arab Labour Organization recently launched a major effort to attract Arabs to replace workers from such countries as the Philippines and South Korea.

During the mid-1970s, the composition of expatriate skills was heavily weighted toward the lower rungs of the education/skill ladder (Table 2.1, column 8). Highest proportions of unskilled or manual workers were found in countries importing the largest numbers of Asians. More recently, however, OAPEC investments have placed heavier demands for skilled operatives, technicians and professionals. According to World Bank estimates, the share of expatriates required for 'professional and technical' jobs will grow from about 20 per cent in 1975 to 28 per cent in 1980 to 30 per cent by 1985.[6]

Turning to the major labor exporters, Egypt and North Yemen were the leaders in and around 1975 (see Table 2.2).[7] Next in line are Jordan, then India and Pakistan. In most cases, 85 to 95 per cent of these emigrants were consumed by two or three OAPEC countries (Table 2.2, columns 4—6). Saudi Arabia, United Arab Emirates, Libya and Kuwait were the major recipients of Arab labor, whereas Asians flocked to the Gulf states. Distance has obviously been a deciding factor here.

Admittedly, migration has had a far smaller impact on the labor force of the big exporters, Egypt, Algeria and Morocco, than it has on the tiny OAPEC countries. In 1975, it constituted about 3.8 per cent of the combined labor force of the oil-poor Arab countries. Addition of the leviathans, India and Pakistan, reduces the figure to a mere 0.6 per cent (see Table 2.2, column 3). Yet, the picture becomes considerably more provocative when countries are considered on an individual basis. Emigration of between 17 and 42 per cent of the labor force in Jordan, Oman and the two Yemens has been beneficial in view of unemployment and low wages at home, but it has also spurred inflation, disrupted seasonal labor reserves and, more recently, resulted in the loss of key skills.

About the best available gauge of benefits to be had by the labor exporting countries is in terms of the volume of remittances they have received from their workers abroad. By 1977, these sums had soared to

Table 2.2 *Emigrant labor from the major labor exporting countries, 1975*

Major labor exporting countries	Total labor force (000's)	Emigrant labor residing in Arab countries		Country of major destination			Cumulative share of 3 countries in emigrant work force (%)
		Number (000's)	As % of total labor force	1st	2nd	3rd	
	(1)	(2)	(3)	(4)	(5)	(6)	(7)
Egypt	11,044	398	3.6	Libya	SA[b]	Kuwait	84
Iraq	2,941	21	0.7	Kuwait	SA	UAE[c]	97
Jordan[a]	652	264	40.4	SA	Kuwait	UAE	79
Lebanon	747	50	6.7	SA	Jordan	Kuwait	69
Morocco + Algeria	7,500	3	0.03	Libya	Kuwait	—	99
Oman	222	38	17.1	SA	UAE	Kuwait	92
Somalia	1,650	7	0.4	SA	UAE	Kuwait	95
Sudan	4,500	46	1.0	SA	Libya	UAE	95
Syria	1,838	70	3.8	Jordan	Kuwait	SA	73
Tunisia	1,622	39	2.4	Libya	Oman	Kuwait	89
Yemen AR	1,426	290 – 600	20.3 – 42.1	SA	UAE	Kuwait	97
Yemen PDR	359	70	19.7	SA	Kuwait	UAE	96
TOTAL	34,501	1,296	3.8	—	—	—	—
India	200,000	154	0.1	UAE	Oman	Kuwait	77
Pakistan	21,035	155	0.7	UAE	Oman	Qatar	83
GRAND TOTAL	255,536	1,605	0.6	—	—	—	—

Sources: ILO Migration for Employment Project (Geneva), ILO funded International Migration Project (Durham University, England), World Bank, national statistical yearbooks, national censuses, ECWA estimates (Beirut: United Nations).

Notes:
a Jordanians and Palestinians.
b Saudi Arabia.
c UAE consists of seven emirates: Abu Dhabi (1975 pop. = 235,662), Dubai (206,861), Sharjah (88,188), Ras Al Khaimah (57,282), Fujairah (26,498), Ajman (21,566), Umm Al Quwain (16,879).

well over US $4,431 million. This represents a three-fold increase since 1973. Adding other major labor exporters to, or in, the region (e.g. Turkey, India, Pakistan) boosts the remittance figure to just over US $6,000 million.

Remittances to Egypt, Jordan and the Yemens have grown most. Between 1975 and 1977 alone, they grew from some US $892 million to US $2,409 million (Table 2.3, column 2). By 1980, they had grown

Table 2.3 *A profile of remittances to selected labor exporting countries, 1975–7*

Country	Value of remittances in 1977[a] (US $ millions) (1)	Ratio of remittances in 1977 to remittances in 1975 (2)	Value of remittances in 1977 divided by	
			Value of exports in 1977 (3)	Value of imports in 1977 (4)
Algeria	309	0.78	5.0	4.0
Egypt	897	2.44	25.4	16.3
Jordan	419	2.50	62.3	26.0
Morocco	533	0.89	29.0	13.0
Syria	92	1.77	6.6	3.2
Tunisia	145	1.15	10.7	7.2
Turkey	943	0.73	40.3	14.9
Yemen AR	914	2.96	801.8	103.6
Yemen PDR	179	3.19	71.9	43.3
TOTAL	4,431	1.33	24.5	13.8

Sources: ILO Migration for Employment Project (Geneva), World Bank, national statistical yearbooks, unpublished data from national planning ministries.
Note: a These remittance figures pertain to remittances of all workers abroad which includes workers in non-Arab countries as well.

by an additional US $1,000 million. For the poorest Arab countries, these remittances are a godsend. Their significance is particularly apparent when compared with export and import earnings (Table 2.3, columns 3–4). Further, the few existing studies on returning emigrants suggest that their personal savings are up to two or three times the value of their yearly remittances (Miller: 1976). It is hard to imagine the crunch that would ensue in North Yemen with an end to migration for employment, especially in view of its dearth of natural resources, arid climate and extreme underdevelopment.[8]

Documenting the problems

By importing armies of labor, the oil-rich countries have attempted to undermine the major constraint to rapid expansion and development of their economies, namely lack of needed human resources. In the process, however, migration for employment has fostered several undesirable side-effects. The most visible problems pertain to skill loss, inflationary effects, failure to channel remittances into productive investments, dependency on expatriates, social tensions and population distribution. The former problems (skill loss, inflation and remittances) are most troublesome among the labor exporters, whereas the latter pertain largely to the oil-rich labor importers.

Skill loss
In view of its effects on underemployment, migration from the oil-poor to the OAPEC countries was largely welcome up to 1975.[9] Between 1975 and 1980, however, the magnet began to become more selective of skilled workers than unskilled or manual labour. As the development programs of the oil-rich OAPEC countries are very similar, they have even become major competitors for exportable Arab skills. As a result, Jordan has complained of a loss of technicians and skilled manual workers (Birks and Sinclair: 1978b); Egypt has complained of a shortage of skilled mechanics and construction-related people (Birks and Sinclair: 1978b); North Yemen has suffered a 50 per cent vacancy rate in government technical departments (Fergany: 1980); even the Sudan, which had pressing problems of underemployment among most skill levels, has complained of a 'brain drain' (Kidd and Thurston: 1977).

Problems of skill loss have been further accentuated by two developments. First, there is a high degree of occupational immobility in the domestic labor markets of the major exporters (Egypt, Syria and North Yemen). This means that skill shortages generated by departing migrants take a long time to be filled by occupational transfers because there is very little internal readjustment within the labor markets. Second, the very capital that has transformed the Gulf, Saudi Arabia and Libya is now beginning to find its way to the oil-poor countries in the form of grants-in-aid.[10] This means that implementation of externally funded social overhead capital projects requires the same kinds of skills that are, of late, in short supply. This is most acute in rural-agricultural areas where the emigration of agricultural technicians, agronomists, irrigation specialists, etc., is a major setback when agricultural projects are undertaken.

Inflationary effects
Labor has been migrating to the OAPEC countries not only to escape

underemployment. Wages have been at least six to ten times those of the exporting countries (Gorham: 1977). How can the sending countries compete if they wish to retain needed skills? The fact is, they cannot. Levels of productivity simply do not permit competitive wages. This is not to say, however, that wages in the oil-poor countries have not been rising. They have had to, simply to attract workers. Even in North Yemen, where over 30 per cent of the labor force is abroad, wage rates of unskilled construction workers rose twelve-fold between 1974 and 1977, and agricultural wages for seasonal labor rose 300 per cent between 1975 and 1977.[11] In Egypt, the Under-Secretary of the Ministry of Labor took me to a construction site where he pointed out that unskilled hardhats were earning more than himself due to shortages of manual and semi-skilled labour. So much for his doctorate!

Further, easy money in the OAPEC countries and remittances in the oil-poor countries have spurred price increases by fuelling demand for basic non-durables almost overnight. According to Table 2.4, average yearly increases in the food index ranged from about 10 to 30 per cent per year. Increases in the general index climbed to 35 per cent per year in Saudi Arabia and to 46 per cent in North Yemen.

Real estate speculation and rental increases have been nothing short of spectacular. North Yemen is the uncontested leader in this respect. According to the United Nations, it is one of the world's twenty-five 'hard core' less developed countries, yet a modest apartment in Sana'a rents for approximately US $500 per month and land speculators have been cashing in on prices in excess of those in Manhattan. In the OAPEC countries, Nakhleh (1977) attributes the severe housing short-ages, rising rents and rapidly rising real estate directly to demand by expatriates. Before the government of Libya had intervened (Resolution 14), rent for three-bedroom flats had risen from US $400 per month in 1976 to $1,350 in 1978. The real problem here is that the impact of inflation is never distributed equally among all population subgroups. Those without an oil lifeline or remittance sources have been hardest hit.

In sum, inflationary wage and price effects are working against national interests in the exporting countries by injecting destabilizing elements into their economies. The problem for policy-makers is that these forces lie largely outside domestic controls.

Channelling remittances
The long-term benefit of remittances on the development of the labor exporters hinges largely on the direction of expenditures. Yet, there has

Table 2.4   *Average yearly increase in cost of living indices, selected Arab countries, 1972–9*

Countries	Time period (1)	Area (2)	Type of index (3)	Average yearly % growth rate Food index (4)	General index (5)
Labor importers					
Iraq	1976–8	Baghdad	CPI[b]	9.7	7.4
Kuwait	1972–8	National	CLI[a]	14.0	11.3
Libya	1975–8	Tripoli	CLI[a]	1.4	9.2
Saudi Arabia	1972–7	Urban[e]	CLI[a]	28.7	35.8
UAE	1972–7	Urban	Housing	—	16.7
Labor exporters					
Egypt	1972–7	Urban	CLI[a]	16.6	11.6
Jordan	1975–7	National	CLI[a]	13.8	27.1
Mauritania	1975–8	Nouakchott	CPI[b]	18.7	16.7
Morocco	1972–7	Urban	CLI[a]	16.0	13.3
Somalia	1972–7	Mogadishu	CLI[a]	22.6	17.8
Sudan	1973–7	Urban[f]	CLI[a]	—	22.0
Syria	1973–7	National	WPI[c]	10.8	12.4
Yemen AR	1972–5	Sana'a	RPI[d]	34.3	41.3
Yemen AR	1972–9	Sana'a	CPI[b]	36.0	46.4

Sources: National statistical yearbooks and special studies.
Notes: a CLI = cost of living index.
b CPI = consumer price index.
c WPI = wholesale price index.
d RPI = retail price index.
e Households with income of US $170–225 per month.
f Low-income households.

been a visible absence of ways to channel remittances into investments that will fuel development of national capacity, spur regional economies, or work to reduce inequalities in the distribution of income. Instead, the poorest labour exporters have become almost hooked on remittances to sustain consumption of goods by producers which might not have evolved otherwise.[12]

Egypt's national development plan (1976–81) claims that 'Growing numbers of Egyptians work abroad for very high wages, if compared with domestic salaries. These individuals return to Egypt possessed of huge purchasing powers which they individually direct not to savings and investments, but to flagrant and luxurious consumption'. A similar point emerges in studies of North Yemen by Swanson (1979a, 1979b). He stresses that there is little evidence of investment in industrial infrastructure. Nor is there evidence that the government is trying to channel remittances into investment or provide the administrative infrastructure to channel privately held resources into private or social investments.[13]

Steps in the right direction have been initiated by the governments of Egypt, Morocco and North Yemen. Egypt has issued bonds to be subscribed to largely by expatriates. The first issue was for 1,000 million Egyptian pounds. Also, a new investment and trading bank has been established, and Egyptians living and working abroad in the United Arab Emirates contributed 50 per cent plus of the working capital of 5 million Egyptian pounds. The Moroccan government, in conjunction with the Banque Populaire, is giving Moroccan workers abroad preferential exchange rates when repatriating their savings. This policy has actually boosted remittances (MEED: 1978). And, in North Yemen, Local Development Associations are emerging as a public response to mobilize privately held financial resources.

Clearly, pressure is on the oil-poor countries to channel and utilize remittances more effectively because this source of external revenue will not be available indefinitely. This applies particularly to the role that remittances could play in stimulating regional economies and reducing income inequality. While 'urban bias' in remittance spending will surely persist, there is also evidence that poor rural areas in Morocco, Tunisia and Egypt are benefiting by remittance spending on the development of farms, needed housing, etc.[14]

Dependency on expatriate labor

An overwhelming concern of the OAPEC countries is national self-sufficiency. Planners are extremely wary of shifting from dependency on oil to dependency on an expatriate labor force.[15] Yet, by putting the development and construction of a vast social overhead capital largely in the hands of expatriates they are doing just that.

The distribution of expatriates by branch of economic activity in Table 2.5 underlines the nature of the problem. Compare the distributions of Kuwaiti nationals and non-nationals in columns 1 and 2. Kuwaitis are found predominantly in the service sector. In contrast, non-nationals predominate in key industries such as manufacturing and construction, and in trade. Indeed, column 3 reveals that 91 per cent of manufacturing workers are non-nationals and that between 84 and 95 per cent of construction and trade workers are non-nationals. A similar situation pertains to construction in Libya (columns 4–6), and to manufacturing, construction and commerce in Saudi Arabia (columns 7–9). Again, we find that the majority of Libyan and Saudi

Table 2.5 *Percentage distribution of nationals and non-nationals by economic activity, and percentage share of non-nationals in each economic sector, Kuwait, Libya, Saudi Arabia, 1975*

Economic activity	Kuwait			Libya			Saudi Arabia		
	% Distribution		Share non-nationals	% Distribution		Share non-nationals	% Distribution		Share non-nationals
	Nationals	Non-nationals		Nationals	Non-nationals		Nationals	Non-nationals	
	(1)	(2)	(3)	(4)	(5)	(6)	(7)	(8)	(9)
Ag. + fishing	4.6	1.7	46.9	24.8	7.9	13.2	51.5	—	—
Mining + quarry.	2.0	1.5	63.4	3.1	2.5	30.0	1.8	4.6	71.0
Manufacturing	2.5	10.5	90.6	3.7	6.2	41.9	0.4	5.6	94.0
Construction	2.0	14.4	94.5	7.5	52.7	77.6	0.0	40.7	100.0
Elect., gas, water	2.3	2.5	72.0	2.0	1.6	27.7	0.6	1.7	73.0
Trade	7.3	15.7	84.0	10.9	4.2	17.0	9.2	16.9	63.0
Commerce	5.3	5.3	70.8	10.0	2.8	11.6	3.6	9.5	72.0
Services	74.0	48.4	61.4	28.4	13.3	14.0	32.9	21.0	38.0
Other	0.0	0.0	0.0	9.6	8.8	—		—	—
TOTAL	100.0	100.0	70.8	100.0	100.0	27.7	100.0	100.0	46.9

Sources: ILO Migration for Employment Project (Geneva), national statistical yearbooks and censuses.

nationals employed in non-agricultural activity are in the service sector. Thus, while expatriates are developing key skills through experience, the same cannot be said of nationals driving taxi-cabs or selling clothing in oversized service sectors.

Admittedly, lack of needed skills among nationals cannot be over-looked when accounting for the differences above. But, what is often overlooked is the disdain for manual-type work among nationals in the oil-rich countries. Certain jobs are deemed acceptable whereas manual work tends to be equated with low class. This attitude stems from high values placed on bartering and trade. Moreover, lucrative jobs in the government sector, and social class or leisure preferences, are being fed by the ease of living off a virtual rent income from oil exports.

To some extent, such attitudes have led to the voluntary under-employment and unemployment of nationals (Knauerhause: 1976), and the use of windfall oil revenues for the development of a narrow range of jobs deemed suitable or attractive to OAPEC nationals. To illustrate the latter point, the Kuwaiti government is trying to employ all nationals in the service industry. By 1980, over 75 per cent of this goal had been attained. The same applies to Saudi Arabia and Libya. Thousands of jobs have been created in government to be manned largely by unskilled nationals. While 'easy money' has permitted this course over the short run, it is clearly working against goals of national self-sufficiency. The relationship between 'easy money' and the motivation to work is elaborated in more formal terms in Appendix 2.1.

Social tensions

The attitudes described above have given birth to a certain degree of discrimination between nationals and expatriates. In addition to occupational discrimination, tensions can be felt in several ways. One is an outgrowth of the desire to maintain an Arab identity. Rights to obtain permanent residence or citizenship are not easily acquired by migrant workers. Indeed, the work camp approach has been adopted toward removing the impact of expatriates on local labor markets, and on national culture and identity. This applies particularly to migrants from East Asia. There is a trend to award construction and develop-ment contracts to companies from Korea, the Philippines and Malaysia which can bring and provide for their own work force during a limited contract period.[16]

An additional problem is that oil revenues have almost exclusively been spent to benefit nationals. Non-nationals who have been building up the country have been largely excluded. For example, in the case of the work camps, migrants are seldom permitted to bring their wives and children with them as this would necessitate provision of services for the benefit of migrant dependents. Further, conditions of employment, housing and sanitation for migrants have been neglected by governments. Not until 1978 did Saudi Arabia really begin to insist upon reasonable working conditions for immigrants. Immigrants have often been barred from taking vocational training or access to highly skilled jobs where on-the-job training may be available. This applies particularly to Yemenis working in Saudi Arabia.

Finally, increasing information on the fortunes to be made in the OAPEC countries, and difficulties in monitoring border crossings, are combining to pit an influx of expatriates against nationals for employment in some saturated sectors. The problem here is that expatriates are often willing to work at considerably lower wages than nationals. This tends to deplete jobs which are deemed socially acceptable. For example, nationals in Oman are beginning to complain of competition from Asians; nationals in Libya and Jordan are now complaining of Egyptians. Further, tensions have heightened in Libya with the influx of Tunisians, Algerians and Moroccans who have recently faced major cutbacks of job offerings in recession-conscious Belgium, France and Germany. This was evident in the expulsion of some 14,000 clandestine Tunisian migrants from Libya in 1976, and the interception of some 40,000 illegal border crossings (République Tunisienne: 1977).

Population distribution
Migration for employment to the oil-rich countries is clearly adding to problems of population concentration. Moreover, it tends to reinforce the flow of internal migrants that typically converge on the largest cities (Tabbarah *et al.*: 1978). While concentration of development expenditures in the largest cities is the major culprit here, expenditures made by international migrants also enhance the growth and 'bright lights' effect of just one or two urban centres. Though it is difficult to gauge the magnitude of this kind of problem, at least one study has revealed that congestion, housing shortages and lack of recreational facilities are the most frequent complaints about concentration of migrants in Kuwait City (El-Awadi: 1978).

At least ten Arab countries have openly expressed their desire to modify the distribution of their populations (Table 2.6, column 2). Planners seek to reduce the domination of single cities in their urban hierarchy. The largest city represents from 50 to 90 per cent of the urban population in Egypt, Libya, Jordan, Iraq, the Yemens, Kuwait,

Table 2.6 Government perceptions of spatial distribution and policy action, Arab countries, 1978

Country	Largest city as a % of 1970 urban Population (1)	Perceptions of spatial distribution			Policy action		
		Excessive migration to metropolitan region (2)	Excessive migration to other urban centers (3)	Unacceptable dispersion of population in rural areas (4)	Active Decentralization within metropolitan areas (5)	Creation of urban counter magnets (6)	Major rural development programs (7)
Labor importers							
Bahrain	100.0	X			X		
Iraq	49.0	X			X	X	X
Kuwait	95.0						
Libya	45.5					X	X
Oman	—				X		
Qatar	100.0						
Saudi Arabia	26.0					X	X
UAE	—						
Labor exporters							
Algeria	32.5	X	X	X	X	X	X
Egypt	78.5	X	X			X	X
Jordan	46.7	X	X			X	X
Lebanon	50.7	X		X			
Mauritania	—	X					
Morocco	26.0	X	X	X			
Somalia	—	X					
Sudan	24.9						
Syria	31.6						X
Tunisia	35.0	X	X				X
Yemen AR	83.6						

Source: UN Population Inquiries (unpublished)

Bahrain and Qatar (Abu-Aianah: 1978). At the current rate of urbanization, city population in the Arab world will double by 1990. Unless there is improved planning to control it, slow it down or guide its redistribution, then social dynamite will lie ahead (Lawless, 1980).

The oil-poor, labour exporting countries are also failing to create incentives for their returning nationals to settle in rural areas or smaller towns because they are allocating a majority of development or aid expenditures to their largest cities. This problem is most visible in North Africa where rural emigration to the cities is followed by emigration abroad and, subsequently, by heavy settlement of returning migrants in the cities (Findlay: 1978). Fortunately, some countries are beginning to take an active stand against these *laissez-faire* developments (see Table 2.6, columns 5–7). Such action will be illustrated in our discussion of policy measures below.

Policy directives

My approach to the problems described above seeks to make planners take a second look at a range of desirable aims that could be achieved by harnessing the construction sector more effectively. Features of the construction and migration relationship that might be encouraged or manipulated to bring about positive effects on migration and employment include the following. First, as a leading employer of migrants in both international and internal Arab labor markets, the construction sector not only aids labor exporting or labor surplus countries by absorbing large numbers of unskilled workers, but could serve as a port of entry for rural labor to the industrial work force, and could provide on-the-job training. The return of these workers (many of whom are temporary migrants) could contribute invaluable skills to the poorer Arab countries which are just beginning to embark on their own construction–development programmes fuelled by OAPEC 'dollars-in-aid'. Second, appropriate planning of construction activity could influence the distribution of migrants both among and within countries. Third, residential construction is already a major recipient of worker remittances in the poorer Arab countries. This subsector and these funds could be organized to underwrite self-help housing and labor-intensive employment in rural areas and small towns. Fourth, the construction sector is a prime candidate for policy intervention. It receives large shares of development expenditures which policy-makers can generally invest as they see fit. Further, it is much easier to influence than many other variables bearing on employment and migration (e.g. wages and salaries), because a host of technical and locational controls exist to guide its behaviour in desired directions.

In addition to the above, I believe that construction could serve as an engine of growth in the poorer Arab countries as well as in the OAPEC group. It is one of the few economic sectors that can be used to attain, simultaneously, several of the 'basic needs' objectives adopted at the World Employment Conference held by the International Labour Organization in 1976.

Now, the claims above assume that the relationship between construction and labor migration is a strong one, that control of this relationship is well within the policy-makers' domain, and that policy manipulation of the relationship could work to alleviate many of the problems discussed in the previous sections. As these assumptions constitute the building blocks of the policy directives that I have in mind, the balance of this chapter seeks to substantiate them.

Construction and employment of migrants
Between 1971 and 1977, construction absorbed between 11 and 58 per

Table 2.7 *Employment in construction in selected Arab countries, 1975–7*

Country	Year	% of non-agricultural labor force employed in construction
Labor importers		
Bahrain	1975	20.1
Kuwait	1975	11.1
Libya	1975	27.4
Oman	1975	58.0
Qatar	1975	14.1
Saudi Arabia	1975	19.7
UAE	1975	33.2
Labor exporters		
Algeria	1977	14.3
Egypt	1976	8.0
Jordan	1975	12.9
Morocco[a]	1977	16.3
Syria	1975	14.1
Tunisia	1975	12.8
Yemen AR	1975	17.2
Yemen PDR	1976	12.9

Sources: National censuses and sample surveys.
Note: a National development plan estimate.

cent of the non-agricultural labor force in the major labor importing Arab countries, and between 8 and 17 per cent in the labor exporting countries (see Table 2.7). By world standards these figures are extremely high. If we apply the rule of thumb that two additional man-years of employment are created for every three man-years on site in building construction, then the role of construction is second only to agricultural or service employment in most Arab countries.

The importance of construction as an employer of migrant labor *per se* is shown in Table 2.8. In the seven major labor importing countries, 40 per cent of all non-nationals were employed in construction. In Kuwait nearly 60 per cent of all new work permits issued in 1977 were for building and construction alone. Further, on average, 81 per cent of all construction workers in the major labor importing countries were non-nationals in 1975. Somewhere in the order of 60 per cent of these were unskilled or manual workers.

Turning to the major labor exporting countries, approximately 75 per cent of migrant workers from the two Yemens were employed in construction in 1975 (mostly in Saudi Arabia). Among Egyptian workers in Kuwait between 50 and 53 per cent were employed in construction, in Libya 50 to 70 per cent, in Saudi Arabia 30 to 35 per cent and in other Arab countries from 34 to 45 per cent (Choucri: 1978). Between 1973 and 1975 some 40 per cent of Jordanian workers abroad were involved in construction. Finally, the proportion of Tunisian migrants employed in building construction was between 30 and 55 per cent in Libya (1971–6) and 90 per cent in Saudi Arabia (1976).

The tendency for migrants to gravitate to construction or for construction to serve as a 'port of entry' to the industrial labor force for rural workers is evident in many other contexts as well. For example, construction has played a major role in absorbing North African workers in Western Europe. In France, migrants accounted for 48 per cent of the growth in the construction labor force between 1966 and 1976. In 1976 about 40 per cent of all migrant workers in French construction came from Algeria, Tunisia and Morocco. A recent study of this sector points to its function as a 'port of entry' and indicates that it absorbs older workers likely to be unskilled (Tapinos: 1978). Migrants contributed 44 per cent of the construction workers in Switzerland (1974) and 22 per cent in the Federal Republic of Germany (1972). It has also been observed that construction is a major urban employer of migrants from rural areas (up to 80 per cent in Khartoum, Sudan). This is important from the viewpoint of its

Table 2.8 *Non-nationals employed in the labor force and in the construction sector of the major labor importing countries, 1975–6*

| Major labor importers | Year (1) | Total labor force (000s) (2) | As % of labor force (3) | Non-nationals in the labor force | | |
				% estimated to be unskilled or manual workers (4)	% employed in construction (5)	As % of all construction workers (6)
Bahrain	1976	83	43.4	82.1	21.4	48.2
Kuwait	1975	305	69.9	64.0	22.9	93.0
Libya	1975	677	32.8	45.4	53.0	77.3
Oman	1976	222	63.3	75.3	86.0	75.7
Qatar	1975	66	80.0	75.1	18.8	97.3
Saudi Arabia	1975	1,800	42.9	59.9	26.3	84.9
UAE	1975	298	85.4	60.5	37.4	82.4
TOTAL		3,451	49.5	60.0	40.1	81.3

Sources: Birks and Sinclair (1978a, 1978b, 1978c and 1980b), World Bank, national statistical yearbooks, national censuses, estimates by the United Nations Economic Commission for Western Asia.

potential effects on the internal distribution of employment and migration (Shaw: 1978a).

The facts above suggest a number of conclusions. First, since employment in construction, or rather employment in manual jobs, is by no means preferred work among OAPEC nationals, it is virtually left to expatriates from the poorer countries. Second, construction absorbs a disproportionate share of unskilled migrants. Third − though this cannot be derived directly from the data − a large share of the migrants are single (or, if married, are unaccompanied by their dependents) and return home within a few years. In other words, expansion of the construction sector in the OAPEC countries has been virtually synony-mous with (i) increasing immigration, (ii) the absorption of unskilled workers from labor-surplus countries, and (iii) opportunities for on-the-job training which could benefit the labor exporting countries via the return migration of needed skills.

Impact on the distribution of migrants

To what extent could official intervention in construction activity influence numbers and distribution of foreign migrants among Arab countries? As a corollary we can ask, 'Might differential rates of con-struction within Arab countries influence the internal distribution of indigenous migrants as well?' This question is critical because (i) Arab governments perceive internal population distribution as their number one demographic problem, (ii) planners are seeking to reduce the dominance of single cities in their urban hierarchy, and (iii) both internal and international migrants tend to converge on the largest cities.

With the aim of answering these questions I have undertaken a number of studies which seek to measure the effect of differences in rates of building activity among several Arab countries on rates of international labor migration to those countries. I have also examined the effect of differences in rates of building construction among cities or provinces in Syria, Morocco, Algeria, Tunisia and Bahrain on their patterns of internal migration. The empirical results, summarized in Appendix 2.2, convey that investments in construction in different places will have a strong, positive effect on migration to those places. Judging from these results, and in conjunction with other work on the subject (Shaw: 1980a), it seems reasonable to conclude that policy intervention in the building sector could significantly influence both the pace and destination of labor migration. Assuming that 'construc-tion could control migration', we must now ask, 'To what extent can we control construction?'

Scope for policy intervention
The magnitude of construction that is being planned by Arab governments is staggering. For all types of government construction, investment approached some US $100,000 million over the 1976 to 1981
period. It will certainly exceed that amount over the 1981 to 1986
period.

On average, some 10 to 30 per cent of the 1976 to 1981 development plan expenditures were allocated for housing alone (see Table
2.9). This commitment is merely a beginning. Between 1981 and 1986,

Table 2.9 *National development expenditures on housing and construction in selected Arab countries, 1974–85*

| Country | Time period (1) | % Share of planned national development expenditures on: | |
		Housing (2)	All construction (3)
Labor importers			
Bahrain	1980–1	20.0	30.2
Iraq	1976–80	16.3	—
Kuwait	1976–81	31.6	38.2
Libya	1976–80	10.6	21.9
Oman	1976–80	15.2	24.2
Qatar	1978	32.1	—
Saudi Arabia	1976–80	4.6	28.8
UAE (Abu Dhabi)	1976–80	19.2	37.0
Labor exporters			
Algeria	1980–4	15.0	21.8
Egypt	1978–82	5.8	7.9
Jordan	1981–5	—	45.0
Morocco	1976–80	15.2	30.0
Somalia	1974–8	5.0	—
Sudan	1976–80	12.0	25.0
Syria	1976–80	9.0	—
Tunisia	1976–81	14.0	—
Yemen AR	1977–82	12.1	15.2
Yemen PDR	1974–9	8.7	22.0

Sources: National development plans.

governments have set housing targets of some 50,000–150,000 units
in each of the smaller OAPEC countries, 80,000 units in Jordan,
146,000 in Libya, 700,000 in the Sudan, 280,000 in Tunisia, 450,000
in Algeria, upwards of 800,000 in Egypt, and 350,000 in Iraq (with an
additional 620,000 proposed for the 1986 to 1990 plan).

Since the enormous funds for this task are in the policy-makers' domain, they represent a readily available means for steering employment opportunities (and hence internal and international migrants) away from the largest cities. Such action is likely to appeal more and more to policy-makers in view of national goals to (i) close the rural–urban gap in housing availability, (ii) promote labor-intensive employment in smaller towns and off-farm work opportunities for farm families (see Chapter 3), and (iii) find an alternative to highly restrictive rural–urban migration policies such as demanding residence and work permits, demolishing squatter settlements, or keeping down urban wages (which usually involves a confrontation with unions).[17]

Of course, a major difference between the oil-rich and the oil-poor Arab countries is that planned government expenditures on building construction (per capita) are several times greater in the former group. This implies a wide differential in the potential influence of a 'construction–migration strategy' between the two groups of countries. Could migrant remittances be used to close this gap?

Though policies to guide remittances into productive investments are few, large shares of migrant remittances are already finding their way into private housing. Further, since many migrants originate from rural areas (e.g. from North Yemen, Oman, Egypt and the Maghreb countries), remittances could promote desperately needed residential construction in areas other than the largest cities. For example, the highest rates of migration in North Yemen in 1975 were from the poorest provinces. Most of these migrants came from farm backgrounds and left their wives or families to manage the farm during their absence. Remittances to these families might be anywhere from five to ten times their yearly farm income. Though North Yemen is one of the world's poorest countries, remittance-fed residential construction is surprisingly high in areas outside the capital, Sana'a.[18]

Clearly, the opportunity exists to develop savings and financing schemes to reinforce these positive effects. During the past decade a good deal of success has been achieved in mobilizing savings of low-income families for housing programs in developing countries (Sweet and Walters: 1976; Vernez: 1976). With a little planning, there is no reason why the private ambitions of a great many migrants to own their own home could not be harnessed to promote national goals of self-help housing, labor-intensive employment and population decentralization. If remittances over the 1976 to 1981 period alone had been channelled into housing construction in the seven major labor exporting countries, they would, on average, have doubled the per capita development funds available in this sector.

As far as specific kinds of policy intervention in the construction sector are concerned, it will suffice to say that a wide range of controls and regulations are already available to guide its locational behaviour. Residential construction is sensitive to variations in the cost of construction materials, the cost of construction loans, demolition rates, land-use zoning, and the price of housing and subsidies (Shaw: 1978a; Strassman: 1979). Further, government intervention in building construction as a means of redistributing population growth and urban development has already met with a good deal of success in a variety of developed and developing countries (Shaw: 1980a).

The contribution of building construction to economic growth
Needless to say, any decision to enlist building construction in the service of distribution and migration policy assumes that employment in this sector will not impede economic growth. Such an assumption might have been heavily criticized during the 1950s and early 1960s. During the early 1970s, however, and particularly after the consensus reached at the HABITAT conference in 1976, building construction found its way back into the heart of development strategy. In many cases, increased World Bank support for housing programs in developing countries has led the way. The traditional preoccupation with housing's high capital/output ratio and the view that housing construction provides little more than a durable consumer good have now been pushed aside as narrow and unfounded (United Nations: 1971; Grimes: 1976; Currie: 1976). Indeed, by shifting the emphasis from growth-related to development-related investments, the World Bank and other institutions are attempting to underline the important role of housing construction in providing or stimulating the expansion of a whole range of infrastructural and social services (Winpenny: 1978; Richards, 1979).

In a wider context, world figures show that construction accounts for up to 50 per cent or even more of gross domestic fixed capital formation, and capital formation in construction accounts for over 10 per cent of GDP (see Table 2.10).

Between 1975 and 1978, construction contributed approximately 56 per cent of gross fixed capital formation in Iraq, 39 per cent in Kuwait, 86 per cent in Saudi Arabia, 41 per cent in the United Arab Emirates, 46 per cent in Algeria, 69 per cent in Jordan, 56 per cent in Morocco, 48 per cent in Syria, 58 per cent in Tunisia, and 70 per cent in North Yemen.

Regardless of the level of development, residential construction represents between 20 and 30 per cent of the gross fixed capital forma-

Table 2.10 *Selected measures of building construction and housing expenditures at different levels of development, 1970–6*

Measure	Level of development[a]		
	Most developed (N = 15)	Moderately developed (N = 16)	Least developed (N = 8)
(1) Construction capital formation as % of gross fixed capital formation	55	←—— 49 ——→	
(2) Construction capital formation as % of gross domestic product	12	←—— 11 ——→	
(3) Residential and non-residential building construction as % of gross fixed capital formation	40–60	35–50	22–30
(4) Ratio of residential to non-residential building construction	1.02	2.10	3.58
(5) Residential construction as % of gross fixed capital formation	20–30	30–40	15–23
(6) % of private final household consumption in purchasers' values allocated to housing expenditures	21	←—— 20 ——→	

Sources: UN *Yearbook of National Accounts Statistics*, national statistical year-books.

Note: a 'Most developed countries' are those with a per capita GNP of US $2,000 or more; 'moderately developed' = US $300–1,999; 'least developed' = less than US $300.

tion and over 40 per cent of total construction (Table 2.10). Between 1965 and 1970, investment in housing accounted for as much as 46 per cent of total construction investment in France and 55 per cent in Italy.

The fact that capital formation in residential construction represents such a consistent share of gross domestic product over a wide range of countries implies that housing is an investment that will be made by consumers at every stage of development. Indeed, housing represents some 15 to 25 per cent of household expenditures in developed and developing countries alike (Table 2.10). Direct payments for housing, including maintenance, absorb about 23 per cent of the average American's income and up to 40 per cent of the income of the poor. Housing is the major focus of saving for all but the highest-income families. It is also viewed as a means of raising economic productivity because it increases incentives for saving and capital formation, and has been recognized by the World Bank as a profitable investment item, yielding a high flow of income.[19]

With many migrant workers available for the construction sector, productivity per worker can be permitted to lag because employment can grow, disproportionately, to make up the difference. This is not to say, however, that productivity is always low. For example, the ratio of the contribution to GDP per construction worker to the contribution per manufacturing and service worker was, respectively, 1.49 and 1.59 in Indonesia (1971), 0.83 and 1.09 in Mexico (1970), 0.93 and 0.80 in Pakistan (1972), 1.58 and 2.01 in Tanzania (1967), 2.18 and 0.77 in Algeria (1974), 1.07 and 1.39 in Tunisia (1966). Clearly, construction is able to hold its own.

As an employment strategy in less developed countries, Strassman (1979) concludes that stressing employment in construction would 'not go against what would happen anyway'. His analysis of twenty-seven developed and less developed countries shows that it would just start the process sooner because the share of the labor force in construction will naturally augment as the country begins to take on characteristics of more developed economies. Further, his work on employment generating effects of housing subsidies in Columbia, Mexico and Venezuela found that subsidies would create about 33 per cent more man—years of work if channelled into areas other than large cities. They would provide 2.5 times more man—years of work if channelled toward families earning less than US $2,000 per year than toward families earning more than US $7,000 per year. The same finding emerged in an input—output study of twenty different construction products (ten of which related to housing); non-luxury housing registered outstandingly high employment potential (Koenigsberger: 1975).

Finally, recent studies on the role of building construction in employment and economic growth suggest the following conclusions: the income multiplier for housing construction in developing countries appears to be about 2;[20] one unit of final demand for housing can lead to as much as two units of aggregate output in the economy as a whole;[21] residential construction provides between two and three years of employment for each new unit: one man-year on the job, one in factories producing building materials and up to an additional man-year in related industries;[22] in terms of 'per unit of value-added' at least two studies estimate equal if not greater returns to construction labor than to manufacturing labor in 'industrialized settings';[23] high growth rates for a number of countries have been spurred by exceptionally high growth rates in construction;[24] and since the capacity of the construction sector sets a physical limit to the acceleration of growth, it can actually serve as a bottleneck to development plans if its capacity is insufficiently planned.[25]

Tying it all together

A most important reason for enlisting construction in policies to influence migration and employment is that it is one of the few economic sectors that can simultaneously contribute to the satisfaction of several basic needs. Construction has increasingly occupied a central position in many employment missions of the International Labour Organization because it utilizes labor-intensive modes of production, spurs the development of indigenous building industries, absorbs large amounts of unskilled labor, and is conducive to the adoption of self-help techniques.

The planning of construction activity on a regional basis, in contrast to its usual *laissez-faire* concentration in primate or largest cities, has also been recognized as a means of correcting serious imbalances in virtually all forms of social overhead capital, and ushering rural people into the mainstream of development by providing infrastructure and employment closer to where they live (e.g. through feeder roads, light agro-industries).[26] In short, government intervention in construction activity holds the potential for tackling distributional problems which have eluded Arab planners during the growth frenzy of the past decade. Its direct impact on international and internal migration, employment generation, labor-intensive production, and the provision and decentralization of social overhead capital, implies that it may be the best available policy tool for influencing the distribution of Arab migration and employment.

In the process, an abundance of national and interregional policy levers are available for tackling the kinds of migration-related problems described in the first part of this chapter. Problems of 'skill loss' to the oil-rich OAPEC countries could be minimized by emphasizing temporary absorption of unskilled workers, promotion of on-the-job training for expatriates (see Chapter 6), and return migration of needed skills to the oil-poor countries. Inroads could be made against population concentration in largest cities and 'urban bias' in development expenditures by decentralizing construction expenditures on social overhead capital, especially for low-income housing. This might go a long way toward reducing migration from small towns and rural areas by providing desperately needed housing and services, promoting off-farm employment, and reducing income disparities in the process. Inflationary real estate speculation and consumption of luxury imports in the cities might be undermined by channelling migrant remittances into productive investments and self-help housing, particularly in outlying areas. Finally, by embracing interregional labor mobility as an incredible opportunity for redistributing wealth, steps could be taken to invest in the long-term development of human capital for the region as a whole. This might include generous educational and social spending for Arab expatriates in the OAPEC countries, training programs where unskilled or illiterate nationals are taught by more qualified immigrants, and bonding arrangements whereby skilled or trained migrants might be obliged to return home with their enhanced experience.

Fortunately, the policy directives proposed here complement many of the planning goals and needs expressed in the current round of national development plans. This applies particularly to acute shortages of residential housing in rural and urban areas, plans to revitalize waning cities or to construct urban counter-magnets, and the obvious necessity of creating rural employment toward stemming the exodus to overburdened cities. Given the lack of consistent national or international policies dealing with labor migration in the Arab world, and the fact that redirecting or tempering such movements has now become a major challenge, it is my conclusion that construction activity should be planned to serve these goals without delay.

Appendix 2.1 Easy money, labor and leisure

From an economic standpoint, the supply of labor is usually examined in terms of responses to changes in the wage rate and to the availability of non-labor income. To analyze these responses, economists conventionally adopt a basic model of the consumer demand for goods. In this model, goods for consumption take the form of leisure and real income (or goods), and it is assumed that the individual prefers more of both goods and leisure. In turn, his pursuit of these ends is constrained by the price of the goods and by a finite number of hours. Unless he receives non-labor income, he must allocate his time to the labor market in order to obtain the income to purchase the goods that he wants. In most cases, the model predicts that hours of labor supplied will respond positively, or at least non-negatively, to positive changes in the wage rate, and negatively to the availability of non-labor income.[27]

To appreciate the effect of 'easy money', such as gifts or artificially high wages, on labor supply decisions, it is necessary to extend the basic model to include a more realistic analysis of the allocation of time. At the macro level, this requires recognition of the role of cultural factors in participation decisions so that the impact of economic development on consumer tastes is not overlooked. At the micro level, it requires a shift in emphasis from the individual as the decision making unit to the household, so that labor supplied by the household head is not treated in isolation from that supplied by other family members.

To illustrate the potential effect of 'easy money' on participation decisions in a changing development context, it is useful to examine labor supply in terms of the real income prospects of different population subgroups. In Figure A.2.1, for example, segment AB pertains to the poorest population subgroups. It could be described as the Malthusian range in that all household members of economically active

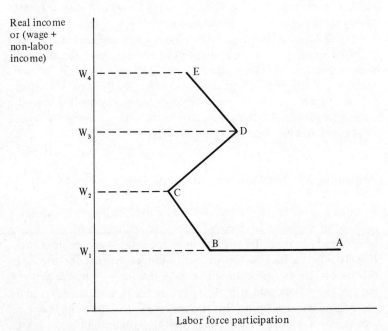

Figure A.2.1 *A secular supply curve of labor force participation*

ages must work at wage W_1 merely to survive. In the Arab world, members of such groups might include subsistence farm households in isolated rural areas. Segment BC, on the other hand, pertains to subgroups that are enjoying rapidly rising incomes (W_1 to W_2). In this case, labor force participation is represented by a backward rising zone (i.e. less labor outlay), on the assumption that tastes are changing slowly. To illustrate, imagine the isolated rural household which receives a substantial 'remittance wage' from a household member employed in a distant, relatively lucrative labor market. Within the real income range of such subgroups, consumption patterns of the household may not have changed, so that the family may send fewer of its members to the market place to work (e.g. as has been observed in agriculture in North Yemen).

Segment CD in Figure A.2.1 pertains to a middle-class subgroup that is experiencing a widening of expectations following, say, improved education, or residence in urban areas that are undergoing substantial socio-economic change. Here labor force participation is likely to increase as real income earning prospects increase because changing tastes require larger incomes to achieve greater combinations of desired goods and leisure activities. Segment DE is drawn to reflect the situation of population subgroups who are receiving artificially high incomes via non-labor income transfers, etc. In this case, the abundance of non-labor income or 'easy money' (i.e. W_3 to W_4) may reduce the motivation to work in view of the fact that income has become freely available to consume desired goods and leisure activities. When economists say that the oil-rich countries are living off a virtual rent income, an implication for the labor market is that wage or price policies may have little effect on labor supply decisions. Population subgroups corresponding to segment DE are clearly evident among the more favored classes in several oil-rich OAPEC countries.

Appendix 2.2 Analysis of the relationship between building construction and international and internal migration

The relationship between building construction and patterns of migration has been examined in two contexts. One is international, involving migration flows among several Arab countries. The other is national, involving migration flows among urban areas or provinces within countries.

Among countries in the international analysis, higher rates of residential building construction are strongly associated with larger inflows of foreign migrant labor. On average, a 10 per cent increase in the rate of residential building construction (holding all else constant) is associated with a 13 per cent increase in the rate of foreign labor immigration.

In the internal migration analysis, higher rates of residential building construction among urban sectors in Morocco, cities in Iraq, and mohafazas in Syria were also strongly and consistently correlated with rates of net migration to them.

Time series data for Bahrain and Kuwait, and evidence for Algeria, tend to be consistent with the results noted above.

International evidence: details

To my knowledge, only one study has estimated the impact of differentials in residential building construction on international migration flows among several countries (see Shaw: 1978a). This pertains to 169 migration flows among thirteen OECD countries in 1971. The elasticity of differentials in residential construction (RC) with respect to differentials in international migration was found to exceed all of the other variables considered, including distance, average wage and salary differentials, and dummy variables capturing the effects of migration policies, commonality of language, etc.[28]

While data shortcomings prevent exact replication of the OECD study for the OAPEC countries, it is possible to analyze migration to ten Arab labor importers 'j' from thirteen suppliers 'i' with respect to variations in rates of residential building. Migration from each country 'i' to 'j' (M_{ij}) is represented by the stock of non-national workers that were employed in the receiving country 'j' in 1975. M_{ij} has been normalized by expressing it as a rate per thousand labor force of the host country 'j'. Of a possible 130 country-to-country migration flows, 123 have been retained after discounting missing observations.[29]

That M_{ij} is represented as a stock rather than a flow implies that it might influence the rate of building activity (i.e. reverse causality). That is, if residential building construction (RC) and M_{ij} influence each other's behavior simultaneously, then it would be necessary to separate their interactive effects by estimating a simultaneous equations model. For the Arab context, however, it is reasonable to assume that RC is largely independent of M_{ij} for at least two reasons. First, M_{ij} pertains to a relatively short period of time as most labor force migration in the region has been a post-oil development (1973/4). In such cases, RC can be assumed to be relatively independent of migration because RC is likely to be influenced more by availability of mortgage funds, interest rates, housing grants, incomes and relative prices prior to the time of

M_{ij} than at the actual time of M_{ij} (Evans: 1969, Shaw: 1978a). Second, as most labor force migrants are denied permanent residence or citizenship, they are not likely to exert an important effect on RC through the demand for housing.

The empirical model to be estimated takes the following form;

$$1 \quad M_{ij} = f(RC_j, RC_i, X_j, X_i, u),$$

where: M_{ij} = the rate of gross migration from country 'i' to 'j'; RC_j, RC_i = rate of residential dwelling starts per thousand national labor force (not total labor force) of country 'i' or 'j'; X_j, X_i = a vector of control variables or other factors thought to influence migration; u = a randomly distributed error term with zero mean and constant variance.

Our estimation procedure makes use of a model that is linear in parameters but non-linear in variables (i.e. log-normal least squares regression). All independent variables are evaluated separately (RC_j, RC_i) rather than in ratio format (RC_j/RC_i), to allow for asymmetries in the effect of origin and destination characteristics. That is, the symmetry assumption, which restricts origin and destination characteristics to be of equal significance in the migration decision, finds little support in the literature. Judging from most econometric studies on internal migration, economic conditions at places of destination consistently out-perform those at places of origin. Allowing for asymmetries in the effects of origin and destination characteristics will permit evaluation of this finding in the Arab context as well.

Variables which have been evaluated, in addition to RC, include:

1 cost of migration, as represented by distance in airline miles between capital cities of origin and destination countries (D_{ij});
2 commonality of culture, as represented by commonality of language ($LANG_{ij}$); $LANG_{ij}$ is represented as a dummy variable with 1 = Arabic is common to both countries, 0 = otherwise;
3 extent of political freedom, as represented by a quantified measure of civil liberties (CL_j, CL_i); the scale for CL begins with 1 = most free, and ends with 7 = least free, (obtained from the series *Freedom in the World*, edited by R.D. Gastil, and published by G.H. Hall of Boston);
4 educational selectivity at places of origin (E_i), represented by the number of male students enrolled in third-level education per 100,000 population;
5 presence of governmental policies at places of origin which aim

to promote migration (PROMO$_i$); PROMO$_i$ is represented as a dummy variable with 1 = PROMO exists, 0 = otherwise.

In keeping with the literature, greater distance (D$_{ij}$) is expected to be negatively related to M$_{ij}$. Commonality of language (L$_{ij}$) is expected to exert a positive influence on M$_{ij}$ through its effects on access to information and reduction of psychic costs to relocating in a new country. Lack of civil liberties (CL) at place of possible destination is expected to have a negative effect on M$_{ij}$ for obvious reasons, whereas lack of CL at place of origin may either provoke M$_{ij}$ (as a means of escape), or restrict M$_{ij}$ if it impedes mobility or access to information on foreign opportunities. Educational selectivity (ED$_i$) is expected to have a positive effect on M$_{ij}$. This conforms with findings in a great many contexts where emigrants tend to be more educated. Finally, promotional policies at country or origin (PROMO$_i$) are expected to have a positive effect on M$_{ij}$ for obvious reasons.

Regression results are summarized in Table A.2.1. Excluding dummy or scaled variables PROMO$_i$, LANG$_{ij}$, CL$_{ij}$, the regression coefficients can be interpreted as elasticities. The difference between regressions I and II is simply that the former contains fewer control variables.

The reported elasticities and student 't' ratios (in brackets) convey

Table A.2.1 *Analysis of international labor migration to the OAPEC countries, 1975*

Independent variables	Symbol	Regression I Reg. coeff.	Regression I Student 't'	Regression II Reg. coeff.	Regression II Student 't'
Residential construction	RC$_j$	1.587	(7.25)	1.307	(6.47)
	RC$_i$	−0.532	(2.73)	0.017	(0.09)[a]
Cost of migration	D$_{ij}$	−2.741	(10.70)	−2.338	(10.03)
Language commonality	LANG$_{ij}$	0.619	(1.42)[a]	1.620	(3.61)
Civil liberties	CL$_j$	·	·	−0.617	(3.28)
	CL$_i$	·	·	−0.820	(3.31)
Educational selectivity	ED$_i$	·	·	0.317	(2.35)
Promotional policies	PROMO$_i$	·	·	0.356	(0.62)[a]
Constant		15.828		19.177	
F ratio		40.746		33.584	
R^2		0.566		0.702	
Sample size		(N = 123)		(N = 123)	

a signifies not statistically significant at the 0.01 level or better.

the following. First, variations in residential construction at places of destination (RC_j) exert a strong positive effect on M_{ij}. As an influence in Arab inter-country migration, RC is second only to distance. While RC_i exhibits a significant negative effect in regression I, it is not significant in regression II. Moreover, the coefficient of RC_i in regression I is far smaller than for RC_j. Thus, in keeping with empirical findings on internal migration, economic opportunities at places of destination seem to out-perform those at origin.

Second, most of our 'control variables' perform as expected. Distance (D_{ij}) exhibits a strong negative effect and its coefficient remains relatively constant in both regressions I and II. Commonality of language ($LANG_{ij}$) exhibits the expected positive effect though it is statistically significant only in regression II. As expected, lack of civil liberties at place of destination (CL_j) exhibits a negative effect on M_{ij}. Futhermore, higher values of CL at place of origin (CL_i) exert a statistically significant negative effect on M_{ij} as well. This implies that lack of CL at place of origin may restrict M_{ij} for the reasons suggested above. Education has the expected positive effect on M_{ij} implying that countries with more educated members produce more migrants. Finally, PROMO carries the expected sign but is not statistically significant, implying that government promotional policies had a negligable impact on M_{ij} during the period under study.

Needless to say, the predictive capacity of our expanded regression is highly satisfactory at $R^2 = 0.70$. Moreover, an analysis of residuals provides no indication of heteroscedasticity meaning that the error term is more likely to be attributable to randomly distributed errors than neglect of an important variable.

Time series evidence

Another means of evaluating the construction:migration relationship is to incorporate the 'business cycle' approach pioneered by Brinley Thomas (1973). For example, drawing on Thomas's time series data between 1968 and 1911, I regressed migration from the UK to the USA against (i) US residential building activity (RC^{us}; positive effect hypothesized) and (ii) UK residential building activity (RC^{uk}; negative effect hypothesized).[30] Constant elasticities for RC^{us} and RC^{uk} were observed to be 0.76 and −0.75 respectively (though RC^{uk} was barely statistically significant at the 0.10 level). As observed in Thomas's own graphic analysis, construction cycles are clearly significant to understanding variations in migration between continents.

While time series data on the OAPEC countries are extremely scarce, the experience of Bahrain between 1971 and 1977, and that of Kuwait between 1967 and 1976, testify to the impact of construction on immigration. In the case of Bahrain, Figure A.2.2 charts increases in

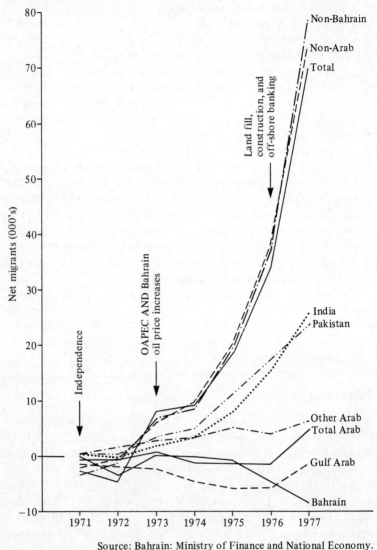

Source: Bahrain: Ministry of Finance and National Economy.

Figure A.2.2 *Cumulative net migration in Bahrain by major events and population groups, 1971–7*

net migration that first accompanied the jump in oil prices and then the boom in construction. In the former case, 10,000 net migrants, attracted largely by employment in petroleum-related activity, entered Bahrain in 1973 and 1974. By mid-1975 and then by 1977, however, cumulative net migrants jumped to 40,000, then to 70,000 following rapid expansion of construction employment.

Kuwait offers an interesting example of the kind of impact that low-income housing might have on migrants. Toward redistributing wealth, the Kuwaiti government commenced a low-income housing program for resident Kuwaitis (including Arabs able to secure Kuwaiti citizenship). Between 1969–70 and 1975–6, government activity in this program was at least double that of any other year during the decade. Correspondingly, resident permits more than doubled during these years from a 'usual' 30,000 to 74,000–100,000. The correlation between construction of low-income housing units and issuance of resident permits during the decade is $r^2 = 0.56$, elasticity at 0.5. These findings are particularly significant in view of the fact that neither yearly changes in oil revenues nor per capita government expenditures correlate significantly with variations in resident permits issued. As other OAPEC countries have offered low-income housing to their nationals as well, this factor could be construed as an important 'missing' variable in the regression analysis above.

Internal evidence: details

In many respects the relationship between building construction among urban areas, and differentials in migration to those areas, has already been summarized for Canada, the USA, UK, USSR, Israel and Brazil by Shaw (1980a). The study on Canadian urban migration is particularly relevant here as variations in urban residential construction were found to be highly correlated not only with the distribution of indigenous migrants among urban areas, but with the internal distribution of recent international migrants as well (see Shaw: 1974b).

Turning to the Arab countries, I found that levels of residential construction were highly correlated with rates of net migration ($r^2 = 0.78$) to the urban sector of eleven governates of Morocco (1960–70).[31] The elasticity was 0.5. In an analysis of net migration to seven cities in Iraq (1970), similar results were found using 'value of city residential construction' as the explanatory variable ($r^2 = 0.70$). However, the elasticity was considerably higher at 1.75.

For Syria (1970), I examined rates of in-migration to the urban centers of twelve mohafazas, specific to four population age groups. My explanatory variables included 'proportion of the urban labor force in construction' (CL) and 'allocation of government development funds per capita to the urban center' (GF) as well as measures of urban unemployment and manufacturing wages. Results of this inquiry are particularly interesting in view of the large share of urban development funds that go to public works, which in turn employ a large share of construction labor. Only CL and GF were statistically significant with elasticities of 0.77 and 0.22, respectively. I also examined the role of CL and GF in accounting for inter-urban life-time migration flows among the twelve mohafazas. Results tend to corroborate the findings reported above. CL was again statistically significant with elasticity of 1.16.[32]

Stock should also be taken of the bold efforts in Algeria to absorb surplus labor and curb rural–urban migration since restrictions were placed on emigration. 'Building and public works' have served as the leading sector by providing 38 per cent of new employment growth between 1970 and 1976. As reported by Bénachenhou (1978), this activity has been planned to influence growth of rural employment and migration with the result that (i) rates of migration to the coastal cities have fallen by 33 per cent and (ii) the share of total city population retained in the interior cities has increased from 51.5 per cent in 1966 to 52.5 per cent in 1973 (see also Sari: 1979). To an extent, employment in 'building and public works' has served a similar function in Tunisia. In 1975, 61,500 were employed in this sector as a means of reducing disparities in rural housing and services, creating non-farm jobs and reducing rural emigration (Tunisia, CMRADR: 1979).

Finally, the government of Bahrain has been successful in using low-income housing programs to redistribute Bahraini nationals to new outlying suburbs, and to promote population growth in some of its traditional villages (Al-Hamer: 1978).

Chapter 3

Energizing traditional agriculture

Introduction

Arab agriculture faces two major challenges over the next twenty years. First, food demand will double as rapid population growth produces an additional 133 million Arabs by the year 2000.[1] Currently, food requirements are being met in eighteen of twenty Arab countries only because huge imports have been financed by petro-dollars, grants-in-aid or government subsidies. For the region as a whole, food imports rose by more than 75 per cent between 1970 and 1978. During the same period, the ratio of agricultural imports to exports grew five-fold, and dollar values of vegetable and animal imports quadrupled. The oil-rich countries imported 22 times more than they exported in 1977, resulting in an agricultural trade deficit of some US $2,990 million. The oil-poor countries imported 1.9 times more than they exported, resulting in a deficit of some US $1,600 million. Policy-makers are particularly anxious to reduce dependency on such imports in view of their vulnerability to high commodity prices and fears that trade arrangements may be disrupted by international tensions.[2]

Second, traditional agriculture must be integrated more fully into the mainstream of modernization. Subsistence farmers, pastoralists and landless workers represent some 14 million out of 19.6 million agricultural workers. In most countries, the majority of these workers are employed on tiny holdings of between 0.5 and 2.5 hectares, their productivity is low, and the transportation and marketing of their cash crops is poorly developed. As a result, disparities in incomes between rural and urban areas are wide (Table 3.1). Moreover, population growth and the inability of fragmented holdings to absorb additional family members are exacerbating poverty conditions by adding to the

Table 3.1 *Rural/urban income disparities, selected Arab countries, 1950–78*

Country	Period (1)	Rural/urban measure (2)	Rural/ urban ratio (3)	Source (4)
Oil-rich				
Kuwait	1972	Avg. monthly $ of ag. workers/urban service workers	0.52	Kuwait: WCARRD (1978)
Iraq	1971 1978	Yearly cash $ of ag. laborer/ industrial worker basic yearly income	0.67 0.53	Issa (1979) MEED (1979)
UAE	1978	Ag. worker/urban laborer basic wage	0.79	UAE (1978)
Oil-poor				
Algeria	1968 1978	Ag. worker/industrial worker basic monthly wage	0.44 0.50	Bénachenhou (1978) Nelson (1978)
Egypt	1958/9 1964/5 1974/5	Rural/urban average total family expenditures	0.55 0.62 0.61	Egypt: WCARRD (1978)
Mauritania	1970	Rural/urban per capita income	0.07	Shaw (1978b)
Morocco	1960 1971	Rural/urban per capita income	0.59 0.45	Nelson (1978) Salmi (1978)
Tunisia	1975	Rural/urban % hhlds with per capita income US $116 +	0.33	ILO files
Sudan	1967/8	Rural/urban average yearly household income	0.36	ILO files
Yemen AR	1975	Rural/urban per capita income	0.24	Shaw (1978b)
Egypt	1958/9 1964/5 1974/5	% rural families below official poverty line[a]	35 27 44	Radwan (1977)
Morocco	1975	% rural families below official poverty line[a]	44	ILO files
Somalia	1970	% rural and nomadic families below official poverty line[a]	70	Shaw (1978b)

Note: a Estimated expenditures needed to assure minimum diet, assuming that two-thirds are spent on food.

stock of landless workers. Landless workers range anywhere from 15 per cent of all *farm* household heads in Algeria to 58 per cent in Egypt and the Sudan. Most are seasonally employed at low wage rates. In the predominantly rural-agricultural economies of Mauritania, Somalia, the Sudan and the two Yemens, the increase in the number of landless workers is necessitating the creation of some 1 million new rural jobs by 1985. This is alarming in view of surveys revealing that rates of rural underemployment have been hovering around 20 to 40 per cent in these countries (Shaw: 1978b). Rural–urban migration is hardly welcome as an escape-valve because unemployment in most Arab cities is already high and migration has been depleting the rural labor force of its youngest, most educated workers.[3]

Policy-makers concede that possibilities of augmenting future food production are tied irrevocably to problems confronting the traditional farmer.[4] Accordingly, most governments have aligned themselves with agricultural development strategies which focus on the poor. Excluding Bahrain, Kuwait, Qatar and the United Arab Emirates, where agriculture represents a small proportion of the labor force (see Appendix 3.1), and funds for investment are enormous, virtually every national development plan incorporates some semblance of the World Bank's 'rural development strategy'. Essentially, this is a production-oriented approach which seeks to provide the necessary and sufficient conditions for achieving productivity increases and real income growth among the poor. To a lesser extent, governments have also adopted the 'basic needs' policy as promoted by the International Labour Organization. Essentially, this is a consumer-oriented approach which aims to provide the necessary conditions for survival through gainful employment. In short, most Arab economies, regardless of unevenness in population size, gross national product, level of development, resource endowments or structure of agriculture, have one thing in common. They have publicly expressed a commitment to alleviate poverty among the majority of their agricultural population.

The first part of this chapter reviews and evaluates this commitment in terms of three major policy interventions. These include agrarian reform, land reclamation and resettlement schemes, and large-scale irrigation and mechanization. This is followed by a brief synopsis of related public expenditures on agriculture. The message of this review is inescapable. Mismanagement of agricultural planning in the past has resulted in failure to ameliorate income and employment in traditional agriculture, incomplete agrarian reform, and 'urban bias' in the allocation of development expenditures.

The policy directives that I have in mind aim at improving employment, labor productivity and equality of economic well-being via (i) modernization of small-scale farming, (ii) expansion of non-farm employment opportunities for the landless and marginal worker, and (iii) encouragement of various facets of agricultural potential that have remained underdeveloped due to neglect or oversight. My approach complements the 'basic needs' or 'integrated rural development' concepts in so far as it advocates a multipronged attack at the grass roots level. I hope to convince the reader that diversionary paths typical of the last ten years have simply delayed the necessity of committing development funds to the integration of the small-scale farmer into the mainstream of modernization.

Major approaches

Attempts to overcome poverty in most Arab countries are visible in the pursuit of one or more of three major approaches. First, wide-scale agrarian reform and development of cooperatives preceded the oil boom in countries exhibiting relatively good agricultural potential. Second, land reclamation and resettlement schemes have been implemented as both pre- and post-oil interventions. For the most part, these have been carried out in the oil-poor countries, though several endeavors accompanying costly irrigation and desalination projects have been undertaken recently in the oil-rich countries. Third, large-scale irrigation/mechanization schemes are predominantly a post-oil development. Over the last seven years, they have been widely publicized in oil-poor and oil-rich countries alike. Expectations of massive bilateral aid have fuelled hopes that these schemes will rescue traditional agriculture in the future.

Unfortunately each approach has enjoyed far less success than was initially expected. Lack of commitment has been the dehabilitating factor in some cases. In others, professional excitement in government ministries over the scale and cost of these schemes has worked to shift attention away from the 'plight of the masses'. A review of each approach helps pinpoint where they went wrong and where their future potential may lie.

Agrarian reform
Between 1958 and 1966, land redistribution and agrarian reform were initiated in Egypt, Iraq, Morocco and Syria. South Yemen, Libya, Tunisia and Algeria followed between 1968 and 1972. In most cases, the Egyptian model served as the blueprint for action. This involved two elements: redistribution of land held by large estates, and organization of beneficiaries into cooperatives.

Though many of the reforms got off to a slow start, most have attained their legislated goals or are in the completion phase. Table 3.2

summarizes accomplishments up to 1978. The symbol 'ns' signifies that land redistribution is not a significant issue, whereas 'no reform' signifies that Jordan and North Yemen have not undertaken land redistribution programs.[5]

In terms of their impact on employment or equality, the reforms cannot be hailed as a success.[6] First, redistributed land was less than 20 per cent of the total arable land base in five of the eight countries (Table 3.2, column 5).[7] In Iraq, Algeria, Morocco and Tunisia, the reforms were largely confined to the redistribution of huge tracts of land which were inherited upon independence rather than the usurping of private land in the hands of nationals. In the case of Egypt, 5.4 per cent of the owners still held 45 per cent of the land by 1970. The average size of the 'large' holdings was 7.3 hectares versus 0.8 for the remaining 95 per cent. In Syria, confiscation was limited to large landholdings of 100 hectares or more. Some 38 per cent of the farms of 10 to 100 hectares in size were untouched, meaning that the reform merely increased the representation of farmers in the 'less than 10 hectare' category. And in Iraq, the old landlords have actually retained the most productive plots (Hummadi: 1978).

Second, in six of the eight countries, beneficiaries represent a mere 1.0 to 18.3 per cent of the total agricultural households (Table 3.2, column 6). Landless peasants have been largely excluded by legislative neglect or because of the sheer size of their numbers. In Egypt, an initial reduction in the concentration of landholders between 1958 and 1965 gave way to a subsequent rise in concentration because (i) land distribution was limited to previous tenants and small farmers, and (ii) later reforms did not distribute land rights to the growing number of landless peasants.[8] In the relatively aggressive Algerian reform, only a small proportion of the potential beneficiaries were satisfied in the 'modern sector' while little was done for the landless peasants in the traditional sector (Kielstra: 1978). Similarly, redistribution of land to descendants of original private holders or occupants neglected landless peasants in Morocco and Tunisia.[9] In short, land reform in the Arab world cannot claim to have had a significant impact on income inequality. Rather, critics of the reforms contend that redistribution of land to a few has created a relatively small class of middle-income agriculturalists.[10]

This is not to say, however, that land reform has been entirely in vain. By undermining the era of large and often absentee landholders, some 800,000 families have been given a chance to extract a better living from the land. Reductions in the concentration of landholdings

Table 3.2 *Assessment of land reform programs, Arab countries, 1952–78*

Countries	Year begun (1)	Redistributed land up to 1978					Effectiveness of reform in reaching institutional goals (7)	Impact on equality in agriculture (8)
		Hectares (000's) (2)	Beneficiaries (000's) (3)	Average hectares per beneficiary (4)	As a % of total arable land (5)	Beneficiaries as % of total agricultural households (6)		
Oil-rich								
Bahrain	ns[a]							
Iraq	1958	1,152	223	5.2	15.5	41.3	Moderate	Moderate
Kuwait	ns							
Libya	1970	71	5	14.2	2.9	3.4	High	Negligible
Oman	ns							
Saudi Arabia	ns							
UAE	ns							

Oil-poor

Algeria	1972	1,538	130	11.8	22.3	18.3	High	Moderate
Egypt	1958	1,048	342	3.1	36.1	10.7	Moderate	Small
Jordan	no reform							
Lebanon	ns							
Mauritania	ns							
Morocco	1957	335	24	13.9	4.5	1.0	Low	Negligible
Somalia	ns							
Sudan	ns							
Syria	1958	1,150	54	13.0	12.7	18.0	Moderate	Moderate
Tunisia	1971	558	75	7.4	18.6	23.0	High	Moderate
Yemen AR	no reform							
Yemen PDR	1958	126	31	4.1	54.8	11.2	High	Small

Sources: FAO, 'Country Review Papers' for the World Agrarian Reform Conference (Rome: United Nations, Food and Agricultural Organization, Mimeo, Restricted), *Middle East and North Africa* (1979/80), Griffen (1975), Kielstra (1978), Radwan (1977), Tuma (1970), Askari and Cummings (1976), national statistical yearbooks and agricultural censuses.

Note: a ns: not a significant issue.

have slightly ameliorated production in Egypt and Syria (Askari *et al.* 1977; Keilany: 1980), income inequality in Egypt (Radwan: 1977), and problems of rural emigration in Iraq (Al-Jomard: 1979). Several thousand cooperatives have also organized small farms into more viable purchasing and marketing agents, and provided desperately needed credit, new inputs and extension services. Between 1961 and 1975, they were largely responsible for augmenting tractor and fertilizer use in the Arab world from approximately 153,000 to 407,000 units and from 641,000 to 2,135,000 tons (more on co-operatives later).

With a renewed commitment to equalizing the distribution of land and credit, these beginnings could be pushed a great deal further. According to the latest round of agricultural censuses, relatively large farms still hold disproportionate shares of arable land. For example, in Syria, 2.5 per cent of the relatively large farms (say, in excess of 50 hectares) hold 29 per cent of the arable land; in Algeria 2.2 per cent hold 47 per cent; in Tunisia 4.6 per cent hold 46 per cent; in Morocco 2.5 per cent hold 27 per cent; in Jordan 8.7 per cent hold 54 per cent; in Iraq 1.8 per cent hold 26 per cent; in Sudan 1.8 per cent hold 15 per cent; in Kuwait 3.1 per cent hold 37 per cent; and in Lebanon 0.2 per cent hold 15 per cent.[11] In Egypt, 12 per cent of the land is still held by only 0.2 per cent of the farms and, with 46 per cent of the total land being rented, the reign of the absentee landlord may again be visible.

Further redistribution could go a long way toward increasing the average size of smallholdings. In Tunisia, redistribution of land on the largest holdings could boost the average size of smallholders who represent 64.3 per cent of all farms from 4.3 to 16.0 hectares. This would compare favorably with an average farm size of 16.4 hectares among 31 per cent of Tunisian farmers in the medium size category (i.e. between 10 and 50 hectares). In Algeria, the average farm size of smallholders who represent 79.2 per cent of all farms could be boosted from 2.7 hectares to 9 hectares. This compares with an average farm size of 16.6 hectares among 19 per cent of Algeria's farmers in the 10 to 50 hectare category. Similar results obtain for Iraq, and for Jordan (which has not undertaken a major reform).

Reclamation and resettlement
The concept of 'reclamation and resettlement' won approval in view of large gaps between cultivated land and soils that have the potential of being arable.[12] For example, the amount of potentially cultivable land divided by actual cultivable land in the five poorest Arab economies is

15.3 for the Sudan, 6.8 for Somalia, 13.3 for North Yemen, 2.9 for South Yemen and 7.6 for Mauritania. In Egypt, reclamation and resettlement is perceived as the sole most important ingredient for long-term survival in view of extreme shortages of arable land per capita. In the Sudan, this approach was expected to stimulate employment and productivity to the point that Sudanese agriculture might serve as the bread-basket for the entire Arab world.

As reclamation and resettlement is a long-term process, it is understandable that details on costs, returns and rates of implementation show slowly. For this reason, convincing arguments in favor of reclamation and resettlement during the late 1960s and early 1970s easily prevailed over the doubts of its adversaries. But, alas, estimates of costs and returns are beginning to emerge with rather discouraging policy ramifications.

In terms of cost, reclamation and resettlement schemes have been two to five times greater than anticipated. Costs in the arid climates of the Middle East and North Africa are considerably greater than in other regions. Per capita costs of reclamation and resettlement in the Sudan and Egypt were between four and ten times those of other African countries.[13] While financing is much less of a constraint among the oil-rich countries, cost estimates of approximately $6,200 per reclaimed hectare and $5,700 per capita in new settlements in capital-rich Saudi Arabia have been sufficiently high to warrant a go-slow approach.[14]

In terms of implementation problems, reclamation and resettlement schemes have encountered endless difficulties with the result that employment and income benefits have been very slow to materialize. To illustrate this point, 300,000 beneficiaries were to be settled on 494,000 hectares resulting from the High Dam water in Egypt. This was to be accomplished by 1970. As time crept on, however, the area target dropped by 31 per cent to 342,000 hectares, of which only 60 per cent were reclaimed by 1970. Further, only 35,290 hectares were settled (17 per cent of the reclaimed land), by 26,000 families (9 per cent of the planned beneficiaries). Between 1971 and 1976, only 9,160 additional hectares were reclaimed and the total number of beneficiaries rose from 26,000 to a rather insignificant 35,000.[15] This is similar to the experience in sub-Sahara Africa (e.g. Nigeria, Zambia, Rhodesia and Ghana). Moreover, incomes have taken a much longer period of time to improve than was anticipated. Wazzan (1975) shows that productivity per unit of land rose slowly on small, resettled farms in Egypt and took about ten years to attain viable growth rates.

Finally, reclamation and resettlement schemes have been undermined by a lack of motivation on the part of beneficiaries. Such complaints are almost universal in the literature. Planners responsible for reclamation and resettlement have failed to appreciate that settlement work requires a good deal of civil and social engineering in the form of layout, dwelling design, roads and irrigation schemes. This is evident in Egypt where difficulty was encountered in obtaining the response and initiative among the newly settled Nubians on the Upper Nile. In forced settlement, as in the Nubian case, the displaced people felt little or no responsibility to achieve adjustment in their new setting because they had merely been 'dumped into it'. The Sudanese approach in the Gezira and Mangel almost avoided popular involvement from the start. The tight grip by officials from outside the region was only gradually loosened as village councils were established in later years to permit the tenants to have a say in the management of their agricultural affairs (Higgs: 1978).

Summing up, reclamation and resettlement schemes have had a limited impact on rural poverty. The future looks bleak if only because the frightening worldwide escalation of costs will probably prohibit such schemes in places where they are needed most.[16]

Large-scale mechanization

Most national development plans have favored large-scale irrigation and mechanization schemes. On the one hand, a preference for dams and extensive irrigation systems has been motivated by a shortage of rain-fed land and the extremities of climate. On the other hand, a preference for large-scale mechanization is an outgrowth of (i) professional commitment to Western or communist models concerned with economies of scale, (ii) the belief that highly organized agri-business or state farms are necessary to enhance worker motivation, employment and productivity, and (iii) government desires to provide highly visible exceptions to the rule of sluggish or diminishing returns to effort on small, traditional holdings.

Much has been made of the productivity augmenting and export benefits to be had from large-scale mechanization. Students of growth underline successes, as measured by rapid productivity increases among a narrow range of export commodities. They rightly contend that these developments can hardly be attributed to traditional agriculture. In contrast, students of development see little improvement, as measured by negligible employment augmenting effects, and the persistence of gross income inequalities and poverty among the masses. They raise the question, 'Economies of scale, yes, but who benefits?'

While empirical impressions on this issue may be preliminary, they tend to convey the feeling that the bias toward 'bigness' leaves much to be desired. First, it is a fact that development funding has been channelled disproportionately into large-scale dams, irrigation and mechanized farming on the perimeter of urban centers. These funds have favored the most prosperous farming areas and a rather small class of middle-income agriculturalists. In Morocco, 60 per cent of the agricultural funds in the 1968 to 1972 plan went directly to such ends. During the 1973 to 1977 plan, investments in the more prosperous irrigated/mechanized areas were three times those in the traditional 'bour'. Yet the bour produced 68 per cent of the total agricultural output, represented 87 per cent of the total land and employed 72 per cent of the labor force.[17] In' the Sudan, the emphasis on large-scale irrigation/mechanization between 1962 and 1971, and a disproportionate allocation of funds to the relatively prosperous East Central Sudan between 1970 and 1975, worked to the virtual neglect of traditional farmers who cultivated 63 per cent of the land. At the extreme, the Southern and Red Sea Provinces, with 23.7 per cent of the rural population, received only 0.3 per cent of the total development funds between 1971 and 1976.[18] In Algeria, investments in the 'sector autogere' generated five times more employment on the fringe of the two largest cities, Algiers and Oran, than in the predominantly rural areas (Bénachenhou: 1978).

Second, large-scale mechanization has fallen far short of its employment expectations. In Algeria, the 'sector autogere' employed only 0.105 workers per arable hectare versus 0.340 for the private, largely traditional sector. Further, increased mechanization resulted in a decline in permanent and total workers from approximately 174,000 and 276,000, respectively, in 1970 to 121,300 and 237,000, respectively, in 1973.[19] In the Sudan, mechanization in the Rahad area and Northern Provinces displaced traditional cultivators and livestock farming without compensating the displaced. Estimated employment effects for seasonal workers were far overstated at between 240 and 335 seasonal workers per 1,000 hectares. Realized employment was only 120 to 170. In Algeria, performance of the 'sector autogere' was even worse at 50 workers per 1,000 hectares. Similar complaints have been made against mechanization in Tunisia (Tunisia, CMRADR: 1979), Morocco (CMRADR: 1979) and Somalia (ILO: 1977a).

Third, by favoring prosperous areas and failing to augment employment, investments in large-scale mechanization may actually be working to increase income inequality. In Algeria, improved productivity on large-scale farms has worked against the relative incomes of temporary workers by boosting incomes of permanent workers disproportionately (Bénachenhou: 1978). In the Rahad area of Sudan, mechanization of cotton holdings increased the income of a handful of farmers while resulting disequalibria in the supply and demand for seasonal workers were used to exploit a 'cheap source of labor'. This led to unemployment and a deterioration of incomes for the landless. Further, in the Habila mechanized farming scheme in Southern Kordofan, 89 per cent of the farm profits were channelled into urban rather than rural areas (Affan and Olsson: 1978).[20] Also, since large-scale mechanization utilizes large inputs of capital, a considerable portion of gains from higher productivity tend to be channelled to urban suppliers. Again, this conflicts with goals of diffusing gains locally. Similar claims against the effects of large-scale mechanization on income inequality apply to Morocco (Griffen: 1975), Tunisia (Tunisia, CMRADR: 1979) and Libya (Allan: 1973).

Summing up, preference for large-scale mechanization is at the heart of a controversy over preferred ways to transform Arab agriculture.[21] By opting for mechanization around big cities because of the inherent difficulties of doing something effective in the traditional sector, planners have unknowingly fed prosperous areas and failed to make inroads into isolated rural areas. With marginal effects on employment, small improvements in productivity per worker or per hectare over small farms, and relatively miniscule investment of profits in rural areas, large-scale mechanized schemes may even be subject to the same kinds of criticisms that were leveled at large landowners during the pre-reform era.

Public expenditures

In view of the problems noted above, agriculture has been assured a higher priority in the allocation of national development funds. Moreover, policy-makers concede that meagre investments during the 1971 to 1976 round of national development plans were partially responsible for widespread failure to attain targeted agricultural growth rates in most countries.[22] Has this assurance fostered larger commitments during more recent rounds of national development plans?

Unfortunately, allocations of public expenditures for agriculture showed little improvement in most countries during the 1976 to 1981 plan period (excluding Libya, Somalia, Sudan and South Yemen). In toto, only 8.7 per cent of all Arab development funds were allocated to agriculture during this period though it employed no less than one-half of the entire Arab labor force (Table 3.3). For all countries combined, this amounted to $219 per year per agricultural worker versus $2,583 per non-agricultural worker. Among the oil-poor countries, most of which are largely agricultural, public expenditures per agricultural worker were only 17.4 per cent of those of non-agricultural workers. In Egypt, with a myriad of problems confronting traditional agriculture, some 5.5 million workers, representing 50 per cent of Egypt's labor force and 29 per cent of the total Arab agricultural labor force, were allocated only $110 per head compared with $1,014 per non-agricultural worker. The commitment to agriculture in this troubled country actually dropped from 17.5 per cent between 1969 and 1970 to a befuddling 8.6 per cent between 1975 and 1980.

In most countries, planned allocations during the 1981 to 1986 round of national development plans appear to comply with priorities set out during the previous plan period. For example, allocations to agriculture will be approximately 1 per cent in Saudi Arabia, 16 per cent in Libya, 12 per cent in Algeria, 10 per cent in Jordan, 14 per cent in Tunisia, 15 per cent in South Yemen and 17 per cent in Syria.[23] For the region as a whole, less than 10 per cent of all development funds will be allocated to agriculture over the five-year period.

It is important to acknowledge that intersectoral comparisons of funding could be misleading in so far as non-agricultural allocations often carry over into the rural agricultural community.[24] This applies particularly to expenditures on health, education and physical infrastructure which are intended to serve the entire population. However, the story does not end here. The figures above pertain to planned investments only. Implementation rates are another matter. Most Arab countries also fare poorly in their implementation of agricultural investments. Moreover, rates of realized investments have been typically lower for agriculture than for other sectors. In Iraq, the ratio of realized to planned investments was 1.4 times higher for non-agricultural than for agricultural investments. In Morocco, this ratio was 1.45 times higher in the mechanized sector than in traditional farming. Ratios of realized to planned investments in agriculture *per se* were only 43 per cent in Algeria between 1966 and 1974, 66 per cent in the Sudan between 1970 and 1977, 50 per cent in Iraq between 1973 and 1975, 71 per cent in Jordan in 1977, and 55 per cent in Syria in 1980.[25]

Of course, financial commitments to agriculture must also take stock of major Arab funding agencies. These agencies are particularly important as they hold the promise of massive transfers of aid from the

Table 3.3 *Labor force in agriculture and average yearly development plan expenditures on agriculture, Arab countries, 1976–81*

Groups	Labor force agriculture (000's) (1)	(%) (2)	% share on agriculture (3)	Development plan expenditures		
				Average yearly expenditure per agricultural worker (US $) (4)	Average yearly expenditure per non-agricultural worker (US $) (5)	Ratio (5)/(4) (6)
ARAB WORLD	19,638	53	8.7	219	2,583	11.8
Oil-rich	3,026	45	6.1	712	9,171	12.9
Oil-poor	16,612	55	15.5	129	740	5.7
COUNTRIES						
Oil-rich						
Bahrain	3[a]	6	1.6	2,000	7,829	3.9
Iraq	1,198	43	18.3	672	2,268	3.4
Kuwait	6	2	0.1	3,767	9,865	2.6
Libya	150	22	16.0	6,560	9,732	1.5
Oman	152	63	1.2	47	6,511	138.5
Qatar	2	4	2.5	6,033	8,404	1.4
Saudi Arabia	1,502	63	1.5	174	19,545	112.3
UAE	13	5	2.4	5,446	22,275	4.1

Oil-poor

Algeria	1,337	35	14.0	191	636	3.3
Egypt	4,896	51	8.6	110	1,014	9.2
Jordan[c]	117	28	15.0	657	1,455	2.2
Lebanon	97	13[b]	na	na	na	na
Mauritania	388	84	na	na	na	na
Morocco	2,475	53	19.4	99	463	4.7
Somalia	1,038	83	36.6	43	372	8.7
Sudan	3,510	78	31.2	67	553	8.3
Syria	896	49	23.3	598	1,885	3.2
Tunisia	731	43	11.6	318	1,827	5.7
Yemen AR	869	76	15.8	73	1,243	17.0
Yemen PDR	258	62	27.7	47	202	4.3

Sources: National statistical yearbooks, agricultural census, national development plans and budgets of ministries of planning or finance.
Notes: a Permanent active labor force as estimated by Ministry of Planning, 1979.
          b Estimate.
          c East Bank.
          na signifies no information.

Organization of Arab Petroleum Exporting Countries (OAPEC), to the oil-poor countries. Again, however, commitments to agriculture take a poor second place to non-agricultural investments. Between 1977 and 1980, the three largest bilateral agencies, the Kuwait Fund for Arab Economic Development, the Saudi Arabia Development Fund, and the Abu Dhabi Fund for Arab Economic Development earmarked only 18.7, 17.1 and 11 per cent, respectively, of their loan commitments to agriculture. While the largest multilateral fund, the Arab Fund for Economic and Social Development, sought to provide an exception with its 1979 policy shift to improve traditional agriculture in the poorest Arab countries, its effectiveness has been curtailed by a lack of increased financial support by its largest subscribers (Kuwait, Saudi Arabia and Libya). The problem here appears to be a political one. Several governments have reduced their commitment to multilateral agencies in favor of bilateral vehicles where their generosity is more visible and clearly aligned with their political interests. For agriculture, this means that financial commitments by the oil-rich OAPEC countries to the Arab Authority for Investment and Development (founded 1976) and the International Fund for Agricultural Development (1977, Rome) are comparatively small.[26]

Summing up, national plan commitments and existing vehicles for interregional aid would appear to be in need of a major overhaul if goals of augmenting food production and waging the war on poverty are to be taken seriously. At present, several Arab governments are repeating a pattern typical of less developed countries in general: they are neglecting their agricultural sector financially.

Policy directives

Thus far, I have sought to convey the view that seemingly intractable problems will surely persist in most Arab countries unless governments launch a program of massive intervention. How else could manpower planners possibly accommodate a burgeoning rural youth, or incomes that barely meet subsistence levels? To my mind, a program of massive intervention would require no less than the modernization of traditional agriculture.

By 'modernizing traditional agriculture', I do not mean extending mechanized farming or expanding tillage into traditional areas to obtain rapid increases in the area sown for export crops. Rather, my emphasis is on boosting production of existing, traditional farm or pastoral units by (i) greater investment in fertilizers and high-yielding varieties,

(ii) organizing unviable units to permit optimal control of pests, use of irrigation and crop rotation, (iii) improving watering holes, grazing rights and health facilities for livestock, (iv) vastly improving facilities for credit, storage, transport, marketing and food processing, (v) greater attention to the development of human capital, (vi) encouragement of off-farm employment opportunities, and (vi) abolition of unfair wage and price controls.

The balance of this chapter elaborates these points by reviewing ten policy interventions of potential benefit to small-scale farmers or pastoralists in most Arab countries.

High-yielding varieties

The most popular vehicle for boosting productivity on traditionally cultivated lands is widespread promotion of high-yielding varieties. The adoption of high-yielding varieties in North Yemen doubled yields per acre for a variety of crops (Table 3.4). Various experiments with a high-yielding variety of Tunisian durum wheat promise a 16 to 25 per cent increase over old wheat varieties with technical neutrality of inputs (Gafsi and Roe: 1979).[27] Experiments with high-yielding variety Mexican wheats also produced yields far in excess of traditional 'soft wheats' (Purvis: 1976).

Yet, in most countries, the application of high-yielding varieties remains much more prevalent among large-scale farms than traditional holdings. In North Yemen, for example, crops dominated by mechanized farming comprise only high-yielding varieties, whereas crops more typical of traditional holdings comprise only 15 to 40 per

Table 3.4 *Returns to high-yielding varieties, North Yemen*

| | Yields per acre | | % of total |
Crop	Without high-yielding variety (1)	With high-yielding variety (2)	area under high-yielding variety (3)
Cotton	600–800 lb	1,400 lb	100
Tomato	4.0 tons	8.0 tons	100
Potato	1.0 tons	6.0 tons	100
Wheat	0.6 tons	1.2 tons	43
Maize	0.8 tons	2.0 tons	20
Sorghum	0.5 tons	1.0 tons	15

Source: Yemen AR Country Review Paper, World Conference on Agrarian Reform (Rome: Food and Agricultural Organization, 1979, Mimeo, Restricted).

cent of high-yielding varieties (see Table 3.4, column 3). This is in keeping with criticisms of the 'green revolution' where the biological (genetic) and physical (culture, fertilizers, water) innovations have been found to be insufficient, as the 'revolution' has essentially benefited the larger, well-to-do farmer.[28]

Possibly, the prevalence of high-yielding varieties on larger farms stems from the implausible idea that biological and chemical technologies should be characterized by scale economies. While certain factors may act to produce a minimally efficient size for traditional farms, it is also true that inputs characterizing high-yielding varieties are perfectly divisible and are equally suited for use by small farms.[29] Most important in applying high-yielding varieties is good management over water, seedbed preparation, seedling rates, date of planting, rate and time of fertilizing and weed control. High-yielding varieties are appreciably more sensitive to these carefully exercised controls. Without them, local varieties may actually outperform the high-yielding varieties. Of course, in selecting an appropriate high-yielding variety, preference should also be given to the most technically neutral variety. This will ensure that farmers with poor factor endowments and aversion to risk will not be detracted from using high-yielding varieties by costly fertilizer requirements, etc.

It is also important to concede that inadequate research on appropriate high-yielding varieties is a major bottleneck hindering growth of productivity in the traditional sector. Agricultural technology tends to be location specific, not only regarding its biological and physical components, but its economic and social ones as well.[30] The development of modern, more efficient technology in other countries (mostly in the West) has been, by and large, unsuitable without appropriate modifications to the widely varying agro-climatic and socio-economic conditions of the Arab region. This point is apparent in the sluggish acceptance of Mexican high-yielding varieties in the Maghreb countries. Though the Mexican varieties were relatively good performers, traditional farmers tended to reject them on palatability grounds. In contrast, newly developed Tunisian high-yielding varieties were favorably received as their gluten characteristics were more acceptable for traditional breads, etc.

Intensifying and diversifying crops
There is considerable potential for increasing cropping intensity in virtually every Arab country. In Iraq, crop rotations are rare because fallow farming continues to dominate the general system of cultivation.

In Egypt, efforts to consolidate and control cropping patterns, determined by cotton, should be expanded to overcome the dehabilitating effect of fragmentation. This technique could be applied to other North African countries as well (e.g. Tunisia).

In the rain-fed and irrigated areas of the Sudan, increases in cropping intensity from 63 to 75 per cent in Gezira Main and from 68 to 93 per cent in Managel brought an additional 220,000 hectares of wheat, 75,000 hectares of ground-nuts and 8,000 hectares of rice into cultivation. By increasing cropping intensity from 60 per cent to say, 85 to 90 per cent in the nationalized pumping schemes along the Blue and White Nile, an additional 125,000 hectares could be brought under cultivation.

Though cereals are the staple among traditional farmers, there is also evidence that diversification of crops to include more vegetables could go a long way toward increasing cash incomes.[31] In Egypt, this is taking place spontaneously as smallholders try (illegally) to compromise between their food requirements and the more lucrative vegetable and fruit cash crops.[32] In Qatar, traditional farmers might diversify their existing fodder and wheat crops to include greater vegetable production which is six to twenty times more efficient in water use.

Improving irrigation

A prerequisite to increasing cropping intensity on small farms is improved management of existing water resources. For example, irrigation efficiency is reported to be as low as 50 per cent in Qatar (Hassan: 1979). In Saudi Arabia, a large potential for expanding the area and intensity of crops hinges on improvements in drainage and distribution of water from existing oases (Saudi Arabia, WCARRD: 1979). The importance of adequate drainage can hardly be overstated. The neglect of drainage in Egypt from the time of Nasser up to 1975 has worked to deteriorate some 50 per cent of Egypt's most productive lands.

The practice of increasing cropping intensity without improving canal maintenance in the Sudan requires immediate attention because problems of water flow and drainage are resulting in productivity declines, especially for cotton (Sudan, WCARRD: 1978). Plans to irrigate another 60,000 hectares in the Jefara plain region in Libya should be delayed because natural water resources have been depleted by pumping from existing underground reservoirs at up to six times the recharge rate.[33] Neglect of agricultural investments in Oman and the resulting emigration of smallholders have allowed rapid deterioration of the inherited 'falaj' irrigation system. These underground and above-ground channels, which flow from inland acquifers in the mountains to the farms of the interior and coastal plains depend on attentive and skilled maintenance.[34] Neglect of irrigation in Bahrain is also responsible for increased salinity. This resulted in the abandonment of 478,000 date palms (compared with 417,000 still in production). Finally, in view of the axiom that limited water supplies from irrigated sources are almost always used carelessly, it would seem wise to limit daily pump operations or the maximum amount of water used per day to ensure that reserves are not depleted and to increase leaching facilities to reduce salinity, even in irrigated water.

With respect to the need to develop new sources of irrigation, this hardly requires elaboration. Dam construction and pumping systems are a number one priority in most development plans. Extensive water resources surveys are being carried out in the OAPEC countries (e.g. by Hunting Technical Services) and development aid is being sought to develop huge water projects in many of the oil-poor countries. Just to highlight a few, crash farm programs in Somalia are in need of aid to tie irrigation projects to the Shabella river. This could extend present cultivable acreage from 21,000 to about 70,000 hectares. Work on the Juba is also underway and the goal for 80,000 hectares could be extended to well over 200,000.[35]

The cooperative as overseer
Cooperatives have a long way to go to realize their full potential. According to Table 3.5, they represent small fractions of agricultural holdings in Algeria, Jordan, Lebanon, Morocco and Tunisia. In North Yemen, organized marketing does not even exist, except for mechanized cotton. In varying degrees, the same applies to cooperative representation among the scattered agricultural populations of Libya, Saudi Arabia and Oman.[36]

Cooperatives also suffer from a lack of capital, and existing capital tends to concentrate in the most prosperous areas. In the Sudan, the working capital of cooperatives in the four poorest provinces was only 8 to 30 per cent of the per capita level in the most prosperous provinces (Shaw: 1978b). In Egypt, the ratio of cooperative credit to the cost of agricultural production stood at 0.24 in 1950, rose to 0.28 in the 1960s and dropped again to 0.24 in the 1970s. As a result, loans have tended to be small or have been biased toward larger farms where security of repayment is greater. In 1972 and 1973, 17 per cent of the debtors with relatively large farms not only held 50 per cent of the available

Table 3.5   *Number and representation of cooperatives, selected Arab countries, 1975–7*

Country	Year (1)	No. of cooperatives (2)	Cooperative members (3)	Ratio of co-operative members to the total no. of agricultural holdings (4)
Algeria	1975	5,847	85,197	0.12
Egypt	1976	4,919	2,921,837	0.92
Iraq	1976	1,852	296,502	0.55
Jordan	1977	129	10,335	0.20
Lebanon	1976	67	4,144	0.03
Morocco	1976	728	23,890	0.01
Sudan	1976	2,800	600,000	0.83
Syria	1977	3,432	267,265	0.68
Tunisia	1977	224	10,000	0.03
Yemen PDR	1976	43	31,000	—

Sources: World Agrarian Reform Country Reports (Rome: Food and Agricultural Organization, 1979), national statistical yearbooks, unpublished reports by individual ministries of agriculture.

credit, but there is evidence that they built up debts in view of the lenient penalty of 6 per cent on outstanding loans (Radwan: 1977).

To increase incentives among smallholders it is imperative to subsidize prices for key inputs, boost credit and improve transportation and marketing services. The government of Oman is organizing fourteen cooperatives to provide free spraying and subsidized fertilizer (sold at half cost since 1978). Saudi Arabia is providing interest-free loans through its Agricultural Development Bank, and selling fertilizer at half price. In Kuwait, farm unions are beginning to take over the transportation and sale of products to bring farm prices in closer alignment with wholesale or consumer prices at city auctions. In Morocco, cooperatives are expanding their transportation and storage means to raise their commercial distribution of smallholder fruits and vegetables from 50 to 100 per cent. In Tunisia, cooperatives are attempting to modernize small farms through supervised credit programs. These insist on select seeds, fertilizers, and modern diversification of crops. And in Egypt, cooperatives are tackling fragmentation by aggregating farms for mechanical ploughing, crop fumigating and pest control. Smallholders in the reform areas have been receptive to this kind of intervention as long as the advantages of large-scale management do not conflict with incentives of private gain to individual farmers.

Energizing traditional agriculture

Animal husbandry

Breeding and fattening of cattle, sheep and poultry could go a long way toward improving incomes in the traditional sector. Not only is live-stock production labor-intensive but it is already in the hands of small-scale farmers or pastoral nomads. In addition, demand generally exceeds supply by a wide margin ãnd the high propensity, with rising incomes, to consume meat products should ensure growth in the future.

Table 3.6 *Cattle and sheep per hectare of pasture land and per agricultural worker, selected Arab countries, 1976*

	Cattle per		Sheep per	
Countries	Hectare of pasture (1)	Agricultural worker (2)	Hectare of pasture (3)	Agricultural worker (4)
Algeria	0.03	0.58	0.23	4.00
Iraq	0.53	1.25	2.12	5.08
Libya	0.02	0.92	0.49	25.26
Mauritania	0.05	5.83	0.08	9.04
Morocco	0.27	1.60	1.35	7.90
Oman	0.08	0.57	0.08	0.57
Saudi Arabia	0.02	0.31	0.16	2.36
Somalia	0.09	2.72	0.24	7.32
Sudan	0.64	6.75	0.64	6.69
Syria	0.06	0.61	0.72	6.76
Tunisia	0.27	2.00	1.08	8.01
Yemen AR	0.14	1.01	0.46	3.26
Yemen PDR	0.01	0.60	1.03	54.40

Sources: Food and Agricultural Organization, *Production Yearbooks*, national statistical yearbooks and agricultural censuses.

Table 3.6 suggests that cattle and sheep production could be expanded considerably. If the Sudan or Tunisia were reasonable bench-marks, we could safely say that beef stocking could be increased several times in Iraq, Algeria and Syria. Several countries are beginning to recognize this potential. Saudi Arabia is importing breeding stock, Syria is developing stock raising on a large scale with World Bank financing, and North Yemen is experimenting with livestock fattening farms. Somalia, Tunisia and Libya have increased the commitment to livestock breeding in their current development plans, and Egypt is heavily subsidizing cooperatives specializing in the breeding and fattening of young steers and cattle.

Of course, plans to upgrade quantity and quality of 'traditional' animal husbandry must also take stock of limitations. First, there is a major role to be played by cooperatives in controlling disease, watering points, rights of grazing, and provision of refrigeration and transport. Second, production of required fodder needs to be monitored. In the Sudan and the Sahel region, the cattle population actually declined due to overstocking (and fires) which precipitated a lack of fodder. While much of the fodder could be high-fiber material grown by local small-holders, it is important to develop fodder crops suited to dry areas and to protect them with fire lines. Locally produced urea could also be developed as a major feed input. Third, pasture and grazing rights must be regulated, destocking enforced· and watering points distributed so that animal concentrations are eased. These problems plague Somalia and the Sudan, where conflicts over grazing rights around watering points and in the highlands have led to insecurity among traditionalists. Finally, planners must take cognizance of the fact that while modern animal processing factories may provide the maximum meat or milk yield, they tend to employ a minimum of labor.

Expansion of poultry production is particularly relevant as small-scale farmers are the major producers of chickens. Chickens are also better converters of grain into meat than are cattle. Prospects for expansion are great in Algeria, Egypt, Somalia, the Yemens and all of the oil-rich OAPEC countries. Poultry production is one of the few forms of animal husbandry that has actually returned a profit in Saudi Arabia. Accordingly, poultry farms doubled between 1972 and 1978.[37] Similar positive results have been found in Bahrain, Syria and North Yemen.

Fisheries
While prospects for increasing employment and incomes through development of fisheries may not be huge, they are sound. Many Arab countries are only beginning to tap their fishery potential. Country reviews presented to the World Agrarian Reform Conference (1979) estimate that employment of local fishermen could be expanded several times in North Yemen (present employment 14,000) and increased by another 6,000 in Tunisia (present employment 14,000 permanent, 8,000 occasional). Government estimates foresee a twenty-five-fold increase in the total catch in Somalia, a five-fold increase in Saudi Arabia (Red Sea), and increases from 10,000 tons (at present) to 20,000 tons in Kuwait, from 10,000 tons to 28,500 tons in North Yemen, and from 20,000 tons to 60,000 tons from inland fisheries in the Sudan. Further, there is good potential for developing intensive

fish farming in the larger irrigation canals in Egypt, expanding river fishing in Mauritania, and tapping deep sea fishing which is currently in foreign hands off Oman, Libya and Mauritania.[38]

Of course, attempts to replace foreign firms will necessitate investments in better equipped boats for deep sea fishing. This applies particularly to Morocco with its fishing limits extended from twelve to seventy miles, and to Mauritania where the fishing grounds are the richest in the world. It will also require relatively heavy investment to improve port and refrigeration capacity and to construct fish processing factories.[39]

Human capital

That most countries are in dire need of improved agricultural extension services, agricultural vocational training, and maintenance personnel, cannot be denied. In some countries, where rural illiteracy reaches 90 per cent, information on new inputs has been supplied to smallholders in written reports only (e.g. Qatar). In other countries, agricultural extension agents, who are charged with extending available technology to small farmers, are often poorly trained or uninformed (e.g. Egypt). And, in almost all countries, the supply and distribution of agricultural engineers, veterinarians, technicians and maintenance personnel lags far behind demand (e.g. by 40 per cent in Morocco).[40]

For the region as a whole, less than 5 per cent of upper-level students are being trained in programs of a technical, vocational or applied nature. Only a small fraction of these are being trained for agriculture. Investments in education have been concentrated in modern urban enclaves to the extent that both rates of illiteracy and shortages of teachers in rural areas are three to five times those in urban areas (see Chapter 6).

It is hard to imagine how such deficiencies could be corrected by the existing system of education within, say, ten to twenty years. As this judgment has been elaborated in Chapter 6, it will suffice to say that I have also discussed ways in which policy-makers might improve on the situation. For example, the advantages of drawing on a cooperative system to upgrade extension or vocational services to smallholders include: (i) infrastructure to teach vocational or agricultural extension courses is often available; (ii) the location of existing or planned cooperatives is generally known and accessible to farmers; (iii) cooperative personnel are more familiar with the needs and problems of different resource areas; and (iv) advisory personnel or vocational teachers can be utilized full-time to serve multiple functions in the cooperative.

Off-farm employment

Policies designed to stimulate off-farm employment have a potentially important contribution to make to farm family welfare in several Arab countries. A survey of farm families in Algeria revealed that upwards of 30 per cent of the farm families reported some off-farm employment income (Bénachenhou: 1978). In the Sudan, off-farm income contributed between 20 and 30 per cent of total farm family income in most areas and up to 50 per cent in two major farm areas (Affan and Olsson: 1978). In Lebanon, about 35 per cent of the farm families derive 50 per cent or more of their total income from off-farm sources (Lebanon, WCARRD: 1978). In Iraq, the 1971 agricultural census found that non-agricultural occupations were prevalent among 10.1 per cent of all farm operators and as high as 23 to 59 per cent in three districts. Off-farm work was most prevalent among smallholders, the young, and those with highest levels of education. Finally, in the tiny agricultural sector of the United Arab Emirates (7,760 holdings), 49 per cent of the farm operators reported dual occupations.

However, agricultural policy in most Arab countries has been slow either to recognize or to nurture the potential benefits of off-farm work. Reasons for this neglect are two-fold. First, national agricultural policies are almost exclusively concerned with increasing returns to farming *per se* and the promotion of full-time farming in the process. Thus, national censuses of agriculture tend to emphasize farm enterprise oriented enumeration to the extent that information on off-farm employment or income remains partial. Second, off-farm employment has traditionally been viewed as a transitory step toward farm abandonment. Accordingly, income from off-farm sources tends to be treated as a by-product of farming, and the emergence of part-time farming has often been treated as an agricultural problem to be done away with.

Judging from the record of off-farm employment in many developed and less developed countries (see Appendix 3.2), it is safe to say that programs to promote off-farm work merit encouragement for at least six reasons. First, in situations of underemployment on farms, off-farm work could help reduce pressure to emigrate to urban areas in search of work. This applies particularly to new labor force entrants. Second, it could alleviate underemployment during slack periods on farms. By providing an alternative source of income this might help to reduce the vulnerability of farm families to wide fluctuations in net farm income due to extremities of climate, market discrepancies, etc. Third, off-farm income could be used to build up capital stock. This applies particularly to young or beginner farmers who have insufficient capital to secure loans. Fourth, as off-farm work tends to be more prevalent among poor families, it could help reduce extreme inequalities in the distribution of income. Fifth, it could serve as an important source of on-the-job training in skills other than farming. Sixth, it could help ease the frustrations of 'educated labor' by bringing rates of return to education in closer proximity to those in urban areas. The problem here is that educated labor tends to emigrate not only because returns to X hours of farm work are low, but because farming may not consume a sufficiently large fraction of the farmer's available time. Allocating time between farm and non-farm activities could work to boost the overall rate of return to education. In view of the conflict between goals to educate rural labor and the reality that educational investments usually emigrate to the cities, Appendix 3.3 elaborates on the relationship between off-farm employment and returns to education.

What kinds of interventions are available to the policy-maker to stimulate off-farm employment? While this question could be the target of endless speculation, I prefer to summarize three cases where Arab governments have sought to stabilize rural-agricultural population by encouraging off-farm work. In each case, investments in building and public works occupy center stage.

In Algeria, 1,000 socialist villages are being planned for the purposes of establishing a better geographical balance between human and non-human resources.[41] Between 1968 and 1976, 33 per cent of all new jobs in rural areas were created through building and public works. Upwards of 60 per cent of the new jobs were created in building and public works in the five most rural districts. Between 1974 and 1977, when employment in building and public works really mushroomed, 216 out of 276 projects were in construction and 19 were on the construction of agro-industries. While it is difficult to say how many of the new jobs were taken by rural non-farm households *per se*, it is known that building and public works became an important employment source for farm family members. In the process, employment generation through building and public works has been attributed with promoting (i) lower rates of migration to the coastal than to the interior cities (lower by 33 per cent), (ii) an actual increase in the share of total city population retained in Algeria's interior towns (from 51.5 per cent in 1966 to 53.5 per cent in 1973), and (iii) surprisingly low rates of rural to urban migration.

A similar strategy has been executed in Tunisia. Anticipating a growth in rural-agricultural labor which would be several times the projected demand, the government sought to create off-farm employ-ment through building and public works in small towns and villages. Between 1972 and 1976, 164,000 rural jobs were created with 61,000 in building and public works *per se*. According to the government, the rate of rural emigration dropped to about one-half the level of natural increase as a result (Tunisia, CMRADR: 1979). Accordingly, the current Tunisian plan intends to push investments in building and public works even further through the construction of some 40,000 buildings in rural areas. This compares with only 20,000 for medium sized towns.

Morocco's Promotion Nationale also tried to mobilize labor in rural areas between 1960 and 1977. Its major goal was to create more days of work in the poorest areas. In total, the equivalent of 200 million man-days, or 100,000 man-years, of work were created each year. Again, building and public works played a key role. Approximately 60 per cent of those working part-time were landowners with the added employment boosting farm incomes by up to 50 per cent (Andria-mananjara: 1976).

Successful though these examples seem to be, it is also true that far more could be achieved with greater financial commitment. Even in the relatively aggressive Algerian program, investments in the first and second plan for building and public works amounted to no more than 1 and 2 per cent of total investments, respectively. Further, very little attention has been given to the potential role that remittances could have on development of rural areas among the labor exporters. Yet, it is known that remittances are being used on an individual basis to develop small farms and spur self-help housing. With government efforts to channel these remittances more effectively, there is no reason why these huge sums (approximately US $3,500 million in 1977) could not be tapped to help underwrite off-farm employment.

That construction represents a viable means for stimulating employ-ment, incomes and economic development, has already been elaborated in Chapter 2. Efforts to modernize traditional agriculture will require construction of new roads, storage facilities, agro-industries, servicing depots, etc. Efforts to help poorer farmers in the broader sense of 'integrated rural development' will also require construction of schools, sorely needed housing, medical facilities and community development centers. Appendix 3.4 summarizes a few examples from the five poorest Arab countries to illustrate how construction could augment off-farm employment.

Restrictive controls

It is important to acknowledge that the policy interventions discussed thus far could not operate successfully in an environment of unfair taxing, or restrictive wage and price controls. Yet, in the face of wide gaps between rural and urban incomes and living standards, it is an anomaly that many Arab governments have held farm gate prices and minimum wages down and have failed to tax remote rural areas more fairly. These are the kinds of conditions that typically force farmers to concentrate upon survival and maintenance of their socio-economic position rather than risk improvement and advancement of position through greater effort. Such behavior is visible not only in Arab agriculture (Hassan: 1979); it is well known to the economics of agriculture in general (Mellor: 1966).

With respect to taxing, remote farmers producing traditional crops in the Sudan were taxed more than prosperous producers of higher-value crops. The latter typically lived in closer proximity to the cities (Affan and Olsson: 1978). Unfair taxing in the Sudan Gezira Board actually precipitated a drop in the incentive to produce on the part of tenant cotton farmers. Their complaint was against unfair revenue sharing (49 per cent of the tax revenues for themselves, versus 15 per cent for local administration and 36 per cent siphoned off by the federal government).

With respect to wage and price controls, stiff measures in Algeria and Iraq between 1964 and 1974 depressed farm gate prices and agricultural wages while intermediaries earned exploitative profits during transportation and urban marketing.[42] In Egypt, the farm gate price of wheat was so distorted in 1977 (so the government could sell subsidized bread in urban areas at 25 per cent of the true cost) that farmers could sell their wheat straw (price uncontrolled) as a 'poor' animal feed for 1.5 times more than the value of a kilo of wheat grain. Being obliged to grow cereals rather than fruits and vegetables (which are actually more labor-intensive but reserved for larger farms) has also locked the traditional farmer into government controlled returns of about $100 per fedan for wheat versus $219 for oranges.[43] Finally, a tapering off of intensive farming on traditional holdings in North Yemen between 1975 and 1977 (Cohen and Lewis: 1979) can also be traced, in part, to pricing policies. These maintained grain price increases at 30 per cent while wages for seasonal workers jumped 300 per cent in a remittance-fed inflationary economy.

The real problem with such controls is that they often operate, covertly, in the service of an industry-led policy of economic development. Such policies have grown out of the theory that, since productivity is generally higher in manufacturing than in agriculture, priority should be given to industrialization. Other sectors have been expected to benefit from 'trickle-down' effects. The policy instruments for achieving this type of strategy have typically included (i) taxation of the agricultural surplus to provide the industrial investment funds, (ii) protection for infant manufacturing industries, and (iii) maintenance of relatively low industrial costs through cheap food and low wages.

Needless to say, the 'trickle-down' theory has been discredited (Griffen and Ghose: 1979). However, many policies designed to serve it either remain in operation or have had a deleterious effect. For example, concentration of development expenditures in modern enclaves, 'growth poles' or largest cities has stimulated rural–urban migration to the point that many cities have grown to overflowing. At times of stagnation, these congested population centers become flash-points of political instability, especially when food staples are not in sufficient supply (Weinbaum: 1980). In such cases, many governments have been pressured to assure a stable supply of food staples (i.e. imply-ing production controls in agriculture) at prices the urban poor can afford (i.e. implying controls on farm gate prices). For agriculture, detrimental effects have been observed in respect of lower incomes, inequality, reduced worker motivation, and lack of employment. To my mind, Arab planners have much to learn from the experience of Egypt where such policies have had a negative impact on poor farmers and the poorest sector of the population (Cuddihy: 1981).

Interregional cooperation and integration
There can be little doubt that attempts to modernize traditional agriculture would receive an incredible boost were Arab governments to formulate interregional policies for integrating agricultural produc-tion and labor markets.[44] While many worthy intentions in this regard have been virtually stifled by ideological and domestic rifts,[45] let us consider a few examples of economic cooperation that could be implemented to good effect relatively quickly.

First, equity and solidarity considerations could work among the oil-rich OAPEC countries to favor importation of surplus agricultural labor from the Maghreb countries and North Africa. Arab labor is already emigrating in vast quantities to serve OAPEC construction. With rising investments in agriculture, particularly in Iraq and Libya, prospects for importing agricultural labor are good. Upwards of 50,000 Egyptian workers are already employed in Iraqi agriculture with another 10,000 needed. A potential problem to be avoided here concerns the increasing importation of Asian labor. It is well known that government preferences for Arab labor are being undermined by private contractors and establishments that have been importing orientals regardless of the overt desire of the governments. This problem is now being taken up by the Arab League and efforts to combat it are being initiated by the Arab Labour Organization (see Chapter 7, concluding section).

Second, the OAPEC countries could help the oil-poor countries to retain their highly skilled and professional agricultural workers. While several countries require medical graduates and other specialized personnel to serve in rural areas (e.g. in Egypt, Iraq), high wages in the OAPEC countries are currently depleting skilled agricultural labor in the oil-poor countries where bonding is virtually non-existent. A sad ramification is that implementation of OAPEC aid for agricultural projects in the oil-poor countries is being constrained because key supervisory personnel are in short supply in rural areas.

Third, Arab countries could place greater emphasis on the importation of cattle from North African countries where the supply is generally abundant and prices are lower. With improved health and marketing arrangements there is no reason why the OAPEC countries could not collaborate to develop a major beef industry. Collaboration is also merited in the production of vegetables and fruits in, say, the Sudan and Egypt for sale in the OAPEC countries. Finally, there are strong prospects for the Maghreb countries to cooperate in establishing canning and processing plants for fisheries. To some extent, the same applies to the Gulf countries.

Fourth, the best examples of economic cooperation may well involve joint irrigation projects. The Jonglei project, an offshoot of Egyptian and Sudanese cooperation, will probably add 150,000 hectares of cultivable land. The huge river basin project between Mauritania, Senegal and Mali is expected to result in another 450,000 hectares of irrigated land. Prospects for cooperative efforts involving the largely untapped water resources of Iraq might well be placed high on the priority list for joint undertakings involving Saudi Arabia.

Finally, the particular problems of Egypt (politically isolated) and the Sudan (poor international credit rating) could go a long way toward solidifying an economic partnership. To some extent this is happening with the Jonglei canal and the construction of the road from Khartoum to Port Sudan. In view of the great infrastructural problems in Sudan's rural areas, and lack of skilled agricultural labor, arrangements might be encouraged to tap Egypt's relatively abundant and underutilized supply of expertise.

Concluding remarks

At a time when references to food shortages, high underemployment, landlessness, poverty and rural exodus are becoming commonplace, it is important to review the commitment to transform Arab agriculture. For this reason, I have sought to evaluate agricultural development strategy, public expenditures and policy interventions of potential relevance to small-scale farmers and pastoralists. My review suggests the following: agrarian reform could be pushed a good deal further through a renewed commitment to equalizing the distribution of land and credit; reclamation and resettlement schemes may continue to have a limited impact on rural poverty due to the high costs involved; large-scale mechanization has favored a rather small class of middle-income agriculturalists due to its concentration on the perimeter of urban areas; the financial commitment to increasing productivity and employment in agriculture needs a major overhaul if the war on poverty is to be taken seriously; and at least ten potential policy interventions could be developed to the fuller advantage of small-scale farmers or pastoralists.

As the possibilities of augmenting food production and problems of traditional agriculture go hand in hand, it is also important that policy-makers confront popular biases that traditional agriculture is stagnant, unproductive and lacking in potential, or that traditional attitudes and tastes will undermine the adoption of new inputs and technology.[46] Mounting empirical evidence is now available to discredit these views. Surveys of long established irrigated farms in northern Sudan reveal that smaller farms are more efficient producers per unit, and per unit labor, than larger, mechanized farms (Ali: 1978). Similar results have been found for traditional Moroccan farmers on the Gharb Plain. Crop by crop, the value added on smaller farms was higher than on the larger holdings (Griffen: 1975). Moreover, mechanization among smallholders in small-scale settlements in the Sudan has yielded production growth rates as high as 20 to 30 per cent per year. These results have prompted numerous smallholder schemes with anticipated growth rates of 16 per cent, compared with only 9 per cent for large-scale farms modelled after the Habilla scheme (Affan and Olsson: 1978).

That existing durra-fallow rotations are now ready for widespread application on a smallholder basis also means that traditional rotations are able to compete with modern rotations on large-scale mechanized farms.[47] Further, in semi-arid areas with light, sandy soils, large-scale mechanization has not lent itself to scale economies. Rather, a flexible system is needed where small-scale farmers retain control since factors of production cannot be centralized or supervised readily, and soil and climatic conditions do not allow easily organized, repetitive processes of production (Adams and Howell: 1979).

Finally, when policies have actively improved the situation of small-holders, production has been nothing but responsive. In post-reform Egypt and Syria, where land redistribution benefited traditional free-holders, production shows a consistent shift toward greater market responsiveness (Askari *et al.*: 1977). And, in the traditional sector of the Sudan, the allocation of labor time to other crops and activities has been highly responsive to price and demand changes (Affan and Olsson: 1978).

In short, it is time to relegate productivity and motivational biases against traditional agriculture to superficial opinion rather than hard fact. Mounting evidence conveys the fact that traditional farmers are responsive to changing markets and that rates of return can compete with those of large-scale mechanization. If there is a lack of worker motivation, it is likely to be attributable to failure to assist with credit, new inputs and amenities or to abolish unfair taxing or restrictive wage and price controls.

Appendix 3.1 Classification of countries by physical resource constraints in agriculture

It is important to acknowledge that Arab countries are extremely disparate in the character of their agriculture. This alone undermines sensible generalization for the region as a whole. To illustrate differences in physical resource constraints, consider the classification of countries by selected characteristics in Table A.3.1.

Of the eighteen countries represented, it is not unreasonable to say that eight have relatively good physical prospects as well as a relatively large share of their labor force in agriculture. These are Algeria, Tunisia, Iraq, Jordan, Syria, Morocco, Lebanon and the Sudan. Somalia would probably fall into this group as well, though it has been excluded from classification in Table A.3.1 due to insufficient data. All of these countries, excluding Iraq and possibly Algeria, can be considered 'oil-poor'.

In contrast to the above, four countries appear to have relatively

Table A.3.1 *Crude classification of physical resource potential of Arab countries, 1975–80*

% of total area with 200+ mm rainfall/yr	Irrigated hectares per worker	% of total land suitable for cultivation					
		<10%			10% +		
		Hectares of arable land per worker			Hectares of arable land per worker		
		<1.5	1.5–3.5	3.5+	<1.5	1.5–3.5	3.5+
<5	<0.5	Bahrain (6)[a] Kuwait (2) UAE (5) Yemen PDR (62)			Saudi Arabia (63)		Libya (22)[a]
	<0.5	Qatar (4) Egypt (51)				Tunisia (43)	Jordan (28) Syria (49)
5–49	<0.5	Oman (63)				Algeria (35)	
	<0.5					Iraq (43)[a]	
50+	<0.5		Yemen AR (76)			Morocco (53)	Sudan (78)
	>0.5					Lebanon (13)	

Sources: National statistical yearbooks, agricultural censuses, Food and Agricultural Organization, *Production Yearbooks*.
Note: a Figures in parentheses beside each country represent percentages of labor force in agriculture.

poor physical prospects as well as a relatively small share of their labor force in agriculture. These are Bahrain, Kuwait, the United Arab Emirates and Qatar. Successful development of agriculture in these countries will probably require a heavy reliance on abundant oil revenues.

The balance of the countries in Table A.3.1 require further sub-grouping. Oman, Saudi Arabia and Libya each have relatively serious physical constraints. However, they can also draw on abundant oil revenues to upgrade opportunities for their relatively large agricultural populations. Next comes Egypt. The combination of some severe physical constraints, population pressure on the land, and shortages of development funds, imply a very difficult challenge for the future. Finally, the two Yemens, each with a relatively large share of their labor force in agriculture, severe physical constraints, and lack of development funds, would appear to face the greatest difficulty of augmenting agricultural production and employment. Possibly, Mauritania should be included with the Yemens, though data are again insufficient for its classification in Table A.3.1.

Appendix 3.2 The record of off-farm employment in agricultural development

The contribution that off-farm employment is making to agricultural development in a wide variety of countries is seldom reflected in development theory, let alone agricultural policy. Accordingly, this appendix summarizes evidence of off-farm employment in developed and less developed countries. It concludes that off-farm employment has, in many countries, made a strong, positive contribution to farm family incomes, farm production, and the reduction of income inequality; that it affords an alternative to rural emigration by reducing underemployment and augmenting rates of return to more educated farm family members; that it is accessible to policy intervention because it is available in various guises during the process of agricultural transition; and that its impact on the structure of farming requires a rethinking of agricultural development strategy in countries which have been slow to recognize its importance.

Magnitudes

The prevalence of off-farm employment and the rapid rise in its contribution to farm family income in several countries has caught policy-makers by surprise. Consider the figures in Table A.3.2. In the 'high-income' countries, approximately half of all farm families had an off-farm source of income. This income derived largely from off-farm employment. In Canada (1970), 49 per cent of the farm families derived more than 50 per cent of their total income from off-farm wages and salaries, or self-employment. Only 41 per cent derived their major source of income from farming *per se*.[48] In Japan (1975), fully 63 per cent of the farm families derived more income from off-farm sources than from farming. Moreover, the pace at which off-farm income has grown in these countries can be appreciated by the fact that its contribution to total farm family income rose from 35 to 73 per cent between 1958 and 1970 in Canada, from 38 to 62 per cent between 1949 and 1969 in the USA, and from 33 to 68 per cent between 1955 and 1975 in Japan.

While data for less developed countries are considerably more limited in quality and geographical coverage, they also suggest that off-farm employment is making a sizable contribution to farm family income. Judging from the data in Table A.3.2, this source may be contributing anywhere from 20 to 50 per cent of total farm family income in the 'middle-income' or 'low-income' countries. Again, this income derives largely from off-farm employment, particularly as government transfers and retirement pensions are much less prevalent in poorer countries.

Of course, the impressions above are based on national or sample averages, implying that interregional variations in off-farm employment are disguised. To illustrate, in Canada (1970), its contribution to total farm family income ranged from 71 per cent in the province of Newfoundland to 47 per cent in Saskatchewan. In Surinam (1960), off-farm income represented between 52 and 65 per cent of total farm family income in the districts of Nikeru and Surinam versus 20 to 30 per cent in others. In Chile (1976), its contribution to total farm family income ranged from 23 to 50 per cent among three districts; in Iraq (1970) its contribution varied from 22 to 59 per cent among three mohafazas; and in North Yemen its prevalence ranged from near zero in the most remote rural districts to 70 per cent of total farm family income in the district of Hojuriyya. These variations are of interest in so far as they convey 'the range of what may be possible' when it comes to promoting off-farm work in areas that are disparate in resources.

Table A.3.2 *Prevalence of off-farm income among farm families, selected countries, 1965–75*

Countries	Year	Farm families or households		Qualifications
		Proportion earning some off-farm income (%)	Contribution of off-farm income to total farm family or household income (%)	
High income[a]				
USA	1969	47	62	National census
Canada	1970	60	73	National census
UK	1964–5	49	–	County samples
Germany	1970–1	60	–	National census
Norway	1970	47	–	National census
Poland	1975	59	–	National census
Spain	1972	48	–	National census
Japan	1975	87	68	National census
Middle income[b]				
Taiwan	1975	–	43	National census
Chile	1976	–	31	Small area samples
Surinam	1965–70	–	59	Small area samples
Iran	1971	24–42	20–33	Small area samples
Low income[c]				
Algeria	1975	30	–	Small area samples
Korea (So.)	1975	–	23	National census
Thailand	1972	–	41	Sample of northern area
India	1968	70	39	Sample of major district
Pakistan	1968	–	23	Small area sample
Yemen AR	1970	32	–	Small area sample
Sudan	1975	–	50	Sample of 2 major areas
Nigeria	1962	32	–	Small area sample
Kenya	1968	50	–	Small area sample
Zambia	1966–8	–	22	Small area sample
Lebanon	1965	30	–	Small area sample

Sources: National censuses, surveys and research studies.
Notes: a Countries with per capita income between US $3,000 and 9,000.
b Countries with per capita income between US $1,000 and 2,999.
c Countries with per capita income between US $0 and 999.

Impact on economic welfare

The impact of 'spontaneous' off-farm employment on earning power is such that it may be doing more to enhance the economic welfare of farm families than agricultural policies which are explicitly intended to do so (e.g. government transfers, price stabilization and support, protective tariffs). To illustrate this point, without off-farm earnings, the proportion of self-employed farm operators in Canada's 'poverty' category would be about 1.5 times its present size (Shaw: 1979b, p. 129). Almost identical results have been reported for the USA by Larson (1976). In terms of income inequality, off-farm employment in Canada is held largely responsible for a drop in the farm family gini coefficient of concentration from 0.52 to 0.43 between 1960 and 1970. The same applies to the USA, where the farm family gini coefficient dropped from 0.47 to 0.41 between 1949 and 1969 (Shaw: 1979d). These declines are truly impressive in view of the comparatively small drop in the gini coefficient for urban families in each country.[49] Certainly, no agricultural policy in either country can claim to have had a comparable impact on the distribution of farm family income.

Impressive results are also evident in several less developed countries. In Taiwan, between 1962 and 1975, the increased prevalence of off-farm employment among poorer farm families produced declines in the rural gini coefficient from 0.34 to 0.30 (Ho: 1979; Chinn: 1979). In Chile, the income gap between smallest and medium sized farms (i.e. 0.5 versus 2–4 hectares), would be eight times larger were off-farm sources of income not available to the smallest farmers (Monardes: 1978). In central Java, the increase in off-farm employment earnings between 1969 and 1973 is credited with reducing the gini coefficient from 0.58 to 0.53 (Soejono: 1977). Again, these studies tend to agree that agricultural policies concerned with returns to farming *per se* have not had a comparable impact on income inequality.[50]

Access to off-farm employment among farm family members is also known to stabilize the flow of family income and to provide a source for 'capital deepening' on the farm. In the former case, access to off-farm work helps reduce the vulnerability of farm families to wide fluctuations in farm prices and net farm income. This is of no small importance to farmers in the oil-poor countries where the intransigence of the climate often succeeds in wiping out an entire crop. It is also important to farmers in developed countries in view of unexpected productivity shortfalls, unexpected productivity increases among importing countries, rapid increases in the cost of almost all agricultural inputs, and ever-changing trade agreements, barriers or restrictions.

As for capital deepening, most small-scale farmers, and particularly those in the poorer countries, have great difficulty in obtaining credit to expand either the size or the technical efficiency of their holdings (e.g. irrigation pumps, fertilizer). Income from off-farm employment can play a key role here both as a direct source of financing and as 'collateral' against which farmers can obtain additional credit from usual sources. For example, in Canada, small-scale farmers have been observed to plough off-farm earnings back into their farms (Shaw: 1979b); in Italy, rising non-farm employment income has promoted increased investment on the farm (Knapskog: 1977); in France, some 15 per cent of all farmers have taken up off-farm work solely to increase their income for farm investment (Laurent and Campi: 1978); and in Wisconsin, USA, 36 per cent of the farmers took up off-farm work solely to finance farm investment (Ryohei: 1978).

Availability

Preliminary studies suggest that the availability of off-farm employment varies substantially according to stages of economic development, regional variations in resource endowments, and existing government policies. In the early stages of development, rural areas and towns provide more non-farm employment than do urban areas. Thus, in African countries, rural areas and towns provide over 75 per cent of all non-farm employment opportunities versus approximately 66 per cent in southern and eastern Asia and 33 per cent in Latin America (Anderson and Leiserson: 1980). In later stages, the organization of production in urban centers shifts non-farm activities to the fringes of larger towns and cities. In such cases, questions of proximity and transportation emerge as deciding factors in the off-farm employment decisions of farm families (Huffman: 1980).

Regional variations in resource endowments are important in so far as they give rise to traditional forms of non-farm activity. In less developed countries, handicrafts and cottage industries tend to supplement farm family incomes in areas which are poor in agricultural resources. Such traditions have been observed in India, Iran and Syria (Guha: 1970). In more developed contexts, farmers in resource-poor areas often maintain ancillary activities which make use of their farm equipment such as the cutting, storage and delivery of wood, light construction work, contract hauling, etc.

Of course, government policies can influence the availability of off-farm jobs through the decentralization of population and industry, the distribution of public works programs, the provision of credit for small-scale industry in rural areas, etc. Thus, the greater prevalence of off-farm employment in Taiwan than, say, in Korea, can be traced directly to government decentralization policies which have promoted jobs in closer proximity to Taiwanese farm families (Ho: 1979). The merits of augmenting rural off-farm employment through public works programs have been realized to the extent that such measures are now explicit in the national development plans of several countries.

The least ambiguous consensus concerning the availability of off-farm work is that the means and the milieu for augmenting this source of employment are well within the policy-maker's grasp. In addition, such action should be embraced as a viable development policy, especially in poorer countries, because non-farm activities tend to be labor-intensive and have been shown to be surprisingly efficient. Most are small-scale, less capital-intensive, and more geographically dispersed (which serves decentralization policy). They tend to offer more opportunities for unskilled and family labor, have greater linkages with the agricultural sector, and have greater export potential than has often been assumed. Moreover, it can be shown that their expansion is conducive to greater employment growth and higher labor income for low-wage workers. The reasons are that the elasticity of substitution between capital and labor tends to be high, wage rates tend not to be pushed up too rapidly, the price elasticity of product demand tends to be high, and technical change, which increases the efficiency of both capital and labor use, tends to be high.

Appendix 3.3 Off-farm employment and returns to education

Off-farm work and multiple jobholding can have an important influence on returns to education and total employment income in cases where (i) a share of the educated farmer's labor is already underemployed or (ii) where education's 'allocative effect' is likely to promote adoption of labor saving technology. That is, shares of underemployed farm family labor will tend to be allocated to rural non-farm labor markets to the point where the marginal revenue product of farm labor equals the net wage of off-farm labor. Its income augmenting effects would be particularly prevalent among young, highly educated farmers whose physical capital is limited and whose human capital cannot, as yet, be fully utilized. Indeed, in cases of underemployment and limited physical capital, any allocation of farm labor off-farm could reasonably be expected to result in improved private rates of return to education on-farm. Of course, efficiency of resource allocation between farm and off-farm labor markets will also depend on the size, diversity and proximity of off-farm work opportunities.

Education can be assumed to bear on off-farm work through its effect on the processing of information about alternative work opportunities and by satisfying employers' credential, 'screening' and human capital requirements. Further, presence of an educated labor force will influence the supply of off-farm work opportunities by exercising a positive influence on the location decisions of non-farm enterprise.

Figure A.3.1 illustrates the interaction between off-farm work, off-farm wage rates, and the rate of return to education on-farm. It

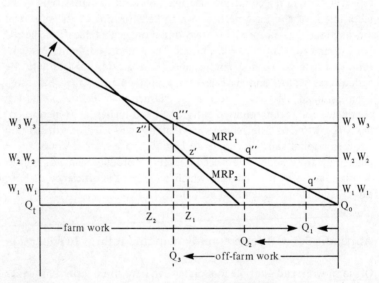

Figure A.3.1 *Returns to off-farm and farm work*

abstracts from seasonal variations in the marginal productivity of labor (e.g. harvest time versus winter months), and assumes (i) that off-farm workers are 'price takers' (implying the horizontal wage lines $w_1 w_1$, etc.), (ii) declining marginal revenue productivity (MRP_1) of increases in one factor of production, (iii) optimizing behavior, (iv) that $w_1 w_1$ is the going off-farm wage rate, and (v) that we are dealing with a limited-capital farmer with a relatively high level of education. At $w_1 w_1$, the point at which the farmer will tend to allocate his time between farm and off-farm work, is represented by q', or from O_0 to O_1.

Now, suppose $w_2 w_2$ represents a minimum agricultural wage which is compatible with the 'going' or minimum urban wage rate and that wages above $w_2 w_2$ (e.g. $w_3 w_3$) represent private wages for semi-skilled and skilled jobs. $w_2 w_2$ could act to shift the farmer's optimal farm/ non-farm allocation from q' to q''; his off-farm labor allocation would increase from Q_1 to Q_2. An increase to Q_3 would depend on whether the farmer's level of education and training qualified for a more highly paid part-time, semi-skilled job (i.e. $w_3 w_3$). In this sense, $w_2 w_2$ would apply more to off-farm work of a temporary nature whereas $w_3 w_3$ would apply more to more permanent part-time jobs requiring a certain minimum level of education.

Assuming all else constant, an increase from Q_1 to Q_2 or Q_3 would increase the rate of return to educated labor on-farm, and in addition improve overall income at no loss to the economy. That is, the division between off-farm and farm work would tend to be consistent with requirements for maximum efficiency. Of course, if the operator's level of education were also increased, and if this promoted labor saving technology, then the negative slope of MRP (with respect to labor) would increase (say, to MRP_2). All else held constant, his new off-farm labor allocation would shift from Q_2 to Z_1 or Q_3 to Z_2 (i.e. depending on whether his off-farm work was temporary or whether he was a multiple jobholder).

Clearly, the process described above assumes that varying degrees of off-farm employment opportunities exist, that minimum wages are in effect and that productivity of human capital is such that wage rates, in excess of the minimum, have been offered to 'educated labor'. While such assumptions are inapplicable to many less developed countries, it is also true that some governments are intervening in rural off-farm labor markets toward creating such conditions. For example, in Algeria and Tunisia, the introduction of minimum wages in agriculture ($w_2 w_2$) has been combined with active development of rural non-farm labor markets toward providing farm families with alternative sources of income. In Algeria, $w_2 w_2$ is now close to the urban minimum wage, underemployed farm family labor is being absorbed both as temporary labor and as multiple jobholders, and out-migration from farm to urban areas is unusually low. In developed countries, such as Canada, off-farm wages above $w_2 w_2$ have long existed and it is reasonable tō propose that off-farm labor markets are beginning to work under competitive conditions toward (i) equating rates of return, in general, close to the

10 per cent benchmark observed in most wage and salary contexts (Shaw: 1980b).

Appendix 3.4 Off-farm employment and construction

To see how construction might augment off-farm employment, consider the following examples which pertain to the five poorest Arab countries.

First, prospects of employment in the construction of feeder roads have hardly been tapped. In the Sudan, government funds for road building do not really plan for feeder roads. In the case of the southern provinces, most settlements are isolated and beyond the reach of public services. Yet, when feeder roads were constructed to serve Kordofan, improved access to markets resulted in an increase in the cultivation of ground-nuts by 2 million acres. In South Yemen, it has been suggested that the construction of feeder roads and storage facilities could probably lead to a doubling of cultivable areas (Yemen PDR; WCARRD: 1978). In North Yemen, the World Bank reported that inadequate feeder roads led to wastage of perishable fruits and vegetables. Of course, to maximize employment in rural road construction, capital-intensive construction must be avoided. This applies particularly to Somalia with its low interest rates and low tariffs on imported machinery, and to the Sudan with its emphasis on paved roads. According to the International Labor Organization mission to the Sudan, dropping these capital-intensive procedures would raise labor in construction by up to 30,000 workers.

Second, construction of storage facilities for agricultural and fish products is a viable avenue for generating off-farm employment. This has been proposed by the ILO mission to the Sudan for ground-nut production among traditional farmers in western Savannah. Storage facilities hardly exist for agricultural products in North Yemen and the same applies to potential fishing industries in North Yemen, Mauritania and Somalia. The construction of fish harbors at Laskorey, Bossasso, Alola and Hobyo in Somalia, harbors in North Yemen, and more supply facilities for fishermen in Mauritania (water, ice, fuel, oil), should also be high on the priority list.

Third, building construction, particularly self-help housing, offers far-reaching employment and redistributive effects in all countries. Some governments have actually committed larger housing subsidies to rural than to urban areas. Of course, construction of irrigation systems and wells to serve herds are top priority in most countries. The International Labour Organization mission to Somalia also underlines greater labor-intensive benefits from construction of floodwater systems than new irrigation systems. Open wells and low-cost tube wells in Somalia, Sudan and South Yemen could be constructed by unskilled labor using simple tools. As an example of a broad-based approach utilizing relatively labor-intensive construction, South Yemen combined the development of five watering points with twenty-three boarding schools, some community-type centers, one hospital and seven health units for Bedouins. Such settlement programs are particularly relevant to the pastoral populations in Somalia and Mauritania where they could provide substantial employment in land preparation and the construction of infrastructure and self-help housing.

Finally, it is important to acknowledge at least one pitfall which has worked to cripple labor-intensive construction strategies in the past. This concerns a lack of people with certain essential skills (foremen, carpenters, designers, irrigation specialists, etc.). These shortages have been a weakness in getting technical development programs underway in each of the five countries noted above. In the first stages of rural construction, select skills may have to be imported in an overseer capacity. On-the-job training and crash programs in vocational training can go a long way to fill these gaps. Most important, however, is that candidates for special training programs need to be bonded for rural service (say, for two to three years) until rural labor markets become sufficiently competitive.

Chapter 4

Appropriate population policy

Introduction

At present growth rates, the population of the Arab world will almost double within twenty years. This implies an additional 138 million Arabs by the year 2000 (Table 4.1). At present levels of labor force participation, the number of jobs must increase by 30 to 40 million merely to keep abreast, and national product must increase by at least 3 per cent yearly to keep per capita income from backsliding.

Proponents of the Malthusian specter avidly point out that growth in the twelve oil-poor countries will be severely constrained because rising child dependency ratios will overburden social overhead capital, deplete the marketable surplus from agriculture, and reduce household savings and investment. Advocates of population control or anti-natalist policies forewarn that unless action is taken quickly the number of inhabitants will far outstrip all available resources (Larsen: 1979). Population control is expected to produce positive results in the form of higher family savings, greater prospects for investing in the education of existing children, transfer of government funds from social overhead capital to investments in 'productive capital', and the release of women for employment in the formal labor force.

On the whole, Arab governments have paid little heed to the Malthusian threat posed above. Sixteen out of twenty governments perceive their rates of natural increase and fertility to be 'acceptable' (Table 4.2). The only countries which perceive their rates of fertility and natural increase to be 'excessive' are Egypt, Jordan, Morocco and Tunisia. Some countries actually perceive a shortage of manpower and encourage population growth to meet future needs (e.g. Libya, Iraq).[1]

Why have Arab governments resisted organized family limitation

Table 4.1   *Demographic characteristics, Arab countries, 1978*

Countries	Estimated population (millions) (1)	Crude birth rate per thousand (2)	Crude death rate per thousand (3)	Crude rate of natural increase (%) (4)	No. of years to double population[a] (5)	Population projection to year 2000 (millions) (6)	Infant mortality rate per thousand (7)	Total fertility rate (8)	% population aged less than 15 years (9)
Arab world	152.5	43	14	3.0	24	291.0	127	6.7	44.5
Oil-rich	26.7	45	13	3.2	22	52.4	112	7.0	46.7
Oil-poor	125.8	43	14	2.9	24	238.6	130	6.7	44.0
Oil-rich									
Bahrain	0.3	43	7	3.6	20	0.7	44	6.7	46.9
Iraq	12.2	42	10	3.2	22	24.4	86	7.2	48.9
Kuwait	1.1	49[b]	5	3.4	21	2.3	44	7.2	44.3
Libya	2.8	48	9	2.9	24	5.3	130	6.8	49.0
Oman	1.5	49	19	3.0	24	2.9	138	7.3	46.2
Qatar	0.2	49	16	3.3	22	0.4	135	7.2	44.4
Saudi Arabia	7.8	49	19	3.0	24	14.9	152	7.1	44.7
UAE	0.8	44	14	3.0	24	1.5	135	5.9	28.2
Oil-poor									
Algeria	18.4	48	14	3.4	21	38.5	145	7.2	44.0
Egypt	39.6	38	11	2.7	29	71.2	108	5.0	40.7
Jordan	2.9	48	13	3.5	20	6.2	89	6.5	49.9
Lebanon	2.9	33	8	2.5	28	5.0	59	4.6	41.6
Mauritania	1.5	45	24	2.1	33	2.4	187	5.9	42.0
Morocco	18.9	45	14	3.1	23	36.9	133	6.8	46.0
Somalia	3.4	48	21	2.7	26	6.1	177	6.1	45.0
Sudan	17.1	48	16	3.2	22	34.1	144	7.0	45.0
Syria	8.2	45	14	3.1	23	16.0	114	7.6	49.3
Tunisia	6.0	36	13	2.3	31	9.9	135	7.0	45.0
Yemen AR	5.0	49	22	2.7	26	9.0	210	6.8	46.8
Yemen PDR	1.9	45	20	2.5	28	3.3	170	6.1	42.5

Sources: Population Division, United Nations, New York; Population Division, United Nations Economic Commission for Western Asia.
Notes: a This estimate is crude because no attempt is made to incorporate effects of international migration.
            b For Kuwaitis only.

Table 4.2 *Government perceptions of fertility and natural increase, Arab countries, 1974–8*

| Countries | Government perceptions | | | | Government policy favors national family planning (5) |
| | Fertility | | Natural increase | | |
	Excessive (1)	Acceptable (2)	Excessive (3)	Acceptable (4)	
Oil-rich					
Bahrain		X		X	No
Iraq		X		X	No
Kuwait		X		X	No
Libya		X		X	No
Oman		X		X	No
Qatar		X		X	No
Saudi Arabia		X		X	No
UAE		X		X	No
Oil-poor					
Algeria		X		X	No
Egypt	X		X		Yes
Jordan	X		X		No
Lebanon		X		X	No
Mauritania		X		X	No
Morocco	X		X		Yes
Somalia		X		X	No
Sudan		X		X	No
Syria		X		X	No
Tunisia	X		X		Yes
Yemen AR		X		X	No
Yemen PDR		X		X	No

Source: United Nations Government Population Inquiries, 1974, 1976, 1978, Beirut: United Nations Economic Commission for Western Asia, unpublished.

efforts? At least three reasons have emerged in my discussions with government officials. First, planners contend that even if population control were carried out vigorously today, this would not stop the predicted doubling of the population over the next twenty years. That is, tomorrow's parents have already been born. Accordingly, they contend that population control *per se* does not represent a viable means of solving existing employment, income and social overhead capital problems.[2] Second, they contend that there is little evidence that population control would ameliorate their most serious problem, namely inequalities in the distribution of employment and income earning opportunities. Simple aggregative 'numbers games' which link reductions in population growth with higher per capita incomes are spurned as being of limited relevance to those at the lowest end of the income distribution where subsistence activity is a way of life. At best, planners argue that population control among the poorest might reduce political threats to government or the *status quo* by relaxing frustration over restricted access to available resources. In other words, they contend that problems connected with population pressure would be greatly reduced were existing resources more equally distributed among the poor. Third, they argue that the motivation to reduce desired family size and, subsequently, fertility is really contingent on shifting socio-economic conditions. They point to studies by, say, Freedman and Berelson (1976) or Mauldin and Berelson (1978) to show that declining birth rates in less developed countries have been only marginally contingent on family planning programs *per se*.[3]

Does this imply that population policy and family planning are dead issues in the Arab world? No it does not. But it does imply that appropriate policy must be guided more by concrete welfare considerations than by questionable claims that population control will rapidly promote economic betterment. What are these considerations? In the most general sense they involve unrestricted access to knowledge about, and the means for, the planning and spacing of births, health care of the mother, problems of sterility and sub-fecundity. This is quite distinct from extremely narrow goals of population control or anti-natalist policies. Such knowledge is recognized by the United Nations as a basic human right, and, in my experience, it is of interest to most Arab planners. Moreover, Arab planners are concerned that the social and economic welfare of the family unit should not be jeopardized by a surge of unwanted births. Should socio-economic conditions in the Arab world change to the extent that the desire for large families should decline, then we can expect that Arab governments would want to help their populace to limit their families,[4] otherwise the welfare of married couples and society at large would suffer.

I believe that an appropriate population policy for countries of the region should begin by acknowledging that the traditional push for population control is outdated. That is, I am in sympathy with the contentious points that have been raised by Arab planners concerning the questionable impact of such policies on economic development. Rather, my focus is on the future social and economic welfare of the family unit *per se*. The proposition that I wish to explore concerns the strong possibility that socio-economic improvements being undertaken by the Arab governments will themselves indirectly give rise to a surge of unwanted births. Were this to happen, the welfare of married couples, and Arab society as a whole, would surely suffer unless planners were to anticipate and prepare for the consequences well in advance.

Before the 1973 oil boom, the above proposition would not have raised much interest. That is, the socio-economic situation in most countries was relatively constant, family size desires were high (i.e. six or more children), and even larger numbers of births per woman (i.e. seven to ten) were needed to overcome the destructive effects of high infant and childhood mortality. Since 1973, however, at least two major developments have had an important impact on population. First, health authorities have waged war on foetal deaths and infant mortality to the extent that losses are dropping by up to 10 per cent per year in most countries. The implication for Arab families is that eight or ten live births will no longer be needed to guarantee a desired family size of five or six surviving children. Second, incredible investments in education are affecting opportunities for women as well as the family size desires of Arab couples. As a result of this, combined with rising household incomes, at least in the oil-rich OAPEC countries, there are good reasons to expect that a more educated populace will press governments for improved knowledge and access to family planning services. In one sense, the wisdom of Islam may have foreseen this development. The Qur'an not only wishes to address 'those who are taught and knowledgeable', but it contains no injunction against birth control.

The aim of this chapter is to consider the possibility that Arab families will increasingly be seeking family limitation techniques as a direct outgrowth of socio-economic investments which are being initiated by Arab governments now. The following sections focus on the relationship between education and declining demand for children by (i) relating changes in literacy and education to a projected decline in fertility, (ii) quantifying the demand for family limitation which will result, and (iii) relating this demand to the broader question of education and population policy. In turn, these points are discussed in terms of a number of qualifications pertaining to stability of the fertility/education relationship over time, and improvements in infant and childhood mortality rates. The policy directive that I wish to advocate is really one of timing in which Arab governments are urged to anticipate the consequences of programs upon which they have chosen to embark.

Education and the demand for children

In the past, questions concerning the future demand for children in the Arab world evoked all kinds of speculation. Most of this derived from a wide literature on fertility transition in the historical development of non-Arab countries.[5] With improvements in data sources, however, we can now ask, 'Does Arab experience *per se* suggest specific variables that can reliably be used to anticipate fertility decline and, thus, subsequent demands for family planning to avert unwanted births?' To address this question, I have examined results of fertility surveys from Algeria (1971), Egypt (1960, 1970, 1973, 1976), Jordan (1961, 1967, 1972, 1976), Kuwait (1975), Lebanon (1959, 1971), Syria (1970, 1976) and Turkey (1968, 1975).

A review of these sources leads me to conclude that the relationship between education and fertility, or more specifically planned investments in the education of Arab women, can be used to anticipate prospective declines in their fertility over the next twenty years. Five reasons can be advanced in support of this claim. First, unlike any other index of socio-economic development in the Arab region, differences in levels of female education are strongly and consistently associated with differences in family size. Available survey data reveal that the average number of live births to married women between the ages of 15 and 49 years drops from about 5 or 6 among those with no schooling, to about 3 or 4 among those with a secondary certificate, and to 2 or 2.5 for those with a university degree. This wide spread in live births by level of education remains fairly constant across several countries in urban and rural settings alike. In addition, measures of literacy or education have been found to be the strongest or most consistent predictors of Arab fertility differentials in several multivariate analyses.[6]

Second, for those familiar with the economic–demographic literature on fertility decline in the process of development, the negative fertility/education relationship over the long term makes sense on theoretical grounds.[7] That is, increased education is thought to influence fertility and overall family size through several 'intervening variables' which themselves are known to be the immediate determinants of fertility.[8] For example, prolonged education tends to delay the age at which females first marry. Thus, the total time 'at risk' of conception during the reproductive cycle is shortened.[9] Higher education also tends to broaden the quantity and quality of tastes for consumer durables, travel, etc. According to the Easterlin hypothesis (1975, 1980), this tends to stimulate a greater demand for additional income.

To meet this demand, educated women are not only expected to choose to work more but are expected to reduce the number of their dependent children because the 'opportunity cost' of staying at home with them is greater (see Chapter 5).[10] Moreover, higher earnings potential among more educated women is expected to reinforce the opportunity cost foregone of staying at home.[11]

In addition to the above, education in the Arab world has been observed to exert an independent effect on fertility regardless of women's employment status, urban or rural residence, occupation of the husband, or family income. Allman (1980), for example, summarizes evidence to show that Arab fertility differentials based on education were detected earlier than differentials based on urban/rural residence. This implies that education can be construed as an agent of change in its own right.[12] Of course, rising educational investments are not likely to occur independently of other aspects of modernization. It has been clearly established that educated women are usually more informed about health care, diet, medical facilities, etc. This alone works to reduce sterility, sub-fecundity, and mortality among their offspring to the extent that large numbers of live births are not needed to attain desired family size. In addition, education enhances awareness, frequency of use, and effectiveness of use of modern family limitation techniques.[13]

Third, discrepancies which have been observed in the negative fertility/education relationship are not likely to detract from the generalizations made above as long as fertility decline is examined (i) in terms of the education of the female (or mother) versus that of the male,[14] (ii) among countries that are relatively homogeneous in culture (e.g. Moslem) versus cross-culturally, (iii) for aggregates versus individuals *per se*, and (iv) in contexts where some education exists and improvements in health and infant mortality are underway.[15] For the most part, such conditions are honored in the application to be undertaken in the second part of this chapter.

Fourth, the merits of using completed education to anticipate future declines in fertility are reinforced by the fact that Arab fertility differentials do not vary as consistently with other indices of development. For example, changes in the composition of the population residing in urban versus rural areas tend not to be an accurate guide of forthcoming changes in fertility because fertility or average family size have often been observed to be similar in both settings (Table 4.3).[16] The same applies to the distribution of employed family heads in agriculture versus non-agricultural industries. In Algeria (1972), for

Table 4.3   *Urban/rural differentials in fertility among married women, selected Arab countries, 1961–74*

Country	Urban	Rural	Type of measure
Algeria (1971)	5.7	5.6	Average children ever born to females married at ages between 17 and 19 years
	2.0	2.3	Average children ever born to females married at ages of 25 and over
Egypt (1960)			
Illiterate	4.8	4.4	Average number of children ever born
Secondary	2.0	2.2	to married females between ages of
University	1.6	1.7	15 and 49 years.
Egypt (1970–3)			
Illiterate	5.3	5.2	Average live births to married women
Primary	3.9	3.1	aged between 15 and 44 years
Secondary +	2.3	2.3	
Jordan (1961)	5.1	5.4	Average children ever born to married women aged between 13 and 50 years
Jordan (1967)			
West Bank	6.1	6.1	Average children ever born to married
Gaza	5.8	5.7	women aged between 15 and 49 years
Jordan (1972)	5.4	4.7	Average live births to married women aged between 15 and 49 years
Iraq (1974)	5.9	4.4	Average children ever born to married women aged between 15 and 49 years
Lebanon (1959)	7.3	7.4	Total fertility rate among Lebanese Moslems
Lebanon (1972)	4.1	4.9	Average number of children per married woman aged between 15 and 44 years

Sources: National censuses and surveys.

example, families headed by workers in industry had 5.1 living children, on average, versus 5.4 for those in agriculture and 5.2 for those in transportation, trade and services. In Jordan (1972), families headed by agricultural workers had 6.3 live births, on average, versus 5.6 for those headed by non-agricultural workers and 5.2 for skilled laborers. In my analysis of child dependency and crude birth rates in Tunisia (Appendix 4.1), the proportion of the population active in agriculture had no effect on fertility.[17]

As for female employment, we would expect some differential in fertility by working status if only because education raises prospects for employment and, thus, the 'opportunity cost' of devoting all a woman's time to child rearing.[18] However, as extended families tend to reduce the burden of dependent children on working women, the differential in fertility by employment status tends not to be consistent. To illustrate the point, in Turkey (1968), Moslem women who had never worked in rural areas had 4.2 live births, on average, versus 3.9 for those employed in agriculture. In Egypt (1976), married women who were not economically active reported 5.4 children (ever born) versus 4.0 for those economically active. For those employed in agriculture, the figure was 3.7 versus 4.6 for those employed in 'industry, transportation and communication occupations'. In Lebanon (1972), the wife's work status before and after marriage was not a significant predictor of the mean number of children ever born, according to a multivariate analysis by Chamie (1981). In a multivariate study of eighteen Arab countries, using 1970 data, Azzam (1979b) concludes that female labor force participation rates do affect the crude birth rate. Finally, in my analysis of Tunisian fertility (Appendix 4.1), female activity rates exert no effect on variations in fertility.[19]

Similar conclusions apply to other variables that might be used to anticipate shifts in fertility (e.g. religion, family income). Differentials frequently do exist, but they are often small or inconsistent across countries. While the average age of females at marriage almost always stands out as a strong conditioner of fertility, it is also true that changes in this variable are usually contingent on extended periods of female enrollment in schools.[20]

Fifth, my use of completed education to estimate future fertility decline has an appealing policy advantage. That is, (i) information on the structure of female enrollments by age is available now, (ii) today's enrollments can be used to estimate completed education among tomorrow's cohort of married women between the ages of 15 and 49 years, and (iii) tomorrow's educational structure can be traced directly to intentional government planning. Thus, the effects of educational investment can be monitored relatively easily, and the consequences of these investments for future fertility can be anticipated. In contrast, had other variables such as 'the distribution of the labor force by economic sector', or 'income' turned out to be useful in accounting for present variations in fertility, they could hardly be used for future estimation because knowledge about their future evolution is, at best, vague.[21]

Now, in order to evaluate the effects of educational investment or, more precisely, increased female enrollments, on future fertility in the Arab world, we must (i) establish the extent to which higher levels of education are indeed strongly and consistently related to lower levels of fertility, and (ii) calibrate the extent to which fertility will fall in the face of an X per cent increase in female educational attainment. These tasks require the application of a statistical technique called 'least squares regression' to analyze variations in fertility performance by level of education. The results of this technique, to be presented in a non-technical language, permit the derivation of a shorthand 'estimating equation' for calculating fertility decline among married women in the future. That is, by feeding the estimating equation with information on the expected educational characteristics of Arab females in the future we can estimate the number of births that Arab couples are likely to seek to avert in the future. The section below describes both methodology and results. It is followed by a discussion of a number of qualifications.

Calibrating the relationship

Data for six Arab countries covering the period 1970 to 1976 have been used to calibrate the relationship between average fertility and average years of completed schooling among married women. Average fertility has been measured as the average number of live births to married women of reproductive age (i.e. 15 to 49 years).[22] For the most part, the empirical measures for completed schooling and fertility are similar for the six countries (see Appendix 4.2).

By pooling small numbers of observations for several countries, the education/fertility relationship has been calibrated using a maximum of thirty-five observations. Combined, these observations are reasonably representative of the Arab region in so far as they contain the experience of a Gulf country (Kuwait), three additional Middle Eastern countries (Jordan, Syria, Lebanon) and two North African countries (Egypt, Algeria). Moreover, the experience of the largest Arab country, Egypt, is represented by thirteen of the thirty-five observations.

The statistical relationship has been calibrated using least squares regression analysis. The results, presented in Appendix 4.3, convey that a very strong inverse relationship exists between levels of fertility and levels of wives' education. That is, approximately 83 per cent of the variation in average levels of fertility among women in our sample countries can be accounted for by variations in their level of education. Moreover, the techniques employed allow us to conclude with a reasonable degree of confidence that an increase of one year in the duration of education of married women will be accompanied by a drop of 0.21 in the average number of live births that they will have over their reproductive period. That is, a woman with, say, ten years of education should have, on average, 2.1 fewer live births over her reproductive cycle than a woman with no education.

The above conclusions are applicable whether the effect of education on fertility is estimated entirely on its own, or in the presence of controls for two additional variables (see Appendix 4.3). The control variables are 'whether government policies pertaining to women's employment are restrictive or not' and 'the level of infant mortality' in each country. The former control variable was considered in the analysis as critics might contend that the effect of higher education on fertility could be cancelled out by the presence of barriers to employment. The control variable pertaining to infant mortality was considered in the analysis to accommodate the notion that increases in education in high mortality contexts have been observed to result in increases, not decreases, in fertility (Cochrane: 1979).[23]

In my view, the fact that the relationship between fertility and education is strong, statistically significant and consistent across countries suggests that the findings reported in Appendix 4.3 can be used as a crude benchmark for the Arab region as a whole. Furthermore, the results in Appendix 4.3 (Table A.4.3, row G) allow us to construct a shorthand estimating equation for purposes of quantifying the number of births that females in the Arab region are likely to attempt to avert in the future as the level of their education increases.

The estimating equation, as derived from the results in Appendix 4.3, is really quite simple. It takes the following form:

Average number
of live births
to married women = $5.45 (E_0) + 4.20 (E_6) + 2.93 (E_{12}) + 2.09 (E_{16})$,
aged 15 to 49 years.

where: E_0 = % of married women aged 15–49 years with no schooling or illiterate,
E_6 = „ „ „ „ „ „ „ „ primary certificate,
E_{12} = „ „ „ „ „ „ „ „ secondary certificate,
E_{16} = „ „ „ „ „ „ „ „ university degree.

Essentially our shorthand equation is a weighting method. It operates as follows. Suppose that all married females between the ages of 15 and

49 years in country X are illiterate. Then, the value of E_0, or those with zero education, would be 100 per cent, or 1.00. As a result, the weighting equation above would tell us that the average number of live births per woman in the cohort of married women in country X would be 5.45 (1.00) = 5.45. In this case, there would not be any entries, or weights, for the educational categories E_6, E_{12} or E_{16}.

In contrast, say that 'tomorrow' (meaning some time in the future) 50 per cent of the married females in the same country X will finish primary schooling and that 50 per cent will complete secondary schooling. According to the weighting equation above, the average number of live births to the married cohort in this case would be 4.20 (0.50) + 2.93 (0.50) = 3.57. That is, there would be no entries for E_0 or E_{16}. The difference between this example and the one above shows up as a drop in the average number of live births between the cohort 'before education' (i.e. 5.45) versus the cohort 'after education' (i.e. 3.57). In percentage terms, the drop is calculated as: 1 − (3.57)/ (5.45) = 34.5 per cent.

Summing up, if we can reasonably assume that the behavioral relationship between education and fertility will remain relatively constant over the short term (e.g. ten years), then the results from our example above imply that the demand for, or use of, family limitation techniques will increase by at least 34.5 per cent among the more educated reproductive cohort of tomorrow.[24] Now, let us apply our estimating equation using real data.

Application

To put our estimating equation to work for a cohort of currently married women between the ages of 15 and 49 years in any single country, we need only establish their current distribution by level of completed education. This is not difficult as approximately 85 to 95 per cent are illiterate in most countries. Thus, according to our estimating equation, an average married woman in 'today's' reproductive cohort in, say, Lebanon or Algeria has 4.45 and 5.50 live births, respectively.

In contrast, to put the estimating equation to work for today's cohort of youth that will be married and bearing children tomorrow is considerably more taxing. First, it is necessary to gauge the amount of schooling that today's female youth between the ages of 5 and 24 years will receive by the time they constitute a large share of the women in 'tomorrow's' reproductive cohort.[25] Second, it is necessary

Appropriate population policy

to adjust the number of females in today's cohort between the ages of
5 and 24 years that will not survive *en route* to becoming tomorrow's
reproductive cohort. Third, it is necessary to estimate the proportion
of those in tomorrow's reproductive cohort that will not marry.

Results of the first requirement are presented in Table 4.4 This
educational distribution is based on UNESCO data and incorporates

Table 4.4 *Expected level of educational attainment among future
married women by 1995, Arab countries*

	% distribution of females now aged 5 to 24 years (1975) by expected level of educational attainment upon reaching ages 24 to 44 years in 1995			
Countries	% no schooling (1)	% completed primary (2)	% completed secondary (3)	% university degree (4)
Arab World	55.3	29.0	13.2	2.5
Oil-rich	55.1	26.7	15.7	2.5
Oil-poor	55.4	29.4	12.7	2.5
Oil-rich				
Bahrain	13.0	41.0	43.6	2.4
Iraq	57.1	25.8	13.6	3.5
Kuwait	12.3	21.0	60.0	6.7
Libya	16.5	56.3	26.0	1.2
Oman	88.9	8.7	2.3	0.1
Qatar	19.2	35.0	45.0	0.8
Saudi Arabia	71.5	17.8	10.4	0.3
UAE	63.3	29.2	7.4	0.1
Oil-poor				
Algeria	50.8	37.6	10.7	0.9
Egypt	47.1	31.1	15.5	6.3
Jordan	31.6	34.7	32.0	1.7
Lebanon	1.4	39.1	52.6	6.9
Mauritania	94.5	4.5	0.9	0.1
Morocco	70.4	16.9	12.1	0.6
Somalia	88.7	9.2	2.0	0.1
Sudan	71.0	22.0	6.7	0.3
Syria	45.1	32.2	19.5	3.2
Tunisia	41.0	46.1	11.6	1.3
Yemen AR	96.5	2.8	0.6	0.1
Yemen PDR	76.8	18.7	4.4	0.1

Source: Calculated using data from UNESCO yearbooks, and Trends and Pro-
jections of School Enrollment in Arab Countries', Paris: United Nations
Educational, Scientific and Cultural Organization, ED 77, Mimeo,
Arab/Ref. 3, 1977, Limited Distribution.

112

the dramatic improvement in the educational infrastructure up to 1975. Thus, in Bahrain, for example, most females entered the primary system, and half of them are expected to terminate at the secondary level. That only 2.4 per cent are expected to continue to university is determined by the capacity and performance of the educational system between 1975 and 1980. As this capacity will surely expand between 1980 and 1995, thus affecting the youngest (but not the oldest) girls in today's cohort, my estimates of educational attainment may be on the low side. If so, this will also tend to underestimate my projected demand for family limitation techniques in the future.

The average number of live births among tomorrow's reproductive cohort in each country is simply determined by entering the figures in columns 1–4, Table 4.4, in our estimating equation. The results of this computation are presented in column 3 of Table 4.5.

The number of today's females that will be alive in tomorrow's reproductive cohort is presented in column 2 of Table 4.5. These figures were derived by applying survivorship rates, calculated from United Nations Model Life Tables, to the figures in column 1. For the Model Life Tables infant mortality rates were used for entry.[26] As virtually all Arab women marry, I determine the average number of live births which will be produced by the reproductive cohort of tomorrow by simply multiplying column 2 by column 3.[27] Results are presented in column 4. In column 5, I estimate the number of live births that would have been produced by the same cohort had their fertility remained constant (i.e. the same as today's largely illiterate cohort). In other words, results in column 5 could be interpreted as the expectations of a 'traditionalist' who does not anticipate any change in reproductive behavior with increased female schooling. The difference between columns 4 and 5 (in column 6) represents the minimum number of births that the more educated cohort of reproductive women tomorrow are likely to seek to avert.

For the Arab world as a whole, I estimate that some 13 million births will need to be averted to accommodate preferences for smaller family size among more educated Arab women. Approximately 3.3 million of these will be to women in the oil-rich countries versus some 9.7 million to those in the oil-poor countries.

Discussion and qualifications

Is the use of a single variable regression to make projections into the future too simplistic? The utility of any explanatory variable for

113

Table 4.5 Estimated live births to be averted among Arab couples in the future, Arab countries, 1975–95

Countries	Cohort of females aged 5–24 in 1975 (000's) (1)	Survivors of 1975 cohort in 1995, now aged 25–44 (000's) (2)	Estimated average no. live births per reproductive couple in 1995 (3)	Total no. live births by the reproductive cohort by 1995 (000's) (4)	Total no. live births assuming no change in education (000's) (5)	Minimum no. live births to be averted by tomorrow's cohort: (5)–(4) (000's) (6)
Arab World	29,078	26,052	4.69	122,295	135,374	13,079
Oil-rich	4,941	4,479	4.66	20,890	24,216	3,325
Oil-poor	24,137	21,573	4.70	101,405	111,158	9,754
Oil-rich						
Bahrain	49	46	3.79	174	234	60
Iraq	2,424	2,249	4.69	10,548	12,216	1,668
Kuwait	225	209	3.50	731	1,103	372
Libya	492	439	4.08	1,791	2,394	603
Oman	172	153	5.29	809	834	25
Qatar	20	18	3.89	70	94	24
Saudi Arabia	1,486	1,300	4.96	6,448	6,986	538
UAE	73	65	4.91	319	354	35
Oil-poor						
Algeria	4,082	3,572	4.69	16,753	18,845	2,092
Egypt	6,482	5,899	4.47	26,368	28,817	2,449
Jordan	537	498	4.18	2,082	2,498	416
Lebanon	480	435	3.45	1,500	1,897	397
Mauritania	283	240	5.36	1,286	1,308	22
Morocco	3,815	3,399	4.90	16,655	18,264	1,609
Somalia	794	676	5.28	3,569	3,685	116
Sudan	3,084	2,739	5.01	13,722	14,719	997
Syria	1,788	1,624	4.47	7,259	8,251	992
Tunisia	1,369	1,246	4.54	5,657	6,087	430
Yemen AR	1,020	892	5.40	4,817	4,863	46
Yemen PDR	403	353	4.92	1,737	1,925	188

prediction purposes, be it one or several, is really determined by (i) the adequacy of the theory behind it, (ii) the degree to which it is known to represent the nexus of factors thought to influence the variable to be 'explained', (iii) the 'goodness of fit' between the dependent and independent variable(s), and (iv) the extent to which the independent variable(s) can be used for future policy projections. With respect to these criteria, and in view of the fact that I have estimated the fertility/ education relationship while controlling for two additional influences, it seems reasonable to conclude that my use of education is defensible.[28]

Of course, I would have preferred to disaggregate education into subvariables to capture its effects on, say, the average age of marriage, or wage and salary opportunities for women. But data are seldom sufficient in quantity or quality to permit such disaggregation for statistical analysis. In addition, data on trends affecting such sub-variables over the future are extremely scarce. This means that a more elaborate multivariate analysis could be used only for simulation with arbitrary manipulation of variables to gauge future fertility decline. In contrast, available data on educational investments and future female school enrollments have allowed me to project future fertility declines in the light of action being undertaken by the Arab governments themselves.

A second qualification concerns the consistency of the fertility/ education relationship over time. Can future fertility be projected using a 'behavioral equation' that has been derived using data which pertain to a past period? The answer is yes as long as (i) the empirical relationship advocating a negative correlation between education and fertility remains relatively constant over time, and (ii) there is no particular reason to anticipate that some epiphenomenal force will disturb the relationship. To my knowledge, the only available data of reasonable quality that might be used to check on the consistency of the empirical relationship pertain to Egypt. Using 1960 census data, the empirical relationship between ten fertility/education observations was entirely consistent with that for thirteen fertility/education observations for the period 1970 to 1976. A pooling of the twenty-three observations produces empirical results that are in general agreement with those presented in Appendix 4.3, Table A.4.3.[29]

Turning to cultural factors, we might also ask whether the impact of rising education on fertility might be undermined, indirectly, by cultural barriers to female employment. After all, the participation of women in the labor force is an acknowledged correlate of smaller family size, and it is known that education and employment interact to contribute to this effect. My view is that restrictions on female employment will be, and currently are being, greatly relaxed in most Arab countries (see Chapter 5). This is evident in both oil-rich and oil-poor countries. To illustrate this point, consider the case of Qatar which has long been associated with Islam's strict Wahhabi movement which spread from Saudi Arabia in the eighteenth century. The government of Qatar is taking considerable pride in adopting a more liberal approach to the role of its women in modern society. The first two Qataris to get Ph.D.s were women, and more and more women are finding jobs, particularly as nurses, teachers and doctors. Consider also the case of Iraq, where an important goal of the government is to increase the involvement and participation of women in the development process. This is evident in the growth of employment between 1972 and 1976 where 29,267 of 133,624 new workers were women. Moreover, relative to past rates of growth, the rate of growth of female employment between 1972 and 1976 was double that for males. And the story goes on with the creation of a large vocational training center for women in Jordan, and the development of a women's union in the Sudan with some 2,759 units and 804 classes operating across the country.

A third qualification concerns timing. To appreciate fully the timing of fertility reduction or the subsequent demand for family planning, it would be necessary to gauge the impact of health-related as well as education-related investments. The significance of health-related investments for fertility or the demand for family planning can be illustrated as follows. Assume that at time 't' Arab couples are just attaining their desired family size. Assume that their desired family size equals six surviving children. Improvements in health, as they bring about a rapid decline in infant and childhood mortality, are likely to motivate couples to cut back on their fertility when 'X + n' live births (e.g. ten) are no longer needed to guarantee their desired family size of 'X' surviving children (e.g. six). That is, with improved infant and childhood mortality rates, the 'surplus' 'n' live births (e.g. four) will no longer be necessary.

Certainly, the Arab world is plagued by high infant and childhood mortality rates (Table 4.1, column 7).[30] With improvements due to massive health-related investments it is reasonable to assume that the demand for family limitation will increase so that the 'n' live births will not cause the desired family size of 'X' surviving children to be surpassed. This point is elaborated in Appendix 4.4. While it is likely to detract from the accuracy of my calculations, it is also true that it will show up as an underestimate of one component of Arab fertility decline. That is, my projections should understate (rather than exaggerate) my case concerning the prospective demand for family planning.

Summing up, if my estimates concerning the demand for family limitation techniques are biased, they are likely to be on the low side. This might present problems were we trying to streamline the efficiency of a well-established system of family planning services. In the Arab world, however, this is not the case. Systems of family planning services are only beginning to evolve. In addition, many Arab planners remain to be convinced that a system of family planning services should be established at all. By understating my case for future family planning, yet showing that the need will be massive just the same, my results convey a minimum effort that will be required to ensure that the welfare of Arab couples is not undermined.[31]

Infrastructure

A rough ordering of countries according to the expected demand for family limitation techniques per married couple is presented in column 1 of Table 4.6. Little effort is required to conclude that the existing infrastructure is completely inadequate to accommodate the projected demand for family limitation techniques in the future. In eleven out of sixteen countries where projected demand has been ranked from moderate to very strong, family planning efforts are negligible (Table 4.6, column 2). Only Tunisia, Egypt, and possibly Morocco, could rapidly expand facilities to accommodate a burgeoning demand. As for modern contraceptive use, most countries are relative beginners (See Table 4.6, column 3).[32]

Assuming that my estimates are reasonable, Arab governments in the 'strong' categories (Table 4.6) are advised to waste no time in boosting their family planning effort. It is the capacity of a workable family planning infrastructure that will be missed when demand for family planning soars. Whereas contraceptive techniques *per se* may be relatively inexpensive and abundant, it is the diffusion of family planning knowledge and health support services that is costly and time consuming.[33] In addition, crucial health support personnel are seldom in adequate supply, particularly in rural areas. Such problems have made a mockery of well meaning programs in several less developed countries. For example, the government of Morocco aimed to reduce the crude birth rate from approximately 50 per thousand in 1968 to

Table 4.6 *Projected demand for family planning versus existing national family planning effort, Arab countries, 1975–95*

Projected demand for family limitation (1)	Existing national family planning effort (maximum value = 24)[a] (2)	Crude estimates of % of married couples using some form of efficient contraception between 1973 and 1978[b] (3)
Very strong		
Bahrain	0	5–10
Jordan	0	25–30
Kuwait	0	15–20
Lebanon	0	25–30
Libya	0	5–10
Qatar	0	5–10
Moderately strong		
Algeria	3	10–15
Egypt	8	14–20
Iraq	0	10–15
Syria	0	10–15
Tunisia	12	15–20
Moderate		
Morocco	4	10–15
Saudi Arabia	0	5–10
Sudan	3	5–10
UAE	0	5–10
Yemen PDR	0	5–10
Weak		
Mauritania	0	0–5
Oman	0	5–10
Somalia	0	–
Yemen AR	0	5–10

Notes: a Values obtained from Mauldin and Berelson (1978).
b Data obtained from International Planned Parenthood, and national surveys.

45 per thousand in 1972. Yet, less than 40 per cent of the married women in cities had ever heard of the IUD by 1971, family planning infrastructure was virtually non-existant in rural areas, and it was difficult to retain medical personnel in rural posts. It is only now that the effects of systematic planning and a reasonable infrastructure are being felt among significant proportions of married women.[34]

Of course, in developing an appropriate infrastructure, family planning should not be equated with anti-natalist policies or family limitation techniques *per se*. On the one hand, care of the mother during pregnancy and improved spacing of children are equally important ways of contributing to the health of Arab women. The key role of midwives could certainly be enlarged to meet this end. By enhancing their training in more modern family limitation techniques, and by certifying their skills, the wait for medical personnel in rural areas could be partially sidestepped. Further, as midwives already have the 'ear' and confidence of Arab women they could play a useful role in disseminating modern family planning knowledge.

On the other hand, population education has an important contribution to make to the welfare of both families and Arab society as a whole in the near future.[35] The problem today is that most couples know little about family planning issues until their family size desires have been exceeded.[36] Accordingly, 'successes' in existing family planning clinics are all to often comprised of women who have virtually completed their fertility cycle.[37] Dynamic health and economic improvements, which are bound to affect sub-fecundity, infant mortality, etc., should be explained to women at the beginning of their fertility cycle so as to enhance their control over their planning of their family. Possibly, this kind of information could eventually be introduced in schools. Rising female enrollments and the predominance of female teachers at the primary level may be rendering the schooling system more suitable for this kind of undertaking. Furthermore, the health and economic situation is changing so rapidly in most countries that failure to familiarize students with the ramifications of these changes on family structure would represent gross neglect. The emphasis sought here has much in common with preventive strategies in modern medicine. Rather than overload expertise and facilities at time of crisis, efforts should be made to educate the populace to avoid crisis-producing behavior well in advance.

As for governments which perceive a shortage of manpower or welcome population growth as a driving force for the future of their economies (e.g. some OAPEC countries), is it in their interests to maintain a strict pro-natalist policy? To my mind, it is not. There is a good chance that the future welfare of their more educated population will be compromised in the process. A more promising way of circumventing this problem would be to encourage pro-migration policies. As argued in Chapter 2, existing patterns of interregional migration should be rationalized to accommodate anticipated population shortages in today's manpower-deficient economies. This would certainly come to the rescue of several so-called 'surplus population' countries (e.g. Egypt, Morocco). It would also give greater substance to the ideals of Arab brotherhood and interregional economic cooperation and integration.

Summary and conclusions

Before 1973, the kind of exercise undertaken here would have offered little of practical worth to governments of the Arab world. High levels of sub-fecundity, foetal deaths, infant mortality and family size desires virtually ruled out the demand for family limitation techniques. Accordingly, most Arab governments showed very little interest in family planning.

Some have erroneously interpreted this resistance as being due to Islamic doctrine or traditional customs. Yet, family planning is far from alien to the Islamic world. Many of the great medical books of Islamic science contained long lists of contraceptive techniques and instructions for their use. Moreover, the Qur'an contains no injunction against contraceptive use. In many respects this is a compliment to the wisdom of Islam. It means that government objectives to improve the socio-economic situation of Arab families need not turn a blind eye to con-comitant increases in the demand for modern forms of family planning.

That the demand for this type of knowledge will increase rapidly over the next twenty years due to investments being undertaken by Arab governments *now*, is the message of this chapter. To my mind, the driving force behind this demand will be two-fold. On the one hand, health-related improvements will reduce the force of infant mortality, etc., to the extent that family limitation techniques will be sought to keep fertility from surpassing desired family size. On the other hand, socio-economic improvements, particularly as they affect female education, will work to reduce family size desires themselves. In focusing largely on the latter, I have combined empirical knowledge about what happens to fertility with increasing female education with a schedule of future female educational attainment. This has been used to predict the number of births that more educated women will seek to avert in the future. For several reasons my calculations tend to under-estimate the number of births to be averted. Thus, it is not unreasonable to conclude that my results prescribe the minimum effort that will likely be required to insure that family welfare is not threatened by a surge of undesired offspring.

My real concern is that Arab governments fully anticipate the 'fertility consequences' of educational programs that are being embarked upon today. The accent is on 'problem avoidance' through employing a preventive approach rather than 'solution by crisis'. An important feature of the preventive approach is to forewarn future couples of the effect of rapid socio-economic development on their future family size and family welfare. To some extent, population education in the formal school system could serve this end. Another important feature is to recognize that the provision of an adequate family planning infrastructure is a slow, step-by-step process. Certification and extension of skills among midwives could go a long way to harness resources which are already guiding the health care of expectant mothers and the spacing of their children.

While the preventive approach may well be constrained by a lack of national funds, international sources could play an important supporting role. Several organizations, including the UNFPA, IPPF and USAID have spent US $48 million in Egypt alone for family planning and health projects during the last five years.[38] The UNFPA, which is the largest source of funds, with a budget of approximately US $125 million, channels most of its funding to the Arab world through sister UN organizations (International Labour Organization (ILO), FAO, WHO) to support integrated projects.[39] The experience of the ILO is that the UNFPA funded projects are well received by Arab governments when they sensibly interrelate population questions with broader issues concerning the socio-economic welfare of Arab families.[40] Distinct from suspicious looking pamphlets touting the biases of population controllers, results of the ILO/UNFPA projects typically evaluate interrelations between population and employment, income, urban growth, nomadism, agricultural settlements, migration, etc. The planned outcome of these projects, called 'Comprehensive Population and Employment Projects', is to synthesize findings on several Arab countries so as to formulate guidelines for national development planning. In my view, the results of these projects could be put to good use in the preparation of a textbook on population and development, written in Arabic, for use in planning ministries and university courses on development. UNFPA funds might be tapped to produce, distribute and communicate this kind of product to good advantage.

Appendix 4.1 Analysis of Tunisian fertility

This appendix examines the relationship between fertility and selected socio-economic characteristics in Tunisian governates. Fertility has been represented by either the crude birth rate (CBR), or the child dependency ratio (DEP). The independent effect of several socio-economic characteristics on variations in either CBR or DEP has been established using multiple regression techniques.

The choice of socio-economic characteristics for the analysis has been directed partly by theory and constrained largely by data limitations. Thus, in accordance with most studies of fertility, I examine the effect of female literacy (a hypothesized + effect), nuptiality rates (a hypothesized + effect), female labor force participation (a hypothesized − effect), value of building construction in each governate as an index of economic growth (a hypothesized − effect), the proportion of the labor force in agriculture (a hypothesized + effect), the proportion of males in each governate that have emigrated (a hypothesized − effect), and the proportion of males in each governate that are unemployed (a hypothesized − effect).

The only variables which were statistically significant and/or consistently demonstrated the expected sign were rates of female literacy and rates of male emigration. Combined, they accounted for nearly 80 per cent of the variation in DEP and 61 per cent of the variation in CBR. Details are reported below.

Details on Tunisian fertility analysis

Variables considered

DEP = child dependency ratio; average number of children aged between 0 and 4 years per female aged 10 years or more.

CBR = crude birth rate; number of births per 1,000 population.

Lit = proportion of females that are literate.

M = number of emigrant males per 100 working males.

NUP = rates of marriage per thousand population.

Additional variables considered are noted below.

Procedure

(i)   The estimated equation and hypothesized signs of variables are as follows:

$\ln \text{DEP} = a - b_1 \ln \text{Lit} - b_2 \ln \text{M} + b_3 \ln \text{NUP} + e$

or

$\ln \text{CBR}$

(ii)   All data have been transformed to log normal.
(iii) Observations are represented by eighteen Tunisian governates.
(iv)   The year of the database is 1975.

Interpretation of results from Table A.4.1
The rate of female literacy (Lit) is the most significant correlate of both DEP and CBR. A 10 per cent increase in the value of Lit is likely to reduce DEP by 4.3 per cent or CBR by 4.0 per cent. Emigration of males (M) is the second most significant correlate of both DEP and CBR. A 10 per cent increase in M is likely to reduce DEP by 1.4 per cent and CBR by about 1.3 per cent. Marriage rates (NUP) are not significantly related to either DEP or CBR, though NUP does carry the expected sign. These findings are in general accord with theoretical expectations and, as is evident from Table A.4.1, the predictive power of the equation is quite high at about 80 per cent in the case of DEP and 61 per cent in the case of CBR.

Additional variables, not reported here, were also considered but they were not statistically significant in the analysis. These included (i) the proportion of the labor force in agriculture (a hypothesized + effect), (ii) value of building construction in each governate as an index of economic growth (– effect), (iii) rates of female activity in the labor force (– effect), and (iv) the proportion of males in each governate that were unemployed (– effect).

Appendix 4.2 Data for the fertility/education analysis

On the whole, the fertility measures for the countries represented in the regression analysis are comparable. This is evident from Table A.4.2. Most of the sample sources have measured average fertility for the country as a whole by sampling urban (U) and rural (R) areas in proportion to the distribution of the national population. Though the Egyptian data of 1970 and 1973 pertain to women in Cairo and in rural areas, respectively, results for both samples are quite similar.

Toward overcoming differences in the age structure between countries (which could affect the fertility measures), the average number of live births to the entire cohort is weighted in the sense that the fertility performance of young or beginning wives is combined with that of older wives. These average figures are noticeably lower than the average completed family size of, say, married women aged 49 years

Table A.4.1 *Regression results for Tunisian fertility analysis*

Independent variables	Analysis of DEP			Analysis of CBR		
	Regression coefficient	Student 't'	Cumulative variance	Regression coefficient	Student 't'	Cumulative variance
Lit (literacy)	−0.427	6.77[a]	74.29	−0.399	2.87[a]	53.49
M (migration)	−0.142	2.13[b]	80.40	−0.126	1.47[c]	59.51
NUP (marriage)	0.120	0.80	80.40	0.723	0.61	60.96
Intercept value	5.17			4.64		
R^2	0.80			0.61		

Notes: a Student 't' is significant at 0.01 level;
        b Significant at 0.025 level.
        c Significant at 0.10 level.

Table A.4.2 *Description of data sources for fertility/education analysis*

Country	Year	Fertility measure	Sample size	Area
Jordan	1972	Avg. live births to married women aged 15 to 49 years	5,214	U + R[a]
Lebanon	1971	Avg. live births to married women aged 15 to 49 years	2,752	U + R[a]
Syria	1970	Avg. live births to married women aged 15 to 49 years	Census	National
Algeria	1970	Avg. children ever born to married women aged 15 to 49 years	12,969	U + R[a]
Egypt	1970	Avg. children ever born to married women aged 15 to 45 years	569	Cairo
Egypt	1973	Avg. live births to married women aged 15 to 49 years	1,234	R[a]
Egypt	1976	Avg. children ever born to married women aged 15 to 49 years	Census	National
Kuwait	1975	Avg. children ever born to married women aged 15 to 49 years	Census	National

Note: a U = urban, R = rural.

who have largely completed their reproductive cycle. As for the possibility that the quality of data may vary from country to country, information on, say, under-reporting is insufficient to quantify the potential magnitude of such errors.

Appendix 4.3 Analysis of the relationship between fertility and education

This appendix quantifies the relationship between the average fertility of married women between the ages of 15 and 49 years, and their level of educational attainment. The results in Part A of Table A.4.3 pertain to the relationship between fertility (F) and education (E) in the absence of control variables. Part B of Table A.4.3. estimates the relationship for all thirty-five observations while controlling for two additional variables.

In Part A of Table A.4.3, regression coefficients have been estimated for countries arranged in groupings A through G. This procedure has been adopted to ascertain if the estimated regression coefficients remain consistent as countries are added systematically to the sample size.

Table A.4.3   *Regression results for education and fertility*

Part A: No control variables

Country group	Sample size (1)	Intercept (2)	Slope (3)	r^2 (4)	Elasticity at mean value $(\Delta F/F)/(\Delta E/E)$ (5)
A 1–2	9	5.38	−0.23	0.88	−0.47
B 1–3	13	5.51	−0.22	0.85	−0.46
C 1–4	16	5.58	−0.21	0.84	−0.46
D 1–5	19	5.45	−0.21	0.83	−0.44
E 1–6	22	5.42	−0.21	0.82	−0.43
F 1–7	29	5.42	−0.21	0.82	−0.42
G 1–8	35	5.45	−0.21	0.83	−0.43

Countries (see Appendix 4.2 for description of data sources):

1	Jordan (1972)	4	Algeria (1970)	7	Egypt (1976)
2	Lebanon (1971)	5	Egypt (1970)	8	Kuwait (1975)
3	Syria (1970)	6	Egypt (1973)		

Part B: With control variables

Independent variables	Regression coefficient	Student 't' value
Education (E)	−0.21	−12.82[a]
Employment restriction (D)	−0.58	− 1.69
Infant mortality rate (IMR)	0.54	1.06
Intercept value = 5.318	$R^2 = 0.84$	No. observations = 35

Note: [a] Student 't' is significant at 0.01 level.

Observe that the r^2 for the 'maximum pooling' in row G is very high at 0.83. The elasticity as *mean value* between fertility (F) and education (E) has been calculated in column 5, and stands at −0.43 for row G.

Admittedly, the number of observations for this exercise is small. For this reason, it is crucial that the empirical relationship is both strong (high r^2) and consistent among countries. According to the results in rows A through G, this criterion is satisfied.

In Part B of Table A.4.3 the relationship between fertility (F) and education (E) has been estimated while controlling for 'whether government policies pertaining to women's employment are restrictive or not', and 'the level of infant mortality' in each country. The former variable has been represented as a dummy variable with values 1 = minimum restrictions on female labor force participation; 0 = all others. Values for the dummy variable (D) have been taken from Azzam (1979b). The latter variable has been represented as the infant mortality rate (IMR). Values for IMR range from 44 to 103 among our sample countries. Reasons for including these variables are given in the text.

Note that the value of the regression coefficient (or slope) for education (E) is -0.21. This value is virtually identical to the slope or regression coefficient reported for education in row G, Part A of Table A.4.3. Thus, the addition of the control variables has not affected the estimated relationship between fertility and education. While neither control variable is statistically significant at the 0.01 level or better, each does exhibit the expected sign. That is, the more countries have minimum restrictions on female employment (D), the less fertility in those countries is likely to be. On the other hand, the higher the level of infant mortality (IMR), the higher fertility is likely to be.

Appendix 4.4 Timing of fertility reduction and family limitation

To appreciate fully the timing of fertility reduction and the subsequent demand for family planning, it is necessary to monitor the effects of at least two influences. One is contingent on the pace of health-related investments. The other is contingent on the pace of socio-economic investments such as education. These components are schematized in Figure A.4.1.

According to Figure A.4.1, the force of infant mortality (IM) and of childhood mortality (CM) is currently working to reduce the cumulative fertility of couples (CF) in the direction of desired family size (DFS) at time 't'. CF may lie anywhere between the total fertility rate and the biological maximum number of children that women can have (say, sixteen to twenty live births). For the moment, we assume that the force of mortality (IM plus CM) is working to hold CF in line with desired family size (DFS_t). However, as the force of IM and CM, as well as problems of sub-fecundity, are eliminated by health-related improvements, the number of children born and surviving will begin to exceed DFS_t. The only way to reduce the excess, or unwanted, births will be to employ some family limitation method.

At the same time that health-related improvements are reducing the

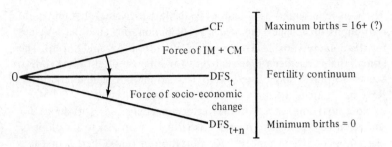

Figure A.4.1 *Shifts in fertility due to two forces*

toll of mortality, assume that socio-economic improvements, such as education, are also exerting an effect. In this case the effect is likely to be felt on desired family size itself. Short of a natural disaster, family limitation methods would also be needed to avert unwanted births towards accommodating the new family size desires (i.e. as represented in the swing from DFS_t to DFS_{t+n} in Figure A.4.1).

More rigorous estimates of the demand for family limitation in the Arab world would require knowledge of future changes in infant and childhood mortality, and the existing gap between cumulative fertility and desired family size, as well as prospective changes in desired family size. While cumulative fertility might be equated with the total fertility rate for estimation purposes (which is about 7 in fourteen out of twenty Arab countries), actual cumulative fertility may well be much higher. This would imply that some form of natural contraception is already at work and is reducing fertility performance near the observed total fertility rate. As for infant and childhood mortality, existing estimates are extremely crude. Further, little is known about their likely rate of decline in the future. Thus, as the force of infant and childhood mortality is relaxed, the extent to which 'surplus' births must be reduced by contraception to attain the desired family size cannot be reliably estimated.

As for actual levels of desired family size (DFS), surveys are so few and far between that behavior of DFS cannot be monitored over time or measured in response to changing socio-economic conditions. At best, available evidence suggests that DFS for ever married women less than 50 years of age is about 4.6 in rural areas in Morocco (1968) and Tunisia (1964), about 4.0 in Lebanon (1971), about 3.6 in Egypt (between 1970 and 1973), about 5.9 in Jordan (1972), about 4.6 in Iran (1970), and about 7.1 and 5.8 in urban and rural areas, respectively, in Iraq (1974). Available evidence also suggests that completed family size is often in excess of DFS.[41] With improved childhood survival, it seems reasonable to assume that the gap between future attainable family size and desired family size will grow. This alone would imply an increase in the demand for family limitation techniques.

Chapter 5

Upgrading women's employment

Introduction

In 1971 the Declaration of Arab states asserted that 'Men and women are partners in life and destiny and they must work together to build a life based on cooperation and equality'. Governments have responded in varying degrees by prohibiting polygamy, allowing judicial divorce, setting minimum ages for marriage, boosting education and establishing minimum wages. By 1975, virtually every national development plan affirmed that women, as well as men, were to be the ultimate beneficiaries of all development objectives. And, by 1980, massive investments in social overhead capital by the oil-rich OAPEC countries and grants-in-aid to the oil-poor countries were working to boost female school enrollments, inject modernizing elements into the household, and enhance job prospects through increased labor demand.

Clearly, women's emancipation is gaining momentum in the Arab world. Thanks to the liberating effects of economic development, the determination of feminist movements, and the wisdom of governments to respond to change, current reforms are making their way into a surprising amount of social and economic territory.[1] Yet, it is also true that many of the reforms achieved to date are only beginning to take hold (Durrani: 1976; Mernissi: 1978). Female employment in government ministries, universities and business remains the accomplishment of a relatively small elite. And marginal increases in the number of women in the formal labor force await sorely needed improvements in the quality of opportunity, the prospects for career development, the equality of wages and participation in decision making (e.g. labor unions, cooperatives).

That literature on Arab development tends to dwell more on the negative aspects alluded to above is well known. Charges that women are 'culturally enslaved', are confined to 'prehistoric roles' or are being 'socially and economically exploited' have spearheaded bold criticism of the canons of Islam and male chauvinism. Yet careful assessment of how Arab women are or should be integrated into economic development is rare. Understanding of the cultural context tends to be shallow, empirical impressions are usually fragmentary or biased, and assumptions concerning the desire of females to participate in the labor force are often unfounded. As a result, the development literature is replete with platitudes, and misconceptions about the Arabic culture have prompted implausible or insensitive policy recommendations.[2]

My discussion about upgrading women's employment begins by dispelling some of the myths about women's opportunities for participation in the Arab economy. This sets the stage for a more realistic consideration of both the barriers and the possibilities open to boosting the quantity and quality of skills that exist or are in demand. Some barriers are simply not amenable to change overnight. In such cases, proposals for dramatic intervention would probably fall on deaf ears. Accordingly, the policy directives that I have in mind incorporate a search for *selective interventions*. These join forces with social and economic changes which are eroding barriers as part and parcel of current national development planning. My aim is to benefit Arab women now without subtracting from the family unit which is so highly treasured in Arabic culture.

Dispelling myths

The Qur'an and Islamic custom
Those who would argue that the emancipation of women requires the demise of religion, because the Holy Qur'an and the Moslem culture are virtually inseparable (at least in theory), have missed the point. Low rates of female employment, education and remuneration can hardly be attributed to Qur'anic doctrine. The coming of Islam in the seventh century AD to what is now the Arab world brought a major improvement in the status of women. In pre-Islamic times, a woman had very limited rights, privacy, status or individuality. In fact, women were looked upon as the most degenerate group in society (Al-Qazzaz: 1978).

Thanks to Mohammed, the position of women was transformed and raised to one of relative equality with men in almost all matters. Mohammed removed the stigma of 'original sin' which held women responsible for the fall of man. Islam restricted the practice of polygamy which had been unregulated. The Qur'an forbade female infant-cide and recognized the woman's full legal capacity to contract her own marriage, to receive a dowry and to own property via inheritance. Mohammed stressed that knowledge and education for both sexes were essential for a good Islamic life, and study of the Qur'an, Hadiths, Sunna and Moslem law (Shari'a) reveals that (i) nothing prevents the Moslem women from participating in political, administrative, religious or social life, (ii) extreme attitudes toward or negative treatment of women are generally deplored, and (iii) there is nothing in the Qur'an that prevents contraceptive use.

The only sexual distinction made under Islamic law aimed to ensure a woman's security and social status. In view of their superior physical strength, men were presumed to be more able to take the leading or protective role in caring for women and children. At the time of a father's death, therefore, two portions of inheritance were received by each son, as against one portion by each daughter. Accordingly, sons were held economically responsible for several dependents (including grandparents). As for a husband's responsibility for the physical well-being of his wife, it was his duty to keep her happy by making her life beautiful (Yusef: 1965). If these duties were not fulfilled, or if the wife was maltreated, she had the legal right to leave him.

Such differences in rights and privileges were hardly intended to give women a lower social status. In fact, many scholars have argued that women suffered less from inequality under Islamic law than under Christianity or Judaism. Furthermore, it is recognized that Islamic law offered less resistance to emancipation than did the civil laws of Europe.[3]

The real problem of Arab women came with the decline of Islamic civilization, the abuse of Islamic law and stagnation in existing behavioral codes.[4] Disregard of Islamic law led to unrestricted poly-gamy, marriage of under-age females without proper consent, and unilateral repudiation of a wife by her husband. The veil had its origins in the uncritical assimilation of foreign court practices during the Umayyad and Abbasid periods, and was adopted as a concession to pre-Islamic customs concerning women's modesty.[5] The same applies to seclusion. This custom was handed down from the court of the Persian empire. Unfortunately, some scholars and theologians erroneously attributed veiling and seclusion to Islam and the Qur'an. This token amount of religious validation managed to extend the life-span of these assimilated practices for several centuries (Esposito: 1976).

It is important to be clear about the original intention behind veiling and seclusion. Their initial role was to protect, honor and distinguish the Moslem in the great palaces and courts where women had considerable nobility as well as the opportunity to join in many activities. However, as these customs spread throughout the Moslem world they had unforeseen and deleterious effects. Poorer women were confined to small houses and were effectively barred from community life. This worked to smother their right to worship publicly in the mosque. Since the mosque in traditional Moslem society served not only as a place for public worship but also as the educational and social center of the community, women's isolation was especially disastrous. Once the woman's place was traditionally accepted as separate from the mainstream of life, her limited function in the family and her resultant low status in society continued for generations.

Clearly, existing behavioral codes for women have been twisted far out of line with original intentions.[6] The greater the effort to realign existing behavioral codes with the wisdom of the Islamic faith, the more we can expect suppression to give way to opportunities for women. This is of no small importance to the planner. Rather than assume that Islam is against the campaign for women, he can expect that Arab educators, theologians and jurists will be motivated by virtue of their faith to be for women's emancipation.

Empirical misconceptions

Studies which convey that Arab women make almost no contribution to the economy, or that their participation in the formal labor force is insignificant, are ill-informed. Yet, many scholars have used fragmentary evidence based on narrow definitions of gainful employment and economic activity to stretch this conviction to ridiculous lengths.[7] As a result, Arab women have been treated as infants in terms of their contribution to the economy. Moreover, policies for upgrading their contribution tend to commence at 'ground zero' with the implication that existing skills, many of which are rather sophisticated, are neglected.

Use of crude activity rates (CARs), as estimated by the International Labor Organization (ILO: 1977b), illustrates my point.[8] These rates suggest that female labor force participation is miserably low (e.g. between 2 and 3 per cent in nine Arab countries). Almost no change is expected by 1985. Closer scrutiny, however, reveals that the CARs underrepresent women's activity. The denominator in this rate includes the entire population, baby boom and all. If we limit the denominator to the economically active labor force only, as in Table 5.1, we find that 11.8 women are employed for every 100 workers.[9] Overall, these

Table 5.1 *Representation of women in the total, in the agricultural and in the non-agricultural labor force, Arab countries, 1971–7*

Groups	Year (1)	Females in the labor force (000's) (2)	Number of females employed per 100 workers in the		
			Total labor force (3)	Agricultural labor force (4)	Non-agricultural labor force (5)
Arab world	1971–7[a]	4,577	11.8	12.6	11.1
Oil-rich	1971–7[a]	739	11.9	18.5	7.8
Oil-poor	1971–7[a]	3,838	11.8	11.5	12.1
Oil-rich					
Bahrain	1971	3	3.9	0.1	3.8
Iraq	1977	544	11.3	37.5	9.0
Kuwait	1975	35	11.4	0.0	11.6
Libya	1973	29	4.2	10.3	2.8
Oman	1975	2	2.8	na	na
Qatar	1975	2	2.7	0.0	2.8
Saudi Arabia	1975	114	6.3	12.8	3.2
UAE	1975	10	3.3	0.0	3.4
Oil-poor					
Algeria[b]	1975	159	4.2	na	na
Egypt	1975	795	7.2	2.3	12.3
Jordan[c]	1975	65	17.1	32.8	9.5
Lebanon	1975	129	17.2	10.6	21.0
Mauritania	1975	17	4.3	na	na
Morocco	1975	691	15.1	13.0	16.9
Somalia	1975	365	22.1	na	na
Sudan	1976	608	13.5	21.0	5.8
Syria	1976	387	21.1	34.2	6.4
Tunisia	1975	507	27.2	36.3	21.8
Yemen AR	1975	49	3.4	4.4	1.4
Yemen PDR	1976	66	18.4	30.4	7.4

Source: National censuses, surveys and estimates in national statistical yearbooks.

Notes: a Totals and rates in these rows are aggregates of countries listed below using available data (i.e. Oman, Algeria, Mauritania and Somalia are excluded).
b Estimate.
c Estimate based on 1975 Labor Force Survey and 1975 Agricultural Census.
na = data not available.

rates translate into 4.5 million females in the formal labor force. Furthermore, recent sources indicate that female activity rates are rising rather rapidly relative to their previously low levels (especially in Jordan, Iraq and Syria).

Now, the revised rates in Table 5.1 are also candidates for criticism. They shroud intra-country and intra-group variations which are frequently very wide. In other words, they do not convey the range of 'what is possible'. Table 5.2 illustrates this point. In Tunisia, the number of economically active females for every 100 active males ranged from 12.6 in Zaghouan governate to 46.0 in Monastir. This compares with a national average of 23.1. In Syria, a high of 22.4 for Hama mohafaza compares with the national average of 12.0. In North Yemen, the high of 46.6 for Sa'adah governate is four times the national average of 11.1. And in Iraq, the number of paid female agricultural workers actually outnumbers males in Thi-Qar, and the national average of 18.7 is exceeded in many mohafazas.[10]

As for intra-group variations, activity rates are three to four times higher among immigrant females in Kuwait, Bahrain, the United Arab Emirates and Saudi Arabia than among nationals. The difference here is attributable to the importation of needed skills that cannot be supplied by underqualified nationals. Religious differentials are also evident. Among the Moslem faction in Lebanon, the proportion of women that had worked before and after marriage was 9.2 per cent for the Druze versus 3.2 per cent for the Shi'a (1971 survey data). The figure for the Druze actually exceeds those for Catholic and non-Catholic Christians (8.1 and 6.9 per cent, respectively).

The above comments do not mention conceptual or measurement difficulties. The question of work in or around the house is central here. Owing to the way in which housework or 'unpaid family assistance' is viewed by most societies, women often consider it as non-work or peripheral to the economic well-being of the family. Women who do weaving or crafts, or who help their fathers, brothers or husbands in the fields are apt to see this work as an extension of housework (Chamie: 1979). When asked whether they work or not, women often respond 'no' because they subscribe to definitions of work similar to those currently used by policy-makers. As Chamie says, 'They might as well have been asked, "Are you a man?".' The seriousness of this measurement problem is demonstrated in a recent labor force survey in Syria. Syrian men were initially asked whether their wives worked. A large number said they did not. However, when asked, 'If your wife did not assist you in your work, would you be

Table 5.2 *Geographical variations in female activity rates, selected Arab countries, 1971–5*

Tunisia by governate	Economically active females per 100 active males (1975)	Syria by mohafaza	Economically active females per 100 active males (1971)	Yemen AR by governate	Economically active females per 100 active males (1975)	Iraq by mohafaza	Number of paid female agricultural workers per 100 paid male agricultural workers (1971)
Tunis	25.3	Damascus City	9.6	Sa'adah	46.6	D'hok	1.1
Zaghouan	12.6	Damascus	4.9	Al Hudaydah	20.0	Ninevah	14.6
Bizerte	16.5	Aleppo	11.0	'Old Sana'a	13.9	Arbil	23.5
Beja	27.3	Homs	13.9	Hajjah	8.5	Kirkuk	7.6
Jendouba	13.2	Hama	22.4	Dhamar	5.2	Al-Sulaimaniya	18.5
Kef	16.9	Lattakia	20.5	Ibb	3.5	Diala	12.5
Siliana	12.0	Deir-ex-Zor	9.8	Al-Bayda	6.0	Baghdad	18.4
Kasserine	28.0	Idleb	10.7	Ta'izz	7.9	Al-Anbar	18.8
Sidi Bouzid	18.6	Al-Hasakeh	8.1			Babylon	47.8
Gafsa	17.5	Al-Rakka	18.1			Kerbela	48.1
Medenine	28.9	Al-Sweida	7.3			Al-Qadisaya	22.9
Gabes	21.5	Dar'a	5.7			Al-Muthanma	14.1
Sfax	15.5	Tartous	17.8			Wasit	12.7
Kairouan	19.0	Quneitra	2.2			Maysan	16.4
Mahdia	43.3					Thi-Qar	123.6
Monastir	46.0					Basrah	16.9
Sousse	30.7						
Nabeul	28.4						
NATIONAL AVERAGE	23.1		12.0		11.1		18.7

Source: National censuses of population and agriculture.

forced to hire a replacement for her?' the answer was an overwhelming yes (Chamie: 1979)!

Another misconception about women's employment is that codes of family honor of women's modesty have succeeded in prohibiting employment outside of farm contexts. Supposedly, women are permitted to work on their farms because they are under surveillance by their fathers or husbands. In contrast, urban work is supposedly denied because it implies exposure to strange men (with all that this is supposed to convey). In his study of 430 farms in Saudi Arabia, Knauerhause (1976) claims that high female labor force participation (26 per cent of the farm work force) would all but disappear if families moved to the city because men would never allow their women to work in 'exposed' environments.

The important point here is not to contest that opportunities for Arab women in industry or business are limited. Rather, it is to ascertain that women have carved out a role in the non-agricultural sector and that this role is sufficiently large as to merit both recognition and development. Table 5.1, columns 4 and 5, reveals that there are nearly as many women per 100 workers, on average, in the non-agricultural as in the agricultural labor force of the region as a whole. More detailed figures by industry for 1975–7 reveal that almost 20 per cent of the manufacturing workers in Jordan and Iraq were women, whereas women represented almost 50 per cent of manufacturing employees in Tunisia. Again, such figures give an idea of what may be possible. They certainly take us far beyond the prehistoric notion that Arab women are confined to the family farm or that attempts to boost their role outside the 'accepted sector' would probably be doomed (see the distributions in Appendix 5.1 as well).

Permitted occupations

One of the most erroneous assumptions about women's work is that dictates of Islamic custom are largely responsible for the concentration of females in the service sector. Women are assumed to gravitate to the occupations of nursing, teaching and household services because they involve the least social contact with males (i.e. as required by 'women's modesty'). Yet, a comparison of employed females in Islamic and non-Islamic countries discredits this rationale.

Table 5.3 compares male and female employment in Arab versus non-Arab, predominantly non-Moslem, African countries. Almost identical proportions of employed females in non-agricultural industries are found in services and industry (largely manufacturing). Were the

137

Table 5.3 *Percentage of male and female labor force in non-agricultural industry, by type of industry, selected regions, 1970*

Region	% males in		% females in	
	Industry	Services	Industry	Services
Arab world	41.4	58.6	26.3	73.7
Arab North Africa[a]	41.6	58.4	30.4	69.6
Middle East	41.3	58.7	23.2	76.8
Africa (excl. Arab North Africa)	46.0	54.0	25.8	74.2

Source: International Labour Organization.
Note:. a Includes Somalia and Mauritania.

cultural interpretation correct, we would not expect to find Islamic women employed in industry at all. On economic grounds, however, similar distributions of employed females between the two groups of countries can be explained by similarities of industrial diversification, including lack of opportunities in a relatively small manufacturing sector. The same applies to the distribution of employed males. They are concentrated in the service sector as well because opportunities in industry are limited.[11]

With respect to specific occupations, the prevalence of Arab women in nursing, teaching and community and personal services (i.e. midwives, domestics) is not that much more apparent than it was in many Westernized developed countries during the 1930s and 1940s. That is, many of these occupations are an outgrowth of informal work carried out by women in their homes.[12] Further, it would be difficult to argue that teaching, nursing or employment as a domestic worker never involves social contact with the opposite sex. Female teachers in many of the Gulf countries have not only travelled long distances from their extended families but are instructing at the secondary level where coeducation is on the rise.[13] Further, work as domestics, especially by the wives of OAPEC immigrants, places women in the very homes of their male employers.

A number of attitudinal surveys also imply that traditional restrictions on women's employment outside the home are relaxing. A survey of Kuwaiti households found that 70 per cent of the respondents were in favor of work for women. Of these respondents 90 per cent chose government employment, particularly teaching, as the preferred field of work (Al-Thakib: 1975). In a survey of rural Lebanese women, over 40 per cent of the total respondents regarded outside employment favorably (ECWA: 1978c). A study of Jordanian households points to a relatively positive attitude toward the employment of women (Abu-Jaber *et al*.: 1977). Only 9 per cent of 189 working women perceived that close proximity to working men posed social problems. Finally, a number of studies in Iraq revealed a generally positive attitude to the employment of women in industry (Iraq: 1973).

Policy directives

My search for appropriate policy interventions begins with an acknowledgment that efforts to increase female participation in the Arab economy need not be concerned about starting from scratch or being brought to an abrupt halt. Canons of the Islamic faith are not against women's emancipation, they are largely for it. Governments are actively taking steps to undermine the suffocating effects of traditional mores by adopting progressive legislation (see Appendix 5.2).[14] Women have carved out a sufficiently important role in the formal labor force to merit much broader development. And, prospects of selective intervention are increasing as restrictive attitudes toward women's employment relax in the wake of economic development.

Now, it is important to acknowledge that not all, or even most, Arab women desire participation in the formal labor force. This premise may seem self-evident. Yet, a surprising number of popular writers have asserted, like Mernissi, that 'any new national economy can not leave 50 per cent of the population (i.e., women) out of the production process'.[15] This kind of remark not only denies the important economic contribution that women make already, it also overlooks the fact that 'wife' and 'mother' roles have a great deal of respect, power and desirability, and that many Arab women prefer devotion to the family which is so highly treasured in Arabic culture.[16] Furthermore, some women may choose not to work because to do so would offend their husband's honor, their family honor, and even their own honor (Pakizegi: 1978). That is, custom prescribes that the husband or father make his wife or daughters financially secure. Essentially, this is an issue of pride and it fosters the attitude that economic security should rule out the need for women to seek economic self-sufficiency. Policy-makers should be quite clear that this attitude is not only propagated by men. Women embrace it as well.[17]

The realities alluded to above are documented in surveys of working women in Kuwait, Jordan and Tunisia. In Kuwait, a substantial share of the women interviewed considered that the home was more important than their job (Al-Thakib: 1975). Among a sample of single working women in Jordan, the majority interviewed planned to quit their job after having children, and in Tunisia, a large proportion of the working women interviewed felt that a financially secure woman should not work (Durrani: 1976). If these attitudes characterize a significant proportion of Arab women, we might well ask, 'Why do women seek employment?', or rather, 'For whom are selective interventions required?'

A review of existing empirical work, including some of my own, reveals that the propensity for women to work can be explained to a large extent by five factors. These include the husband's or father's economic situation, the level of the woman's education, the extent to which household males have emigrated for work, the rate of male unemployment in the general labor market, and the number of dependent children. As women tend to work for different reasons or under different conditions, it is important to identify subgroups of employed women for which different policy interventions are likely to be of greatest benefit.

Husband's or father's economic situation
In agricultural contexts, economic security is hardly the rule. Poverty and income inequality are so widespread among farm families in most Arab countries that prospects for hiring male labor to help during planting or harvesting are largely ruled out. In such cases, women have no choice but to play an important and irreplaceable role in the operation of the farm. They also tend to work as seasonal labor on other holdings or to be engaged in cottage crafts. These activities contribute an important source of family income, especially during slack seasons in farming or at times of poor harvest. In other words, women may work more in rural than urban contexts, not only because 'women's modesty' is less threatened, but because economic necessity demands it.[18]

In urban contexts, family employment is usually limited to the male household head. Pressure is not likely to be placed upon wives or daughters to work unless the husband or father is unemployed or his earnings are insufficient to meet family needs. A survey of 100 working women in Tunis revealed that 82 per cent worked only because they had to for economic reasons, not for the love of the job. Their principal economic reasons were unemployment of the husband or inadequate family income (Durrani: 1976). A study of 1,290 married women in Libya found that unemployment of the family head was a leading determinant of whether wives were working or not (El-Huni: 1978). Unemployment of the household head had a greater impact on female employment than marital status, presence of dependent children, or overall family size. And in both El-Huni's study and an analysis of some 5,000 women in Khartoum by Sheehan (1978), participation rates were observed to decline with higher levels of family income. These findings agree with results of studies in a number of other less developed and developed countries as well.[19]

The subgroup I am concerned about here is women who are working out of dire necessity. In farm contexts, this often means (i) working as seasonal labor at wage rates substantially below those received by men, (ii) being exploited by intermediaries who purchase cottage crafts at ridiculously low prices, or (iii) being excluded from any sort of welfare coverage due to their part-time or marginal work.[20] In cities, it often means employment in undesirable jobs: namely, as factory workers or as domestics. Factory jobs are the last resort. As Maher (1978) observes, living conditions at the edge of the city, where factories are typically located, are dismal, salaries are poor, and benefits are negligible.

Interventions to benefit this subgroup will be quite different from those concerned with, say, the career development of highly educated women. In urban areas, policy-makers should seek (i) minimum wage legislation, (ii) equal remuneration for women and men doing similar factory or household work, (iii) workman's compensation in case of injury or sickness, (iv) on-the-job or in-service training to enhance promotion, (v) maternity leave, and (vi) child-care or day-care facilities. In rural areas, additional efforts are needed (i) to organize the transportation, marketing and financing of cottage crafts on a cooperative basis, and (ii) to include seasonal or in-house workers in social security provisions.

Education

For growing numbers of highly educated Arab women, the relationship between education and employment is strong. Activity rates among females with, say, a university education are likely to range from five to ten times higher than among women with, say, primary education only. In Kuwait, for example, activity rates among Kuwaiti females who had obtained a university degree were 83.0 per cent in 1975 compared with 48.0 per cent for those who had obtained a secondary diploma, 5.6 per cent for those with primary education, and only 1.0 per cent among the illiterate. As an indication of growing employment opportunities for educated women, the figures above compare with activity rates in 1965 of 50 per cent for Kuwaiti women with a university degree, 30 per cent with a secondary degree, 2 per cent with primary education and 1 per cent among the illiterate.

Not unsimilar findings have been reported in several other studies. Chamie's (1979) study of married Lebanese women revealed that 38 per cent of university graduates were employed versus only 4 per cent of primary graduates. Among single women, the figures were 82 per cent and 40 per cent, respectively. Esposito's (1976) study of Egyptian women revealed that 69 per cent of those with university education were working versus only 6 per cent of those with education below medium levels. Youssef's (1977) study of female labor force participation in urban Syria revealed that 55.5 per cent of those with higher or university education were working versus only 4.3 per cent of those with primary education. Sheehan's (1978) study of female labor force participation in Khartoum revealed that 37.5 per cent of those with secondary school education were working versus only 9.2 per cent for those with no schooling. Finally, El-Huni's (1978) study of married Libyan women revealed that the probability of a woman with 'higher than high school education' being in the labor force was 37 per cent greater than for a woman having 'less than high school' education. The latter was 52 per cent greater than for women having no schooling.

Turning to cross-sectional analysis, the effect of education on female activity rates is not likely to emerge as strongly, simply because high average levels of illiteracy tend to vary little among aggregated geographical units. This is evident in my analysis of average female activity rates (FAR) among eighteen Tunisian governates where the correlation between literacy levels and FAR was both low ($r = 0.29$) and statistically insignificant (see Appendix 5.3). Similar results obtain in an analysis of female activity rates in eighteen Arab countries where literacy differentials were barely statistically significant (Azzam: 1979a).

In one sense, the survey studies and the cross-sectional analyses noted above pertain to two groups of women that have different policy needs concerning education and employment. The first is a comparatively small, privileged group who are either seeking a career as an extension of their training or are in demand as a result of their skills (or both). As distinct from the subgroup discussed in the previous section, we can assume that the majority of these women have chosen to work. Many are front-runners of feminist movements in the employ-ment arena or are active supporters of progressive legislation.[21] Their main concern is with career development and wider representation in specialized fields. Only recently have universities begun to expand the choice of academic programs open to women. Most have been educated in literature and the social sciences with professional job prospects limited to the liberal arts as teachers, to administration as secretaries and typists, or to management. The challenge for policy-makers here is to augment general education with certification of more specialized skills in the academic institutions themselves, in vocational schools, or via in-service training. Certification of this type should enhance prospects for promotion. It could also work to counteract under-employment of women due to the general or ambiguous nature of their educational credentials.

The second group is one in which the education–employment relationship is waiting to come of age. As the dramatic rise in female enrollments 'today' replaces intolerable levels of illiteracy 'tomorrow', preparations should be made for a tidal wave of relatively educated women that may be demanding meaningful jobs.[22] At the very least, policy intervention for this group should attempt to match the quantity and quality of women's education with the future needs of the economy. For example, supply/demand estimates for selected skills among women should take stock of a possible 'brain drain' of educated labor from oil-poor to oil-rich countries, or possibilities of return migration should the oil-rich countries seek to replace female expatriates with nationals (e.g. teachers). Furthermore, the totally inadequate representation of females in vocational schools (i.e. less than 10 per cent of all vocational students) needs a major overhaul if women are to be better represented in semi-skilled or technical occupations.

Emigration of labor

By 1980, ambitious development plans in the oil-rich countries had attracted upwards of 2 million migrant workers from the oil-poor countries (see Chapter 2). A large majority of these are males and their emigration has boosted the demand for employable females in urban wage and salary contexts. In agriculture, emigration of male household heads has shifted responsibility for operating family farms to wives. Migrant remittances are also spurring employment of female family members in cottage crafts. In the case of migrating women, the largest proportion have taken jobs as teachers or nurses. In such cases, labor

143

shortages in the oil-rich countries have fuelled women's emancipation by absorbing educated women who otherwise might have remained jobless (especially in Egypt), and promoting women's travel.

In a study of eighteen Arab countries, Azzam (1979a) demonstrates that a significant empirical relationship exists between the emigration of labor and activity rates of females left behind.[23] My analysis of female activity rates in eighteen Tunisian governates confirms this finding though the relationship is just statistically significant (see Appendix 5.3). In Jordan, the effect of emigration on the employment of women has been observed in both urban and rural contexts by Anani (1978). The government has actively sought to augment female enrollments in technical and vocational schools so as to prepare women for middle-level job vacancies. In the process, female crude activity rates jumped from about 4 per cent in 1974 to over 14 per cent by 1980. In the Sudan, activity rates of rural women are reported to have risen in the high out-migration provinces of Darfur and Kordofan, where women have been left to operate farms and take over animal husbandry and handicrafts (Sudan, WCARRD: 1978). Finally, in North Yemen, the effect of emigration on female employment in farm contexts has been reported by Ross (1977). With approximately 40 per cent of the male labor force abroad, responsibility for management of farms has been left to women. As for migrant remittances, it is known that they are finding their way into housing, though we can only speculate about the extent to which they are or could be harnessed to develop self-employed family business. Efforts to channel these enormous funds are only beginning to take shape (see Chapter 2).

The subgroup I am concerned with here consists of women who face new opportunities due to mushrooming interregional growth or government programs which seek to reduce dependence on non-Arab expatriate labor by employing Arab women. Such women are being confronted with the challenge of working in occupations or at skill levels that are usually reserved for men. Recently, they have been solicited by private business and government programs which have communicated the advantages of women's participation in the economy as, say, secondary school teachers, medical or agricultural technicians, hotel management personnel, senior clerical workers, sales workers in department stores, packaging agents in industry, etc.[24]

In urban wage and salary contexts, these women are the front-runners of a long-established feminist push to achieve female representation in all branches of the occupational spectrum. Accordingly, policy-makers should take stock of the kinds of resistance that are being experienced by women who assume jobs typically reserved for men. On the one hand, this is an educational issue. Employers and their male employees should be prepared for the important role that female employees are being asked to contribute to the development of the overall economy. On the other hand, strict monitoring of sex discrimination practices is required, particularly in small factories and stores where women are known to receive less pay than men (UNICEF: 1972; ECWA: 1978b).

In farm contexts, women are finding they have the full responsibility for running the farm, but without the full command over resources needed to do the job. The problem for policy-makers here concerns sex barriers to women's representation in cooperatives, problems of obtaining credit and failure to obtain legal responsibility for their farm land, buildings or machinery.[25] And in both urban and rural contexts, on-the-job or in-service training for women newly employed in semi-skilled jobs could go a long way toward enhancing their productivity and prospects for promotion.

Possible restraining factors
While high rates of male unemployment and child dependency may restrain female employment, they are not as amenable to policy intervention as the considerations discussed above. If large numbers of male household heads are jobless, and if male honor is threatened in the process, we can hardly expect policy-makers to be overly excited about expanding the stock of employable females. This problem is most acute in the oil-poor countries where high rates of unemployment and visible underemployment are symptomatic of slow growth and development (Shaw: 1978b).[26] Thus, rates of male unemployment may be the most significant explanatory variable in my analysis of Tunisian female activity rates, but it is largely policy-empty (see Appendix 5.3). That is, the policy-maker is well aware that the demand for women in the Tunisian labor force is hampered by economic malaise in the overall economy; what he does not know is how to stamp out this malaise. Resolving this question requires nothing less than workable employment and development strategies.

As for child dependency, advocates of population control or family planning have long argued that declining birth rates, fewer dependent children, or smaller family size, will automatically release women for participation in the labor force. While seemingly self-evident, this rationale assumes that an increase in the available supply of employable women (freed from child-care) will be matched by an equivalent

145

effective demand. This neglects the point made above concerning male unemployment. Second, it fails to recognize that child dependency is much less of a burden on employed women in extended family contexts. This is visible in agriculture where day-care of children is shared among several women (Youssef: 1979). It shows up in empirical studies where the presence of children has an ambiguous effect on the participation of Arab females in the labor force. In Jordan (1976 household survey) female employment in urban households is not affected by family size until households surpass five persons (implying three or more children). In urban Khartoum, participation rates for women with one child aged between 0 and 4 years are only slightly higher at 5.4 per cent than for women with two or three children aged between 0 and 14 years (5.2 per cent), or two or three children aged between 0 and 9 years (4.7 per cent) (Sheehan: 1978). In Libya, the correlation between female employment and dependent children is significant for women with children aged between 0 and 6 years, but not for children aged between 6 and 15 years. Nor is overall family size significantly correlated with female employment (El-Huni: 1978). Finally, my cross-section analysis for Tunisia (Appendix 5.3) reveals no relationship between female activity rates and dependent children aged between 0 and 6 years, or crude birth rates.

The point I wish to make, then, is that attempts to urge population control in the push for women's employment may be irrelevant in the Arab context. A wiser course of action would seem to be to acknowledge cultural preferences for large family size; heed shifts in these preferences as they accompany economic development; and provide day-care facilities and other forms of maternal support for women who choose to work while having dependent children.[27]

Legislative inroads

Some Arab countries have been extremely attentive to the kinds of selective interventions discussed thus far. This is visible in recent constitutional reforms pertaining to equality between men and women (see Appendix 5.2), on the ratification of International Labour Organization conventions, and in the provision of maternity benefits for working women.

A total of fourteen International Labour Organization conventions pertain specifically to working conditions among women. Tunisia, Syria and Libya have been most supportive of these conventions. As of January 1979, each had ratified 64 per cent (Table 5.4, last column).

Table 5.4 *Ratification of ILO conventions regarding women, by the Arab countries, as of 1 January 1979*

Country	Convention number (x = ratified)[a]						% of total women's conventions ratified[b]
	81	100	111	118	129	135	
Algeria	x	x	x	—	—	—	57
Bahrain	—	—	—	—	—	—	0
Egypt	x	x	x	—	—	—	43
Iraq	x	x	x	x	—	x	57
Jordan	x	x	x	x	—	—	43
Kuwait	x	—	x	—	—	—	29
Lebanon	x	x	x	—	—	—	57
Libya	x	x	x	x	—	—	64
Morocco	x	—	x	—	—	—	43
Qatar	x	—	x	—	—	—	21
Saudi Arabia	x	x	x	x	—	—	50
Sudan	x	x	x	—	—	—	36
Syria	x	x	x	x	x	x	64
Tunisia	x	x	x	x	—	—	64
Yemen AR	x	x	x	—	—	—	29
Yemen PDR	—	—	—	—	—	—	0
UAE	—	—	—	—	—	—	0

Source: International Labour Organization.
Notes: a The convention numbers imply the following:

81 concerns inspection of work in the industrial and commercial sectors.
100 concerns equal remuneration for women and men on similar jobs.
111 concerns sex discrimination in employment and promotion practices.
118 concerns equality of treatment in social security matters.
129 concerns labour inspection in agriculture.
135 concerns female representation among workers' representatives.

b A total of fourteen conventions pertain specifically to working conditions among women.

Next in line are Lebanon, Iraq and Algeria with ratification of just over half. Among the balance of the Arab countries, support has been moderate in Egypt, Jordan, Morocco, and nil in Bahrain, South Yemen and the United Arab Emirates.

By most standards, conventions 100 and 111 are of greatest importance. Each pertains to inequalities in remuneration and sex discrimination in employment and promotion matters. The governments of Bahrain, Kuwait, Morocco, Qatar, South Yemen and the United Arab Emirates have failed to ratify either one or both of these conventions. Convention 118 is also high on the priority list. It relates to social security coverage, compensation for sickness or injury, pensions, etc. Only six countries have ratified this convention.

Two important, yet highly neglected conventions concern the inspection of working conditions for women in agriculture (No. 129) and the inclusion of women among workers' representatives (No. 135). Ratification of convention 129 by Syria only, when so many countries have ratified convention 81 (pertaining to industry), is ludicrous in view of the importance of agricultural employment in Arab development. As for convention 135, it is hardly reasonable to entice women into the labor force or to expect them to assume responsibility for family farms without giving them a voice in workers' unions or co-operatives. Excluding Syria and Iraq, which have ratified No. 135, this would appear to be an ultimate denial, on the part of most countries, of equality as guaranteed by recent constitutional reforms.

One of the most progressive conventions concerning women's employment has to do with maternity protection. International Labour Organization conventions recommend eighty-four days of maternity leave with pay equivalent to 66 per cent of full salary. Also recommended are medical insurance coverage, paid sick leave in the event of problems during birth, established breast feeding times while on-the-job, and the provision of nurseries in larger establishments. While Arab Labour Organization (ALO) conventions are not as demanding (only forty-nine days of maternity leave), they do recommend leave with pay equivalent to 100 per cent of salary.

The extent to which maternity conventions have been formally adopted by individual countries is reviewed in Table 5.5. Most governments have honored or exceeded the ALO's recommended 'duration of maternity leave', though none has complied with the ILO standard of eighty-four days. With respect to compensation during maternity leave, Bahrain, Oman and the United Arab Emirates provide zero compensation. This is in keeping with their ratification performance noted above. In contrast, Iraq, Kuwait, Lebanon, Syria and the Sudan provide 100 per cent of salary coverage.

Possibly, the most progressive aspect of the maternity convention has to do with provisions for breast feeding and nurseries. Such provisions have been adopted by Iraq, Jordan, Libya and Saudi Arabia. This is a strong indication that efforts are being made by some governments to help working mothers to be as unhampered as possible during their early stages of childbearing.

To sum up, by assessing the performance of Arab governments in ratifying international conventions, I have sought to single out countries where the fight for women's emancipation is making very real progress. Countries which are definitely in the lead in this respect include Lebanon, Iraq, Libya, Syria and Tunisia. Among those failing to ratify the international conventions, some have initiated their own brand of progressive legislation, though such efforts have tended to be piecemeal and poorly enforced.

Conclusion

The popular notion that Arab women are handcuffed by tradition and inertia is due for revision. The liberating effects of economic development, progressive legal reforms and determined feminist movements are constantly augmenting the quantity and quality of women's opportunity. With massive investments in social overhead capital in oil-rich and oil-poor countries, and the dramatic increase in female school enrollments, the next decade will witness growing proportions of women ready to enter employment.

Planners are in a good position to prepare for this onslaught now. Proposals to mobilize educated women to meet labor shortages in several oil-rich and oil-poor countries are increasingly being considered as a means of tackling the kinds of problems discussed in Chapter 6. Moreover, Arab women have already carved out a sufficiently important role in the formal labor force to merit broader development. Improved statistical coverage is enabling the identification of several subgroups that are working for different reasons or under different conditions. For each subgroup, it will become increasingly possible to match policy intervention with clearly discernible needs to bring about crucial changes in working conditions and opportunities.

Over the next few years, attention to women's emancipation should be given particularly high priority for at least two reasons. First, development in several Arab countries is unfolding at such a rapid pace that possibilities for exploiting female labor are likely to increase as the number and diversity of establishments expands. Failure to legislate desirable practices, monitor conditions and certify qualifications now will enable undesirable practices to become firmly entrenched. As any good planner knows, rectifying an entrenched practice 'tomorrow' is a much more difficult task than correctly prescribing the course at the outset. Second, Arab women must be protected against loss of their traditional sources of power as their allocation of time shifts between household roles and formal employment. The merits of employment should be communicated just as strongly as the merits of family work. In cases where women are enticed into the labor force, this should be the responsibility of government and private enterprise. It is also an

Table 5.5 *Comparative schedule regarding aspects of maternity protection, selected Arab countries*

Source	Duration of maternity leave	Before delivery	After delivery	Wages payable during leave	Payable grants (bonus)	Medical and delivery expenses	Sick leave due to delivery	Nursing hours (breast feeding)	Nurseries
ILO conventions	84 days		42 days	66% of salary		Medical insurance coverage	To be specified by country	Convention No. 103	To be established by employers
ALO conventions	49 days		35 days	100% of salary		Medical care & treatment			
Bahrain	42 days			0% of salary					
Egypt	50 days		40 days	70% of initial wage					
Iraq	70 days	30 days	42 days	100% of salary			Max. of 9 months	2 periods, ½ hour each	In establishments employing women
Jordan	42 days	21 days	21 days	50% of salary			Sick leave	3 feeding periods	In establishments employing women
Kuwait	70 days	30 days	40 days	100% of salary			100 days with no pay		

Country								
Lebanon	40 days	30 days	100% of salary					Establishments with 50 or more females
Libya	50 days	30 days	50% of salary	25 dinars	Complete medical care	90 days at 50% salary	1 hour per day, up to 18 months	
Oman	42 days		0% of salary			Sick leave		
Saudi Arabia	70 days	28 days	50% of salary		Medical & delivery costs	Maximum 6 months	1 hour per day	Establishments with 50 or more females
Sudan	56 days	28 days	100% of salary				1 hour per day for 1 year	
Syria	60 days	40 days	100% of salary			6 months maximum	1 hour per day for 18 months	In establishments with 100 or more employees
Tunisia	30 days		50% of salary			15 days over 12 weeks	1 hour per day for 19 months	
Yemen AR	70 days	40 days	70% of salary					
UAE	45 days		0% of salary					

Sources: International Labour Organization, Arab Labour Organization, and unpublished tables prepared by Henry Azzam, Beirut Office, International Labour Organization.

educational issue. Within the school system, the textbook stereotype of Arab women in 'wife' or 'mother' roles only is due for revision.

Finally, too many writers have fallen into the trap of using sensationalism to promote the cause of women's emancipation. Catch-alls implying that Arab women are 'culturally enslaved', and outdated assertions that 'any new national economy cannot leave 50% of the population (i.e., women), out of the production process', are trite. What is needed is a more careful, sensitive, appraisal of how women are and should be integrated into the labor force, as well as of the possibilities for increasing the effective demand for employable women. While the first part of this task requires statistical information which is in short supply, notable improvements in monitoring and reporting have been underway since 1970. A few arduous data gathering missions, in lieu of 'easy-to-reach' international estimates, could go a long way to improving on the naive consensus that Arab women make almost no contribution to their economy. And with respect to increasing effective demand for women in employment, more attention needs to be given to growth and planning problems in the overall Arab economy. This is especially evident in my Tunisian analysis (Appendix 5.3), where male unemployment, or rather, malaise in the economy, overshadows any other determinant of women's employment. In other terms, championing the cause of women in an economic void is hardly realistic or helpful. Conditions which are likely to reduce slack in the labor market need to be identified and planned for so that effective demand for women in specific occupations can be meaningfully estimated. This kind of undertaking would go a long way toward complementing the kinds of selective interventions proposed here.

Appendix 5.1 Females in the labor force by economic activity

(See Table on top of page 153)

Appendix 5.2 Select governmental decrees bearing on women's emancipation

Algeria

The 1976 National Charter and Constitution charges women with full participation in social construction and national development. It does

Table A.5.1 *Percentage distribution of females in the labor force by economic activity, 1971–6*

Country	Year (1)	Agriculture (%) (2)	Mining (%) (3)	Manufacturing (%) (4)	Electricity, gas, water (%) (5)	Construction (%) (6)	Trade restaurants, hotels (%) (7)	Transport communication, storage (%) (8)	Real estate, insurance, business services (%) (9)	Community, social personal services (%) (10)	Activities not adequately described (%) (11)
Arab world[a]	1971–6	45.5	–	–	–	–	–	–	↓ 24.3	↑	–
Oil-rich[a]	1971–6	39.3	–	–	–	–	–	–	↓ 36.4	↑	–
Oil-poor[a]	1971–6	46.1	–	–	–	–	–	–	↓ 22.7	↑	–
Oil-rich											
Bahrain	1971	0.2	0.0	2.4	0.1	0.4	3.7	2.6	1.9	85.9	2.8
Iraq	1977	64.9	0.4	8.9	0.2	0.9	3.0	0.9	0.9	15.8	4.1
Kuwait	1975	0.2	0.1	0.3	0.1	0.6	0.4	3.6	→ 95.3	↑	0.0
Libya	1973	38.5	0.9	4.6	0.3	0.6	1.5	1.0	1.4	50.4	0.8
Oman	na	na	na	na	na	na	na	na	na	na	na
Qatar	1975	0.0	0.0	0.0	0.0	0.0	0.0	0.0	→ 100.0	↑	0.0
Saudi Arabia	1975	66.4	↓	↓	11.5	↓	↓	↓	22.1	↑	0.0
UAE	1975	0.4	2.0	1.1	0.2	2.5	4.6	3.3	5.7	80.2	0.0
Oil-poor											
Algeria	na	na	na	na	na	na	na	na	na	na	na
Egypt	1975	16.1	0.2	10.4	0.6	0.6	7.4	2.2	1.9	40.9	19.7
Jordan	1975	32.8	0.5	18.5	1.5	0.1	1.7	3.3	16.5	23.7	1.4
Lebanon	1975	21.9	0.0	20.8	1.2	0.0	19.6	0.0	4.0	32.1	0.4
Morocco	1971	40.2	na	na	na	na	na	na	na	na	na
Somalia	na	na	na	na	na	na	na	na	na	na	na
Sudan	1976	87.9	0.0	2.9	0.1	0.1	1.9	0.3	na	5.9	0.9
Syria	1975	80.9	0.1	6.2	0.2	0.3	1.0	0.4	0.3	9.8	0.8
Tunisia	1975	55.3	0.2	29.4	0.1	0.2	0.3	0.2	1.5	11.0	1.8
Yemen AR	1975	87.2	0.0	1.3	0.0	0.3	2.7	0.1	0.1	8.3	0.0
Yemen	1976	79.5	0.0	3.2	0.1	0.0	0.4	0.1	0.1	7.8	8.8

Source: National censuses.
Notes: a Totals and rates in these rows are aggregates of countries listed below with available data.
na Data not available.

not merely list the rights of women but places them on an equal footing with men in all spheres of economic and social life.

Egypt

The Egyptian National Charter states in Article 36: 'Women must be regarded as equal to men and must therefore shed the remaining shackles that impede their free movement so that they can play a more constructive role in the society, economy and policy.'

Jordan

The constitution guarantees equal working and educational possibilities for all citizens with no discrimination by sex.

Lebanon

The constitution says that women have the right to equal pay when they do work equal to that of men. Article 44 of the Work Code ensures that salaries for women cannot be below the official minimum wage.

Libya

Section 4 of the Constitutional Proclamation specifies for every citizen the right to work. The word 'citizen' applies to men and women alike; they are considered to be equal.

Syria

Article 45 of the constitution stipulates that the state shall provide women with all the opportunities that would enhance their position and allow them to play a more active role in political, social, cultural and economic life.

Yemen AR

The constitution, promulgated in 1970, lays down equal legal rights and obligations for men and women.

Yemen PDR

Family Law No. 1 proposes dramatic increases in female education and in the equality of rights between men and women.

Appendix 5.3 Analysis of Tunisian female activity rates

This appendix examines the relationship between female activity rates (FAR) and selected socio-economic characteristics in Tunisian governates. FAR has been represented by the number of working females aged 15 years and over per 100 working males. The independent effect of several socio-economic characteristics on variations in FAR has been established using multiple regression techniques.

The choice of socio-economic characteristics for the analysis has been directed partly by theory and constrained largely by data limitations. Thus, in accordance with most studies of female activity rates, I examine the effect of female literacy (a hypothesized + effect), the proportion of males in each governate that have emigrated (a hypothesized + effect), the proportion of workers in each governate that are engaged in agriculture (hypothesized effect uncertain), levels of male unemployment (a hypothesized − effect), and rates of childhood dependency (a hypothesized − effect).

While the presence of dependent children could exert pressure on females to work (especially if males are absent), I use this variable in the traditional sense to reflect the demands of household duties on the woman's time. As for the uncertain effect of employment in agriculture, this is in keeping with findings in the literature which tend to be inconsistent.

Only three variables were statistically significant and/or consistently demonstrated the expected sign. These were rates of male unemployment, male emigration and labor force in agriculture. Combined, they accounted for about 55 per cent of the variation in female activity rates. Details are reported below.

Details on analysis of Tunisian female activity rates

Variables considered

FAR = number of working females aged 15 years and over per 100 working males

U_m = number of unemployed males per 100 working males
Lit = female literacy rates
CD = number of children aged between 0 and 4 years divided by the number of females of labor force ages
M = number of emigrant males per 100 working males
AG = number of economically active workers in agriculture per 100 total economically active workers

Procedure

(i) The estimated equation and hypothesized signs of variables are as follows:

$$\ln FAR = a - b_1 \ln U_m + b_2 \ln Lit - b_3 \ln CD + b_4 \ln M \ (+ \text{ or } -) \\ b_5 \ln AG + e$$

(ii) All data have been transformed to log normal.
(iii) Observations are represented by eighteen Tunisian governates.
(iv) The year of the database is 1975.

Table A.5.2   *Regression results for Tunisian female activity rates*

Dependent variable	Regression coefficient	Student 't'	Cumulative variance
U_m (unemployment)	−1.16	2.19[a]	0.425
Lit (literacy)	0.10	0.13	0.439
CD (child dependency)	0.51	0.25	0.440
M (migration)	0.59	1.37[b]	0.470
AG (% in agriculture)	−0.32	1.39[b]	0.547
Intercept value	3.32		
R^2	0.55		

Notes: a Student 't' level is significant at the 0.025 level.
b Significant at the 0.10 level.

Interpretation of results from Table A.5.2

The rate of male unemployment (U_m) is the most significant correlate of female activity rates (FAR). A 10 per cent increase in U_m will probably reduce FAR by 11.6 per cent. The proportion of the labor force engaged in agriculture is negatively correlated with FAR. It is the second most important variable in the analysis and adds almost 8 per cent to the cumulative variance, though its elasticity is small at −0.32. The rate of male emigration (M) from any governate has a positive effect on FAR, though the relationship is just significant at the 0.10

level and its explanatory power is small. Finally, literacy levels (Lit) and child dependency (CD) are not significantly correlated with FAR.

In addition to the results reported above, it is worthy of note that a two-stage least squares regression was also estimated. This procedure was adopted as another variable (V) was added to those in the equation above, and it was known that V and U_m were related (r = -0.72). V represents the value, in Tunisian dinars, of total building activity divided by the number of working males for each governate. While there was good reason to expect that V would bear directly on male unemployment via the employment of males in the construction industry, it was not known if V would also bear directly on female employment. As it turned out, V was not significant when added to the equation above, and thus the two-stage least squares procedure was dropped.

Chapter 6

Manpower and educational shortages

Introduction

Over the last decade, labor market disequilibriums have been chronic and, at times, wildly distorted in virtually every Arab country. Shortages of literate or educated manpower have been so acute that thousands of vacancies have existed side by side with structural unemployment.[1] Employers have been forced to offer abnormal salaries merely to attract skills from abroad. While shortages are most visible in the capital-rich countries, acute scarcities in the oil-poor countries are hampering development projects as well.[2] In one case, to ensure completion of construction contracts in Egypt in 1978, German and Swiss crane drivers and welders were imported at salaries twenty to thirty times those of their Egyptian counterparts (i.e. US $4,350 to 6,520 per month)!

Shortages can be put down to five factors. First, development plans in the oil-rich countries are extremely ambitious with respect to manpower requirements. Before 1976, this led to the importation of about 1 million unskilled or manual workers to erect social overhead capital (see Shaw: 1979c). Between 1975 and 1980, it required an additional 900,000 skilled expatriate workers merely to manage and operate the new infrastructure. Large shares of these imports were expected to be 'professional, technical and kindred workers', 'clerical workers', 'operatives' and 'skilled and semi-skilled workers' (see Table 6.1).[3] Between 1980 and 1985, the World Bank (1979b) projects that approximately 1 million more expatriates will be added, with an even heavier representation of more highly skilled workers. Not surprisingly, the oil-rich countries are competing fiercely for these workers because

Table 6.1 *Expatriate manpower required by Saudi Arabia, Kuwait and Bahrain, 1975–80 (000s)*

Occupation	Saudi Arabia[a] (1)	Kuwait[b] (2)	Bahrain[c] (3)
Managers	6.1	0.7	—
Professionals	7.8	—	0.3
Technicians and sub-professionals	49.9	11.7	1.6
Clerical workers	90.4	4.8	3.8
Sales workers	65.5	1.5	
Service workers	98.1	40.3	
Operatives	26.3	18.6	5.5
Skilled workers	54.8	9.3	
Semi-skilled	99.7	—	6.0
TOTAL	498.6	86.9	17.2

Sources: a Saudi Arabia, Second National Development Plan, 1975–80, Ministry of Planning.
b Kuwait, 'Estimates of Manpower Supply and Demand in 1975 and 1980', Planning Board (in Arabic).
c Socknat, J.S., 'Projections of Manpower Demand and Supply 1971–1986 for Bahrain' (Mimeo).

their development programs are similar with respect to skill requirements.

Second, grants-in-aid from the oil-rich to the oil-poor countries have fuelled the demand for key operatives to man selective industrial projects. For example, Sudan's national development plan covering the period 1977 to 1983 envisages a demand for 23,950 highly skilled workers, and estimates a supply of only 13,690. Egypt's national development plan foresees possible shortages of up to 370,000 high-level professionals, managers, and administrators, and 304,000 skilled workers between 1978 and 1982. In North Yemen the national development plan projected a need for 76,970 professional and skilled workers between 1976 and 1981, half of which would have to be sought abroad. Deficiencies in these countries have also been exacerbated by attractive wages in the oil-rich group.[4] These have acted like a huge magnet to lure away the most educated and experienced workers.

Third, the Arab region has long been suffering from a brain drain. Over the last twenty years tens of thousands of highly skilled personnel have emigrated to Europe and North America.

Fourth, governments have been increasingly motivated to nationalize their labor force and Arabize their educational systems. This has fuelled the demand for Arab nationals to replace expatriates. The primary manpower goal in this effort is to increase Arab representation in the key productive sectors of research and development, teaching, manufacturing and construction (in which expatriates now predominate). The primary educational goal is to protect the Arabic language and culture from succumbing to Western influence.[5]

Fifth, shortages in most sectors stem from inadequacies on the supply side. These pertain to the quality and distribution of Arab education itself. In the oil-poor countries this is, and threatens to remain, one of the most visible symptoms of underdevelopment. The same applies to the oil-rich countries, though impressive improvements in infrastructure and personnel are beginning to close the most glaring gaps.

Unfortunately, neither petro-dollars, enthusiasm nor impatience can hurry the long and arduous task of upgrading a totally inadequate educational infrastructure to meet the needs of these rapidly expanding economies. The challenge is truly enormous. Al-Wattari (1979) maintains that high-level manpower required for the Arab world by the year 2000 will be somewhere in the order of 13 million. To achieve this target, he calculates that the Arab states would have to build approximately 250 universities with 15,000 students enrolled in each, and some 600 higher technical institutes with 3,000 enrolled in each.

If Al-Wattari's estimates are at all reasonable, then the cost of such a program would be approximately US $150 to 175 billion at 1972 prices or between US $260 and 325 billion at 1980 prices. This amount, in 1980 prices, is seven to nine times greater than all educational investments during the 1976 to 1981 round of national development plans (i.e. about US $37 billion; see Table 6.2, column 1, row D). While expenditures of, say US $37 to 50 billion during each of the next four development plan periods (between 1980 and the year 2000) would amount to a whopping US $148 to $200 billion, it is also true that the majority of these funds would have to be devoted simply to imparting basic reading and writing skills to the rapidly growing population. Moreover, such expenditures on new primary and secondary facilities would require a vastly expanded operating budget. By the year 2000, operating expenditures of approximately US $44 billion between 1976 and 1981 (Table 6.2, column 1, row B) would probably have to be doubled to accommodate this goal as well.

Where, then, do we begin? My point of departure is that education in most Arab countries is being pressed to produce technical or applied skills that neither its infrastructure nor its personnel can possibly hope to accommodate over the next ten to twenty years.[6] Moreover, were

Table 6.2 *Education shares in current government expenditures and national development plan expenditures, 1976–81*

| Item | Approximate cumulative expenditures for the period 1976–81 in US $ billions | | |
	All Arab countries (N = 20) (1)	Oil-rich (N = 8) (2)	Oil-poor (N = 12) (3)
A Approximate value of current government expenditures	287	212	75
B Approximate amount from (A) on education	44	28	16
C Approximate value of national development plan plan expenditures	250	178	72
D Approximate amount from (C) on education	37	29	8

Sources: National statistical yearbooks and national development plans.

policy-makers to orient entirely to this pressure, other important functions of education would be neglected in the process. These pertain to the preservation and extension of the Arabic culture. In other words, exclusive emphasis on secondary school or university curricula to carry the flag of modern technology and development would mean neglecting many long-term societal goals. Accordingly, this chapter suggests an interim approach to the accommodation of pressing demands for more highly skilled Arab manpower without unduly neglecting the cultural content of Arab education in the process.

The policy directives that I have in mind propose that shortages of crucial skills could be significantly reduced over the next decade by (i) drawing on the skills, education and know-how of currently employed expatriates by persuading them to conduct on-site training courses, (ii) enticing skilled Arab emigrants to return to their home countries to conduct university, technical or extension courses, and (iii) 'bonding' recent graduates for service in underprivileged areas. In my view, viable alternatives to this approach are virtually non-existent. To support this conviction, the first part of this chapter reviews in-adequacies in existing educational infrastructure. Specifically, five problems are expected to hinder the integration of manpower and educational policies in the near future. These include inadequacies in the quantity, quality, content and distribution of education, and the ever-present 'brain drain'. This stock taking lays the groundwork for policy directives which advocate an interim solution.

Stock taking

Quantity
Formal schooling has a long way to go to ensure basic reading and writing skills in the Arab world. According to Table 6.3, the majority of the population in most Arab countries had no schooling in the mid-1970s. An additional 10 to 30 per cent had not completed primary school. At the most plebian level, illiteracy means an inability to read simple instructions and it is a handicap in self-directed learning. This has emerged as a daily problem in building construction where the inability to read operating instructions which accompany new power tools and prefabricated components has led to industrial accidents, errors and continual delays.[7] At more sophisticated levels, lack of technical or university skills means that the process of 'spontaneous' learning-while-doing is severely cramped in advanced industrial settings (e.g. installation of refineries, irrigation projects).

Of course, dramatic improvements in the educational infrastructure during the mid and late 1970s will greatly alter the educational profile of the future. This applies particularly to the oil-rich countries. Educational expenditures per capita and per student in the Arab world grew from about three times higher to about ten times higher than all less developed countries between 1970 and 1975. During this period, such expenditures promoted annual growth rates of 5.8 per cent in primary enrollments. As a result, a large majority of primary aged children (both males and females) are now enrolled in Arab schools.[8]

While the growth in primary enrollments is commendable, it is also true that the expansion of primary school infrastructure is a relatively easy task when compared with the development of higher institutes. That is, curriculum is relatively standardized, equipment is simple, and primary teachers can be trained quickly (e.g. within two or three years of leaving secondary school). In contrast, requirements for vocational, technical or higher institutes tend to be prohibitive (e.g. modern laboratories, computers, workshops). Thus, proportions of students at the higher levels in the oil-rich countries are only about one quarter of the levels in developed countries (DCs). (See Table 6.4.) They are about one half the DC level in the oil-poor countries. Exclud-

Table 6.3 *Educational attainment of population aged 10 years or over, selected Arab countries, 1971–6*

Country	Age of population group	Year	% distribution by educational attainment				
			No schooling (1)	Some primary (2)	Primary certificate (3)	Some secondary or certificate (4)	Some higher institute or diploma (5)
Kuwait	10 +	1975	44.6	14.7	22.1	17.3	1.3
Libya	15 +	1973	60.8	21.6	9.6	7.4	0.6
Saudi Arabia	10 +	1974	68.6	18.9	12.5	→	→ 4.8
UAE	10 +	1975	47.5	24.7	7.7	15.3	4.8
Algeria	25 +	1971	84.4	13.0	2.3	→	0.3
Egypt	10 +	1976	56.6	25.1	16.1	→	2.2
Syria	25 +	1970	68.6	25.9	4.2	→	1.3
Syria	15–64 LF[a]	1976	33.6	31.9	17.3	13.5	3.7
Tunisia	25 +	1975	82.7	9.7	6.4	→	1.2
Tunisia	15–64 LF[a]	1975	53.1	31.6	13.8	→	1.5
Yemen AR	15–64 LF[a]	1975	71.8	7.3	18.8	→	2.1
Yemen PDR	10 +	1974	72.8	22.1	5.1	→	→

Sources: ' National censuses of population, manpower surveys and national statistical yearbooks.
Note: a LF = those in the labor force only.

Table 6.4 *Distribution of students by level and percentage of female students, Arab countries, 1976–8*

Countries	% distribution of enrolled students in each level			% of female students in each level		
	Primary (1)	Secondary (2)	Higher (3)	Primary (4)	Secondary (5)	Higher (6)
DCs	56.1	32.6	11.3	48.8	50.0	43.9
LDCs	74.7	22.0	3.3	42.9	36.2	32.7
Arab World	72.1	23.3	4.6	38.0	33.8	32.8
Oil-rich	75.5	21.8	2.7	38.2	31.7	26.6
Oil-poor	71.2	23.8	5.0	37.9	34.3	34.0
Oil-rich						
Bahrain	71.8	26.8	1.4	43.2	49.0	52.6
Iraq	75.4	21.5	3.1	35.3	29.5	27.7
Kuwait	81.6	16.8	1.6	45.7	48.0	32.5
Libya	76.0	22.4	1.6	46.6	33.5	15.8
Oman	99.5	0.5	0.0	28.4	29.4	—
Qatar	89.3	7.9	2.8	47.6	36.8	57.4
Saudi Arabia	71.8	25.1	3.1	36.7	31.1	26.0
UAE	77.8	22.8	0.0	46.3	42.7	—
Oil-poor						
Algeria	83.0	15.3	1.7	40.0	34.1	23.2
Egypt	60.7	32.6	6.7	38.8	35.3	29.8
Jordan	63.2	33.8	3.0	47.1	43.2	41.0
Lebanon	70.0	25.0	5.0	46.3	41.7	—
Mauritania	90.0	10.0	0.0	27.8	11.7	—
Morocco	74.1	24.1	1.8	33.4	32.6	19.5
Somalia	93.3	5.6	1.1	36.4	24.9	10.7
Sudan	78.4	20.2	1.4	37.0	32.2	16.0
Syria	67.6	28.0	4.4	40.1	29.4	25.1
Tunisia	81.4	16.6	2.0	39.3	33.8	26.2
Yemen AR	90.6	8.6	0.8	10.1	11.0	10.2
Yemen PDR	80.9	17.5	1.6	33.4	22.5	19.6

Sources: National statistical yearbooks and published bulletins of ministries of education.

ing Egypt, discrepancies are wide with proportions as low as 1 per cent for at least five countries. Moreover, years of cumulative education and experience are also needed to ensure a supply of good quality instructors. In other words, expansion at the higher levels must not only confront infrastructural problems, it must await the preparation of students who have passed through secondary as well as primary levels.

Quality

Efforts to upgrade the quality of education are largely dependent on the volume of public funds available for educational investment. According to Table 6.5, the magnitude of such funds varies substantially

Table 6.5 *Total expenditures on education per capita, per enrolled student and as a percentage of current government expenditures, Arab countries, 1970–5*

	Expenditure on education					
	US $ per capita			US $ per enrolled student	As % of all public expenditures	
Countries	1965 (1)	1970 (2)	1975 (3)	1975[a] (4)	1970 (5)	1974 (6)
DCs	140	268	636	1,227	—	—
LDCs	7	19	47	110	—	—
Arab world	14	51	102	324	—	—
Oil-rich	24	197	226	1,085	—	—
Oil-poor	11	21	77	134	—	—
Oil-rich						
Bahrain	37	87	150	496	20.0	9.5
Iraq	18	30	119	142	20.4	8.9
Kuwait	132	346	674	1,616	11.8	14.7
Libya	81	227	384	816	13.9	12.2
Oman	4	18	162	419	—	—
Qatar	119	335	492	2,049	—	7.0[b]
Saudi Arabia	19	471	284	3,637	9.8	8.2
UAE	—	110	—	1,335	—	18.6
Oil-poor						
Algeria	19	37	124	211	12.9	14.3
Egypt	10	17	61	98	14.6	17.6
Jordan	11	18	64	88	9.3	9.4
Lebanon	15	25	59	110	16.8	20.5[b]
Mauritania	7	—	223	—	26.6	—
Morocco	9	27	94	210	16.8	20.5[b]
Somalia	2	7	57	97	7.6	10.0[b]
Sudan	5	10	80	110	12.6	14.8
Syria	11	26	52	115	9.3	8.5
Tunisia	21	34	97	173	22.8	22.6
Yemen AR	0.3	2	19	24	—	6.3
Yemen PDR	4	6	40	60	13.0	14.7

Sources: National statistical yearbooks; UNESCO, *Statistical Yearbook.*
Notes: a This column pertains to all students enrolled in the primary, intermediate, secondary and higher levels.
b 1973.

between oil-rich and oil-poor countries.[9] On a per capita and per student basis, they are about eight times greater in the oil-rich countries. They also vary widely among countries in each group. Thus, in the oil-rich countries, per student expenditures in Kuwait are about six times those in Iraq. In the oil-poor countries, per student expenditures in Algeria or Egypt exceed those in North Yemen several times over.[10]

Differences in these investments are reflected in pupil/teacher ratios. To some extent, these ratios can be used as an index of educational quality in that teachers can only spread themselves so far.[11] According to Table 6.6, columns 1—3, primary school teachers in the oil-poor

Table 6.6   *Student/teacher ratios, Arab countries, 1976—7*

Countries	*Number of pupils per teacher in each level*		
	Primary *(1)*	*Secondary* *(2)*	*Higher* *(3)*
DCs	21	16	14
LDCs	34	21	15
Arab world	35	27	19
Oil-rich	24	17	17
Oil-poor	39	31	19
Oil-rich			
Bahrain	19	21	9
Iraq	27	28	21
Kuwait	30	4	7
Libya	21	14	15
Oman	31	2	—
Qatar	18	2	11
Saudi Arabia	21	16	15
UAE	14	8	—
Oil-poor			
Algeria	41	27	10
Egypt	35	43	24
Jordan	45	7	25
Lebanon	—	—	—
Mauritania	22	24	—
Morocco	48	30	26
Somalia	35	27	6
Sudan	36	24	15
Syria	33	20	55
Tunisia	38	20	7
Yemen AR	39	18	41
Yemen PDR	30	24	10

Sources: National statistical yearbooks and published bulletins of ministries of education.

countries had, on average, fifteen more students than their oil-rich neighbours in 1976–7. At the secondary level, teachers in the oil-poor countries had fourteen more students, on average.[12] Again, wide differentials exist among countries at all levels. Anyone familiar with classroom teaching will understand that forty-eight students per primary teacher in Morocco is an uncomfortably large number (Table 6.6). The same applies to forty-three students at the secondary level in Egypt, or fifty-five students at the higher institutes in Syria.

An excessive student load reduces the teacher's ability to disseminate information because attention per student is less in the classroom and in the monitoring of assignments. Combined with motivational problems and a lack of alternative opportunities for students, these realities are manifest in extremely high rates of student failures, repeats and drop-outs (See Table 6.7). Thus, in 1975 'repeaters' made up 25 per cent of grade 1 students in Morocco, 45 per cent of grade 5 students, 32 per cent of grade 10 students, and 40 per cent of grade 12 students. In Tunisia, a 1973 survey revealed that only 27 per cent of the grade 6 students could understand a French newspaper.[13] Only 23 per cent were adequate in arithmetic. In Iraq, a study of university education between 1963 and 1972 revealed that 49 per cent of the students failed

Table 6.7 *Performance of a typical cohort of primary level students, selected Arab countries, 1970–6*

Country	% receiving primary certificate (1)	% receiving primary certificate without repeating (2)	% receiving primary certificate after repeating (3)	% dropping out or incomplete (4)
Bahrain	70.6	19.4	51.2	29.4
Iraq	67.0	17.6	49.4	33.0
Libya	85.1	55.7	31.4	14.9
Qatar	88.4	18.4	70.0	11.6
Saudi Arabia	77.2	20.8	56.4	22.8
Algeria	64.2	26.8	37.4	35.8
Egypt	77.2	54.9	22.3	22.8
Jordan	83.3	63.5	19.8	16.7
Morocco	69.7	10.4	59.3	30.3
Sudan	77.2	53.8	23.4	22.8
Syria	80.2	45.5	34.7	19.8
Tunisia	65.3	14.3	51.0	34.7

Source: UNESCO (1977a).

their preparatory BA exams (Al-Kufaishi: 1977). Similar problems concerning drop-outs or underqualified teachers have been reported for Bahrain (Mahmoud: 1978), Libya (Kerdus: 1979) and Saudi Arabia (Ghamdi: 1977; Al-Abdulkader: 1978).

The above point ignores the quality of information that teachers themselves are imparting. This depends on the quality of their education or, more broadly, on their human capital. This is a controversial topic in several countries because both teacher training and motivation are suspected to be far below acceptable levels. Again, Morocco serves as a good example. By 1975, approximately 30 per cent of all primary teachers were unqualified. This ranged from 20 per cent in Rabat City to 80 per cent in the largely rural province of Ouarzazate. In North Yemen the staffing of new schools in 1974 and 1975 was difficult enough to necessitate the employment of approximately 15 per cent of primary teachers, as 'contract' or 'part-time' teachers, who had themselves dropped out of primary school. While the situation is likely to have improved during the last few years, a special report on education in Egypt (the largest producer of teachers) claims that the proportion of underqualified teachers in preparatory and secondary schools has dropped from 70 to only 58 per cent, and from 79 to 66 per cent, respectively, between 1967 and 1975 (MEED: 1978).[14]

In short, expansion of enrollments at the higher levels must not only await primary and secondary graduates, it must await adequately prepared graduates. In the oil-poor countries there is no question that quality is low. To assume that vastly greater expenditures in the oil-rich countries can eliminate this problem over the short term is hardly realistic.

Content

Closely related to the subject of quality is the breadth of subjects available to students. Arab education has been severely criticized for its failure to produce technical or applied skills in industry, management or agriculture.[15] For the Arab world as a whole, less than 5 per cent of all students are enrolled in applied programs. Comparable figures for developed countries range from 15 per cent for Canada to 45 per cent for the Federal Republic of Germany. At the university level, disproportionate proportions of students are graduating in the literary arts or humanities. For example, 85 per cent of the university students were enrolled in arts in Qatar in 1976–7, 70 per cent in Libya in 1975–6, and 57 per cent in Iraq between 1963 and 1972. Egypt has often been ridiculed for its excessive number of university graduates (51,000 in

1975), many of whom have had to be absorbed into a largely over-staffed civil service.[16]

Table 6.8 shows students enrolled in vocational or technical schools as a percentage of all students enrolled at the secondary level or above. Excluding Bahrain, the oil-rich countries fare poorly in this respect.

Table 6.8 *Student enrollments in vocational and technical schools, selected Arab countries, 1973–8*

Countries	Year	No. of students enrolled in vocational and technical schools (1)	Students in (1) as % of all students enrolled in secondary levels or above[a] (2)	% of students in (1) that are females (3)
Bahrain	1976–7	1,760	10.4	24.0
Iraq	1976–7	28,365	4.7	20.3
Kuwait	1977–8	2,084	4.6	42.6
Libya	1977–8	4,990	2.5	0.0
Qatar	1975–6	82	2.5	47.6
Saudi Arabia	1977–8	5,169	5.9	0.0
Algeria	1977–8	11,798	1.6	19.8
Egypt	1976–7	403,541	18.0	35.0
Jordan	1976	9,437	12.6	26.7
Somalia	1977–8	3,607	25.4	24.5
Sudan	1976–7	12,104	4.3	24.4
Syria	1977	23,300	4.2	—
Tunisia	1977–8	50,887	21.7	—
Yemen AR	1977–8	522	3.8	0.0

Sources: National statistical yearbooks and published bulletins of respective ministries of education.
Note: a Students in 'secondary levels or above' consist of those in preparatory schools (i.e. after primary certification), secondary schools and all higher institutions.

While the oil-poor countries with a relatively strong educational tradition fare best (Jordan, Egypt, Tunisia), the production of vocational or technical graduates in Egypt outranks that of all other countries combined by a ratio of nearly three to one. Though several countries are making a gallant effort to expand technical education it is also true that results will be marginal over the next ten years. For example, enrollment in industrial and commercial institutes in Saudi Arabia was expected to grow by 300 per cent between 1976 and 1981. While the graduation of some 13,000 to 20,000 students may comprise an impressive 15 to 20 per cent of new labor force entrants in any one year (say, in 1981), it comprises only 6 per cent of the labor force entrants between 1976 and 1981 and less than 1 per cent of the entire Saudi labor force.

Distribution
The distribution of educational opportunities is plagued by severe inequalities within as well as between Arab countries. Development expenditures in rural areas or in districts far removed from cities tend to compare poorly with those in urban areas. Variations in literacy or school enrollments are alarming as a result. As an illustration, rates of illiteracy in the most urban districts of Tunisia (Tunis) or Syria (Damascus City) are between one-half and one-quarter of those in many other districts (Table 6.9, columns 1–3). In the Sudan (1973), illiteracy ranged from 41.5 per cent in urban Khartoum to 88.7 per cent in the province of Upper Nile to 96.1 per cent in Bahr el Ghazal. In Algeria (1975), only 6.7 per cent of the school-age children were not enrolled in school in urban Algiers versus 35 per cent or more in several other districts (Table 6.9, column 2). In North Yemen (1974), 95 per cent of all secondary school students were enrolled in three districts with 52.5 per cent of the population (Sana'a, Ta'izz and Hudaydah). The remaining provinces, with 47.5 per cent of the country's population had only 7 per cent of all secondary students (Ibb, Dhamar, Ma'reb, Al-Bayda, Sa'adah, Al-Mahwit).

Needless to say, such inequalities are highly correlated with inequalities in the distribution of skills. This fact alone is a major pitfall in the implementation of development projects in the most disadvantaged regions. Again, 'urban bias' in educational expenditures is a culprit here.[17] It is exacerbated because the few who do obtain a reasonable education tend to migrate to more prosperous urban areas where salaries and amenities are more attractive. In short, the standard rural problems of inadequate funds for educational development, of retaining qualified teachers, and of attracting graduates to local employment is denying education its most heralded attribute in the development forum, namely the capacity to effect the redistribution of wealth by upgrading human capital among the poor.

Brain Drain
The emigration of highly skilled labor from the region has long inhibited the integration of manpower and educational policies. More recently, labor migration within the region has become problematic as well. The brain drain applies not only to older, more experienced

Table 6.9 *Regional variations in illiteracy and school enrollments in Tunisia, Algeria, Syria, 1975*

Tunisia (1975) (by governate)	% of population aged 10 years + that are illiterate (1)	Algeria (1975) (by wilayat)	% of school-age children not enrolled in schools (2)	Syria (1975) (by mohafaza)	% of male labor force in each mohafaza that:	
					Are illiterate (3)	Have more than primary education (4)
Tunis	37.5	Alger	6.7	Damascus City	14.4	26.9
Zaghouan	59.7	Annaba	35.7	Damascus	28.8	13.3
Bizerte	56.3	Aures	38.8	Aleppo	37.4	12.4
Beja	63.8	Constantine	27.7	Homs	22.7	17.5
Jendouba	66.8	El-Asnam	46.1	Hama	28.1	15.2
Kef	59.9	Medea	46.4	Lattakia	27.5	18.3
Siliana	70.4	Mostaganem	43.7	Deir-ex-Zor	53.7	11.1
Kasserine	66.2	Oasis	24.0	Idleb	37.0	12.7
Sidi Bouzid	69.2	Oran	21.1	Al-Hasakeh	55.2	7.5
Gafsa	56.3	Saida	34.7	Al-Rakka	57.4	5.8
Medenine	58.8	Saoura	36.6	Al-Sweida	21.2	15.3
Gabes	59.6	Setif	34.0	Dar'a	32.7	14.5
Sfax	47.4	Tiaret	43.2	Tartous	23.7	20.7
Kairouan	73.8	Tizi-Ouzou	19.5	Quneitra	32.7	5.9
Mahdia	62.4	Tlemcen	28.3			
Monastir	46.2					
Sousse	50.5					
Nabeul	53.2					

Sources: National censuses or manpower surveys.

people, but to recent university and technical graduates. To date, the magnitude of the problem can only be partially appreciated using available empirical data.[18] For example, between 1962 and 1977, the USA, which is one of the largest recipients of Arab skills, absorbed some 18,200 professional, technical and kindred workers, of whom 2,500 were engineers, 3,700 medical professionals, and 1,100 natural scientists (see Table 6.10). The important features in Table 6.10 are not

Table 6.10 *Immigrants from the Arab world to the USA in the professional, technical and kindred worker group, 1962–77*

Time period	*Average no. of immigrants per year in each broad occupational category*			
	Professional technical & kindred (1)	*Engineers (2)*	*Medical professionals (3)*	*Scientists in natural and life sciences (4)*
1962–7	598	99	66	42
1968–71	1,453	183	275	134
1972–6	1,410	196	351	59
1977	1,805	251	527	41
1962–77	1,141	160	236	70
Total number 1962–77	18,256	2,560	3,776	1,120

Source: Department of Immigration and Naturalization, US Government Microfiche, 1970–80.

only the absolute volume of emigration but also the average number of professional and technical emigrants per year. Between 1972 and 1977, when labor requirements in the region were expanding drastically, the average number of emigrants per year exceeded that of the 1968 to 1971 period (except for natural scientists).[19] In other words, the boom in the oil-rich countries has not slowed down the loss of skills through emigration.[20]

In Table 6.11, the same conclusion emerges for countries taken individually. In 1977 (column 3), the proportion of Arab emigrants to the United States in the professional category ranges from 13.5 per cent in Qatar to 34.5 per cent in Libya. In the oil-poor group, proportions of professional emigrants are as high as 18.7 per cent in the largest labor exporter, Egypt, and 33.3 per cent in Algeria.

While it is true that emigrants send remittances to their home countries, these benefits are much more welcome when limited to

Table 6.11   *Total and professional Arab immigrants admitted to the USA by country of birth, 1972–7*

		Immigrants to USA 1972–7		
		% in professional, technical and kindred category		
Country	Total no. (1)	1972–6 (2)	1975–6 (3)	1977 (4)
Arab world	70,698	12.6	11.4	11.9
Oil-rich	11,740	14.0	12.1	15.7
Oil-poor	58,958	12.3	11.3	11.4
Oil-rich				
Bahrain	116	62.5	31.7	28.6
Iraq	6,848	7.3	5.1	7.5
Kuwait	2,342	16.9	18.6	14.3
Libya	667	40.4	34.8	34.5
Oman	60	42.9	26.6	18.2
Qatar	79	35.7	45.2	13.5
Saudi Arabia	1,424	25.1	25.4	28.3
UAE	204	33.3	8.8	22.2
Oil-poor				
Algeria	238	35.3	18.9	33.3
Egypt	10,763	28.6	29.4	18.7
Jordan	14,771	6.8	5.6	6.8
Lebanon	23,066	10.1	8.7	9.7
Mauritania	14	44.4	66.6	20.0
Morocco	1,133	14.3	16.1	11.3
Somalia	80	12.5	9.7	18.8
Sudan	197	17.7	21.4	5.1
Syria	4,823	16.3	17.2	11.7
Tunisia	201	28.0	26.9	15.4
Yemen AR	3,279	0.6	0.7	1.4
Yemen PDR	393	0.3	0.0	7.7

Source: Department of Immigration and Naturalization, US Government Microfiche, ASI 1980.

unskilled or manual workers. That is, manual skills can be replaced more easily than can specialized combinations of skills and experience. This applies particularly to isolated projects (e.g. in rural areas) where loss of key personnel or failure to recruit needed skilled maintenance workers has forced delays and even shutdowns.[21]

Why the emigration of workers with key skills should continue in the face of a development boom is difficult to explain. In addition to the causes examined above, an ECWA (1978a) study cites political instability, dissatisfaction with working conditions and salaries, inadequate research facilities and rigidity of public administrations. In addition, higher educational credentials, especially from study in the USA, often aid the professional to qualify for entry to more advanced developed countries. Whatever the predominant cause, it is clear that efforts to integrate the plans for Arab manpower and education will be constantly undermined unless something is done to remedy the loss of skills.

Summing up

While education in most Arab countries has undergone remarkable improvements during the last decade, its capacity to accommodate demands for high-level manpower remains totally inadequate. This condition will surely persist over the next ten or twenty years because deficiencies in the quantity, quality and distribution of education must await:

1 sufficient numbers of graduates who have passed through a vastly expanded primary and secondary school system,
2 systematic expansion of vocational schools or institutes of higher training (technical or university),
3 substantial improvement in the quality of teacher training, and,
4 correction of extreme inequalities in the distribution of educational investments between urban and rural areas.

In addition, there is no reason to expect that the emigration of highly qualified people to more developed countries will not continue to undermine efforts to integrate educational output with future manpower needs.

In view of the above, Arab planners have been searching for interim measures that will help meet skill requirements in ways that Arab education cannot (UNESCO: 1977b). In a few countries, aggressive policies have sought to stamp out illiteracy through mandatory adult extension courses (Iraq, Libya, Sudan), or by rural literacy campaigns (Somalia).[22] In others, policies to prevent the brain drain have sought to bond the highly skilled for urban or rural service (e.g. medics in Egypt and Iraq). In still others, policies to promote learning-while-doing have sought to enforce large companies to train their Arab work force (Bahrain, Saudi Arabia). Such examples are imbued with worthy intentions, innovative ideas and some prospects of success. Yet, no attempt has been made to combine or go beyond such examples to produce a more comprehensive approach. Such is the concern of the balance of this chapter.

Policy directives

By emphasizing deficiencies in Arab education, I have sought to provide the foundation for an interim approach by indicating the gaps that must be filled. The policy directives that I have in mind propose that not only are resources to fill these gaps available but measures to harness them appear to be well within the grasp of policy-makers. Specifically, I submit that Arab skills could be greatly augmented over the next decade by (i) mandatory on-site instruction by expatriates, (ii) reversal of the brain drain and employment of returning emigrants in teaching posts in extension, technical and university programs, and (iii) bonding of technical or university graduates whose education has been government financed. In turn, augmenting the supply of skilled Arab nationals could help reduce problems of structural unemployment, boost labor force participation rates, and help stabilize employment during cyclical fluctuations in the aggregate effective demand for labor.

On-site instruction

Courses in technical or applied skills usually require instruction in simulated working environments (e.g. in vocational or technical schools). Where better to undertake this effort than in short courses or apprenticeships in the working environment itself? In the oil-rich countries, this working environment is being built from the ground up. Its construction and operation are largely in the hands of highly qualified expatriates who have the experience to manage substantial numbers of workers, the knowhow to instruct subordinates about the technology employed, and access to site and facilities needed for demonstration. In many cases, these highly qualified expatriates are surrounded by barely skilled Arab subordinates or associates. With few exceptions, the process of learning-while-doing is not being developed and extended to them.

The reserve of qualified expatriates to serve this function is enormous. Almost 1 million skilled expatriates were imported during the 1976 to 1981 round of national development plans in the oil-rich countries. By 1985 the number is expected to be in the order of 2 million (World Bank: 1979b). Such numbers exceed the total number of instructors in higher Arab institutes by at least twenty to one. By 1981, some 150,000 of these expatriates were in the 'professional, technical and kindred' category. This figure alone exceeded the total number of instructors in higher institutes by a ratio of four to one. As many of these expatriates are Arab, and as much of the instruction in applied skills can be passed on by demonstration, language is not a major problem.[23]

The potential to harness expatriate 'know-how' is at the finger-tips of policy-makers because Arab and non-Arab foreigners must apply for work permits. In granting these permits, governments could oblige foreign contractors or Arab employers to make provision for on-site instruction of their Arab employees. Fulfillment of this obligation could be monitored by government or union labor inspectors. In addition, a quota system could require employers to ensure that X per cent of their Arab employees were (i) enrolled in the on-site courses, and (ii) were certified upon completion. Of course, such quota systems should apply to all Arab employees, not just Arab nationals of the host country. An aim of the quota system should be to benefit unskilled Arab expatriates from oil-poor countries as well.[24]

Certification is crucial to the success of on-site training schemes. It provides an important incentive to complete the training or apprenticeship because it enhances future occupational mobility. The process of certification should strive to standardize general skills, though variations in course content between companies or expatriate instructors may work against this. By the teaching of general skills, I mean on-site instruction that increases the marginal product of the trainee (e.g. an apprenticeship) by the same amount in the firm providing the training as in any other enterprise. By contrast, completely specific training, such as the operation of an individual firm's wage payment system, raises the individual's productivity only with respect to the firm providing the training.[25] Thus, specific training is largely non-transferable. Such considerations are important to Arab expatriates who will be returning to their country of origin. Accordingly, differences between general and specific training are examined in greater detail in Appendix 6.1.

Returns to on-site instruction could be enhanced by the voluntary participation of expatriate or foreign employers. At the individual level, it is well known that expatriates in many Arab countries feel socially isolated outside their working environments. This applies particularly to contract workers or to those who have come without their families. In extreme cases, such as in self-contained ARAMCO or construction camps, non-working hours tend to be consumed by boredom. What better way to resurrect a sense of purpose than to invite the 'knowledgeable' to assume the role of 'teacher'. In return, expatriates performing teaching functions could be awarded certificates documenting the type and duration of the training they gave. This effort would certainly receive a boost were foreign governments or funding agencies to encourage, subsidize and formally recognize on-site instruction as a form of foreign aid or technical assistance. A useful beginning in this respect would be to enumerate expatriate skills in each country (e.g. via establishment surveys); formally to elicit the participation of qualified expatriates; to prepare 'how-to-do-it' manuals for distribution to participating companies; and to prepare applied manuals as supportive material for instructors.[26]

Finally, economic returns to on-site instruction may actually exceed those to formal schooling.[27] First, the applied nature of the training allows students to be absorbed into the production process almost immediately. Second, problems of job search upon school graduation are reduced because trainees are taught to do tasks which are in demand, and they are in close touch with local labor markets during their training. Of course, the extent to which such benefits will be realized will also depend on the degree to which those who receive training, and in particular vocational type training, are encouraged to go onward into training-related employment.

Merits of on-site instruction are just beginning to be taken seriously by Arab planners. In Bahrain, the government is attempting to introduce a training levy on firms employing more than 200 workers and on banks and hotels with more than 50 employees. The only way to escape this levy is for employers to train more than 5 per cent of their work force. As might be expected, local and overseas businessmen have objected to both the levy and the training on the grounds that it will discourage investment in Bahrain or will constitute a heavy burden on established companies. But the government has been determined to forge ahead in its effort to reduce foreign domination of its work force, and to ensure skills and jobs for underemployed Bahrainis. The process of 'Bahrainization' is described in greater detail in Appendix 6.2.

In Egypt, on-site training schemes have been implemented to fill the void left by skilled Egyptians abroad. The Ministry of Manpower is running six-month crash courses for 7,000 trainees, and 1,000 more are going through upgrading programs. A further 30,000 are in three to four year apprenticeship programs. In addition, the ministry is attempting to describe and standardize 4,000 employable job skills that have evolved through combinations of education, on-site training and experience.

177

Manpower and educational shortages

Finally, in Saudi Arabia, where the development of indigenous manpower is acknowledged to be the kingdom's most important challenge, the government aims to award domestic contracts to foreign-owned companies that agree to employ and train the largest numbers of Saudis as part of this workforce. The Saudis would like to replace the maximum number of foreign workers with their own in a minimum length of time. During the current five-year-plan, emphasis is to be placed on training Saudis to take over from expatriates in banking, commerce, the oil industry, manufacturing and farming.[28]

Instruction by return emigrants

Zahlan (1978, 1981) estimates that some 17,000 Arab engineers, 7,500 natural scientists, and 24,000 medical doctors are residing in the Western world. As of 1975, these magnitudes were roughly 2.2 times the total number of science graduates in engineering, 1.7 times the total number of science graduates, and 5.0 times the number of medical graduates. Their sum is 6.0 times larger than the total number of teachers in higher institutes in the oil-rich countries and 1.4 times larger than those in the oil-poor countries. Their estimated capital value represents a loss of some US $10,680 million to the Arab world.[29]

Were governments able to reverse the brain drain and entice highly qualified emigrants to return to their homelands to take up teaching posts, rapid strides might be made to accelerate the staffing of extension, vocational, technical and university programs. Soliciting emigrants for such employment could go hand in hand with the Arabization of education in that return emigrants would be Arab by nationality and Arabic speaking, and they would be familiar with the strengths and weaknesses of Arab education. In addition, they would have benefited by experience abroad and many would bring invaluable teaching and research experience with them.

The question is, how to lure them back? One answer lies in the distinctive policy that has been pursued by Iraq. For emigrant Iraqis with the equivalent of an M.A. degree or more, Law 154 provides the following incentives for their return:

1 a piece of land and a loan to build a home,
2 tax exemption for one year,
3 a grant of a month's salary if the returnee gets married in Iraq, plus an advance equivalent to six month's salary,
4 transportation costs of his personal and household effects and their entry free of duty,

5 the travel expenses of the professional and his dependents from abroad to Baghdad,
6 a number of other incentives related to the recognition of his previous experience abroad.

Table 6.12 summarizes results of these inducements over an eighteen-month period in 1974 and 1975. The return of some 700 professionals amounts to one third of the total number of highly qualified professionals residing in Iraq with the equivalent of an M.A. degree or above. This is certainly an encouraging number. Moreover, most of the returnees were graduates of Western universities who had specialized in sciences which were badly needed in Iraq. An important lesson to be learned from this experience is the willingness of emigrant nationals to return. While the financing of similar approaches may be more difficult in other countries, there are few policies, to my mind, which are more deserving of international funding and encouragement.

Bonding
Failure to bond technical or university graduates for service in their home country may be one of the weakest aspects of manpower development in the region. This applies especially to the large numbers of students who are receiving government bursaries to pursue studies at Arab institutes or universities abroad. Widespread loss of these graduates through emigration cannot help but defeat costly attempts to cut crucial labor shortages. It also robs the country of an important source of formal and informal instruction.

The potential for loss is particularly high among students studying abroad. Their numbers have grown dramatically as Arab governments have sought to expand the top echelon of their labor force. From Saudi Arabia alone, the number of students enrolled abroad has grown from 2,000 in 1975 to over 12,000 in 1980.[30] While for many of these students there is some stipulation to return, binding work or service contracts are infrequent. As a result, contacts made while abroad, or affinities developed for foreign cultures, often succeed in promoting future emigration.

While most governments take this problem seriously, few have taken aggressive steps to curtail it. As exceptions, the experience of Iraq and Syria serve as good examples. In response to a study entitled 'non-returning Iraqi Graduates: 1958–70', the government restricts undergraduate study abroad, forbids Iraqis to work abroad in the United Nations Organizations (except for limited cases), and requires that

Table 6.12 Qualified personnel returning to Iraq in response to Law 154 by degree, specialization and country of study, 1974–5

PART A

Degree	Country of study									
	USA	UK	Federal Republic of Germany	France	Other Western	USSR	Other Socialist	Arab countries	Other	Total
Ph.D.	115	177	34	16	15	17	19	19	–	412
M.A.	94	120	1	1	5	8	1	7	1	238
High diploma	3	5	46	–	–	–	–	1	–	55
TOTAL	212	302	81	17	20	25	20	27	1	705

PART B

Degree	Field of specialization						
	Science	Medicine	Engineering	Agriculture	Humanities	Petroleum	Total
Ph.D.	137	70	81	47	71	6	412
M.A.	33	19	106	15	62	3	238
High diploma	1	39	12	1	2	–	55
TOTAL	171	128	199	63	135	9	705

Source: Compiled from detailed records of the Iraqi Commission for Qualified Personnel, up to November 1975. See ECWA (1978a).

travelling physicians and engineers submit a guarantee to return. Equally severe measures have been adopted in Syria. In response to a government inquiry which found that 57 per cent of high-level manpower in the sciences did not reside in Syria during the 1956 to 1970 period, the government restricts members of twenty-four selected professions from leaving the country (except with a permit from the government or the trade unions if the individual works in the private sector). Also, university graduates are not handed their degrees until several years of work have been completed in Syria. A professional leaving Syria and failing to return is subject to economic penalties, including the confiscation of his property.

Such policies may well be criticized on the grounds that they infringe individual freedom and opportunity. It is also the case, however, that the emigration of sorely needed skilled people places a heavy burden on economies that are just starting out on the long road to development.[31] At a time when crucial foundations are being laid for future industrial development, loss of key skills can actually halt development projects in their tracks. More than one writer has observed that recent graduates are so concerned with maximizing their personal social status that they neglect the long-term development goals and needs of Arabic society.[32] In my view, a restructuring of educational values, the expansion of course curricula to include information on Arab development needs, and the short-term bonding of higher-level graduates could go a long way to correct this problem.[33]

Correcting inequalities

It is not unreasonable to propose that on-site instruction, the employment of emigrants as teachers, and bonding could all be put to good use to correct inequalities in the distribution of education and skills. Prospects for on-site instruction in remote areas are good because projects are increasingly dotting the countryside. Return emigrants could serve decentralization goals if they were channelled into technical institutes in smaller cities and towns.[34] And, by bonding graduates for service in outlying districts, crucial services and skills (e.g. those of doctors, nurses, teachers, agricultural engineers, veterinarians) could be extended to populations needing them most.[35]

Of course, distributional problems are not only internal. They are growing between countries as well. Interregional migration benefited the oil-poor countries up to 1975 but it started to work to their disadvantage between 1975 and 1980 when it became more selective of the highly skilled. Mandatory agreements to return, incentive schemes (as in Iraq) and bonding could play an essential role here. For example, Egypt continues to pursue an 'open-door' policy which permits the emigration of tens of thousands of highly skilled professionals to the oil-rich countries. At the same time, shortages in rural areas or small towns are chronic, and the labor market is susceptible to fluctuating rates of emigration and return migration (i.e. leading to shortages one year, surpluses the next). At the very least, the government should consider restricting the emigration of skilled people who are in short supply and extend its monitoring system to include emigrating graduates of vocational and higher institutes, as well as government secondees and people officially contracted to work abroad.[36]

Laissez-faire attitudes about retaining staff in technical institutes or universities are also a problem. The slow process of building up adequate staff in institutes of higher learning cannot maintain momentum if it is to be depleted overnight. For example, according to Ali (1977), faculty losses from the University of Khartoum reached alarming proportions between 1973 to 1976 (an estimated 20 per cent or more). Most of these left for the oil-rich countries. Failure to bond such personnel or to impose agreements to return (as in Syria) is making a mockery of the government program to promote self-sufficiency in research and development.

Independent government efforts to correct these distributional problems cannot operate in a void. They must be complemented by integrated manpower policies for the region at large. To date this crucial notion has received little more than lip-service. Yet, economic growth is becoming all the more unbalanced as physical and human capital rush to places of greatest economic advantage. True, governments of the oil-rich countries have sought to offset this polarization through bilateral and multilateral aid. But awarding loans or grants-in-aid means little when the personnel to implement them are absent. By integrating supply/demand requirements on a regional basis, acute shortages in countries of greatest disadvantage could be taken stock of and the emigration of people with crucial skills could be checked. While this kind of policy might be a source of inconvenience to rapid expansion in the richest countries, its contribution to the region as a whole, in the form of more balanced growth, should far outweigh this loss.

Conclusion

For all its remarkable progress, education in most Arab countries will be incapable of meeting demands for skilled or highly qualified manpower for some time to come. Improvements must await a vastly expanded primary and secondary school system, systematic expansion of vocational and technical institutes, substantial improvements in the quality of teacher training, correction of extreme inequalities in the geographical distribution of educational investments, and checks on the ever-present brain drain. No amount of enthusiasm or impatience can ignore the magnitude of the challenge that lies ahead. This applies particularly to the long, arduous process of constructing and staffing technical institutes and universities to the point where they can provide quality education for sufficiently large numbers of students. For the oil-rich countries, this implies continued reliance on expatriates. For most of the oil-poor countries it implies the usual: doing without. For the region as a whole, it implies that 'Arabization' of the labor force is at least ten to twenty years off.

Severe shortages require equally severe measures to overcome them. Governments recognizing this have gone so far as to send tens of thousands of students into rural areas to teach the illiterate; have forced adults to take extension courses in basic reading and writing skills; have imposed training levies on companies toward educating Arab nationals in applied skills; and have restricted emigration of the highly skilled. On the whole, however, no attempt has been made to synthesize various approaches in the form of a general strategy.

Essentially, the policy directives proposed here suggest an interim approach. They consist of three elements; (i) mandatory on-site instruction by expatriates, (ii) employment of returning highly qualified emigrants in teaching posts in extension, technical or university programs, and (iii) bonding of technical or university graduates for service in areas needing them most. Feasibility of such policy action is enhanced by the fact that resources for implementation are available now and measures to harness them are in the policy-makers' domain.

To my mind, the most problematic aspect of human resource development in the Arab region, and the greatest challenge for the policy directives considered here, concerns distribution. Inequalities in the distribution of education and skills are so great and so persistent within and between countries that commitments to solve them should be a priority. For this reason, the proposed policy directives could also be geared to counteract the typical 'urban bias' in educational investments, the *laissez-faire* development of human resources in modern enclaves, and neglect of the human capital needs of the poor.

Appendix 6.1 General versus specific on-the-job training

On the whole, training and certification of general skills are likely to have a more marked impact on the age profile of returns to the trainee than investments in specific training. General training is also more suited to the needs of trainees in contexts of high employment turnover (e.g. Arab workers in the OAPEC countries who must return to their home country). In contrast, advantages of specific training tend to be more discernible for indigenous firms and workers that do not face high employment turnover (e.g. among Arab nationals in the OAPEC countries), or for policies which seek to stabilize short-term fluctuations in labor supply and employment.

Although most forms of training actually fall between general and specific training, their differential effects on wage rates can be illustrated as in Figure A.6.1.[37] Part A indicates the situation when the training is general, Part B when the training is specific.

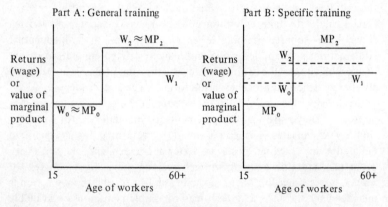

Figure A.6.1 *A comparison of age profiles of returns to general versus specific training*

In Part A, the horizontal line W_1 gives the wage and marginal product of the untrained worker over his life cycle. The stepped line gives the wage and marginal product of the worker who undergoes training. During the training interval, his wage and marginal product, W_0, can be seen to be lower than it would be if he chose alternative employment. Earnings are thus forgone by the individual, and this represents his investment. Following the training period, however, general skills and marginal product are increased to MP_2. Precisely because the skills acquired are general, the wage the trained man can command, W_2, also increases to this level. Over this period, W_2 is greater than the untrained wage rate, W_1. This represents the return on the investment.

Part B represents the case of specific training. As before, the horizontal line marks the wage and marginal product of the untrained individual. The stepped line again marks the marginal product of the worker who undergoes training. However, this line now refers only to his marginal product within the firm in question. His marginal product outside the firm is assumed to be unaffected – it remains at W_1. The wage rate of this individual does not follow the course of the stepped line. Instead, his wage rate will be more akin to the horizontal line. Hence, W_1 will tend to be close to W_2. In fact, W_2 will probably exceed W_1 somewhat, because the employer is likely to raise the wage rate of the trained employee so as to reduce his probability of resignation. Correspondingly, the wage received during the training interval will be somewhat less than W_1. In sum, general training investments can be expected to have a more marked impact on the age profile of wage rates than specific investments.

This is not to say, however, that specific training does not have its positive side. This can be demonstrated with respect to its likely effects on employment stability among an indigenous labor force. When firms invest in the specific training of their employees, their labor becomes a 'quasi-fixed factor'. The cost of labor to the employer thus becomes partially variable and partially fixed. The fixed cost, comprising hiring and training costs, represents an investment by a firm in its labor. As such, these costs introduce an element of capital into the use of labor.

The existence of fixed costs in the case of labor has important empirical implications. Labor in which the employer has invested firm-specific training is less likely to be laid off in the event of a drop in product demand. If such labor is laid off, the firm will lose the opportunity of amortizing the hiring and training costs it had incurred. Thus, among higher paid, more skilled individuals who have received higher firm-specific investments, we would expect the demand for their services to fluctuate less over the business cycle than that for their lesser skilled counterparts.

The notion of fixed costs also has clear implications for labor input utilization during recession or cyclical fluctuations in product, prices or demand. In the down-swing, employers will tend to reduce hours per man rather than lay off workers, thus reducing the ratio of output to workers. In short, fixed costs attached to the employment of labor break the link between wages and marginal profit, at least in the short term.

Appendix 6.2 Bahrainization

The labor ministry's battle for Bahrainization dates back to the country's independence in 1971 (*The Economist*: 1980). But the latest scheme is its most determined attack yet on foreign domination of the business sector.

The Ten Thousand Scheme, as it is called, is an ambitious plan for the 1980s to train 10,000 Bahraini nationals for promotion to key positions currently held by expatriates. It aims to provide day-release training, free of charge, for 10,000 Bahrainis over the next ten years, in business, engineering and computer studies, including administration, accountancy and a range of management and clerical work, with the avowed intention of replacing foreigners in all the better paid jobs.

Several companies have already been Bahrainized as regards capital ownership, but their staff and management have remained intact. In July 1980, for example, the government took a 60 per cent share in the Bahrain Petroleum Company's refinery; by October, Gray Mackenzie Bahrain was reformed as Bahrain Maritime and Mercantile International with 52 per cent of the capital held locally (*The Economist*: 1980). In both cases, however, all the expatriate staff were kept on.

The labor ministry tried in 1982 to impose Bahrainization by insisting that companies replace expatriates with Bahrainis when their contracts end. Resistence to this policy has generally been attributed to a misplaced sense of Western cultural superiority. A measure passed in March 1980, to make it harder to obtain or renew work permits for foreign employees, backfired by affecting the thousands of low-paid unskilled Asian workers whom the Bahrainis are not eager to replace. A revised measure in September froze overseas recruitment specifically for the jobs Bahrainis were to be trained for – though, at the same time, companies were reassured that they could still employ expatriates if no suitable Bahrainis were available.

The government has also set up a comprehensive training plan for Bahraini civil servants, who are similarly overshadowed by expatriates. It has already taken steps to expand training facilities for the important hotel and catering industry. The Higher Vocational Training Council is encouraging firms to develop their own training schemes, as many have already done, and companies are being exempted from course fees as an incentive to send their Bahraini employees for training organized by the labor ministry.

Some companies argue that their own private training schemes already fulfill their obligation to help develop Bahraini manpower. Other firms have objected that they have no Bahrainis on their staff and so none of their employees is eligible for the scheme. The answer to this response has been that they should create extra jobs for unemployed Bahraini school leavers and graduates, nominated by the labor ministry, for immediate enrollment under the Ten Thousand Scheme, and continued employment thereafter. A minimum wage of US $320 per month has been set and the work permit freeze has been extended to include any companies resisting this latest move. Finally, unemployed youngsters have been invited to register for appointment to these new jobs, with 131 doing so in the first two days of the offer.

Chapter 7

Summary and conclusion

Overview

Disparate as the Arab countries may be in terms of their political economy, population size and resources, all have one thing in common. Deficiencies in the quantity, quality and distribution of human resources are perceived to be the single most important bottleneck to progress in the region. This means that policies to broaden employment, augment skills and tackle chronic distributional problems are in great demand. It implies a need to consolidate empirical information toward tipping the balance away from a preoccupation with growth-related and in favor of development-related population, manpower and employment issues; to identify population-related or manpower-related problems that will become more fully entrenched if neglected at this early stage of Arab development; and to propose remedies or policy guidelines which are sensitive to the problems as perceived by Arab governments themselves.

To remedy deficiencies in human resources effectively, policy-makers must be quite clear about what the deficiencies are, how they have arisen, and how they are being perpetuated. With this in mind, I have singled out five broad problem areas which are having an important bearing, either directly or indirectly, on Arab human resources. These are the flourishing construction boom, the poor performance of agriculture, the swelling population, the sluggish integration of women into the development process, and deficiencies in manpower and educational planning.

These problem areas are not intended to subsume the entire gamut of human resource issues confronting Arab development. Nor is my attempt to sketch out policy directives intended to serve as a panacea or 'blueprint for action'. Rather, each problem area has been selected in view of its relevance to long-term development goals, and in light of my personal knowledge or experience of the situation. My aim has been to document each problem area by drawing on a wide variety of empirical studies and data sources so as to familiarize the reader with the breadth and complexity of the issues involved; to consolidate a vast amount of empirical information, relevant to the study of human resources, in one volume; and to lay the foundation for appropriate policy action by indicating gaps that must be filled. By sketching preliminary frameworks for policy action, I have sought to make policy-makers, planners and students of Arab development take a second look at the possibilities open to them of achieving, at a stroke as it were, a range of desirable population, employment and human resource aims.

While the policy directives recommended in this book differ greatly in scope, methodology and timing, they have been designed with several broad guidelines in mind. They seek to increase labor force participation rates and reduce problems of structural and demand deficient unemployment. They are concerned with augmenting the quality of human capital, as well as the supply price or return to a given unit of labor. They aim to correct inequalities in the distribution of employment and income earning opportunities, and they attempt to improve on human capital by utilizing resources or 'building blocks' that are already in the policy-makers' domain. Finally, by emphasizing the plight of poor peoples in both urban and rural areas, they strive to complement United Nations' policies to deal with 'basic needs' and 'integrated rural development'.

Problem areas and policy directives

Construction has occupied the center of the stage in my inquiry because it has been the leading economic sector in the oil-rich countries since 1973. My concern has been to harness construction in ways that will alleviate the population-related and employment-related problems which accompanied the investment frenzy between 1973 and 1977, as well as those which will result from the resurgence of construction contracts during the 1981 to 1986 round of national development plans. I have been particularly concerned with evaluating the extent to which construction might be harnessed to manipulate or redirect flows of both international and internal migrants. I have focused on labor migration because it is largely through the *laissez-faire* interaction of migration and the construction boom that problems such as wage disparities, inflation, income inequalities, loss of of skills, and imbalances in population distribution have become increasingly serious. I have seized upon construction because it has been the driving force behind migration, and it would appear to offer the potential of serving as an engine of growth and development in the oil-poor as well as in the oil-rich countries.

Specifically, I have sought to demonstrate that construction could serve as a key policy variable in Arab migration and employment for at least five interrelated reasons. First, it is a leading employer of migrants in both international and internal Arab labor markets. Second, the employment of migrants in construction typically aids labor exporting or labor surplus countries by absorbing large numbers of unskilled workers, offering a port of entry for rural labor into the industrial work force, and providing on-the-job training. The return of these workers, many of whom are temporary migrants, could contribute invaluable skills to the poorer Arab countries which are beginning to embark on their own construction—development programs fuelled by OAPEC 'dollars-in-aid'. Third, the appropriate planning of construction activity could influence the distribution of migrants both among and within countries. Fourth, the construction sector is a prime candidate for policy intervention. It receives large shares of development expenditures which policy-makers can generally invest as they see fit. Further, it is much easier to influence than many other variables bearing on employment and migration (e.g. wages and salaries), because a host of technical and locational controls exist to guide its behavior in desired places. Finally, the construction of houses is already a significant recipient of worker remittances in the poorer Arab countries. This subsector, and these funds, could be organized to underwrite self-help housing and labor-intensive employment in rural areas and small towns.

Just as construction has been the leading sector, agriculture has been the undisputed lagging sector. Physical constraints have dictated such tiny portions of arable land per worker that one wonders how agriculture could ever become self-sufficient, let alone produce a marketable surplus. While much has been made of the promise of Western-style ranches or Soviet collective units, especially in the Sudan, Algeria and Egypt, the fact remains that a large majority of the agriculture population is locked into micro-scale subsistence farming. In short, problems confounding Arab agriculture are so horrific that references to high unemployment, landlessness, rural exodus and wide disparities in income are beginning to fall on deaf ears.

My concern has been to focus on traditional agriculture, representing some 14 million of 19 million workers. I emphasize the modernization of small-scale farming, the expansion of rural non-farm employment opportunities for the landless and marginal worker, and the encouragement of various facets of agricultural potential that have remained underdeveloped due to neglect or oversight. Specifically, I have sought to demonstrate that prospects for boosting productivity and employment lie in greater attention to high-yielding varieties, intensifying and diversifying crops, improving irrigation, extending cooperative services, small-scale development of animal husbandry, and the expansion of fisheries. Moreover, I have advocated a thorough 'weeding of the garden' in respect of unfair agricultural pricing policies, incomplete agrarian reform and 'urban bias' in development expenditures.

Population growth features strongly in my inquiry because it is the acknowledged driving force behind the demand for jobs and services which are considered to be in short supply in many countries. At present growth rates, the population of the Arab countries will almost double by the year 2000. At present levels of labor force participation, employment must grow by some 30 million to 40 million jobs merely to keep abreast and national product must increase by at least 3 per cent yearly to keep per capita income from backsliding.

On the whole, Arab governments have paid little heed to the Malthusian threat implied above. There are several good reasons for this, one of which is that the demand for family planning services was minimal in most countries prior to the 1973 oil-boom. Since 1973, however, at least two major developments have been exerting an important impact on population. First, health authorities have been waging war on foetal deaths and infant mortality to the extent that losses are dropping by up to 10 per cent per year in most countries. The implication for Arab families is that ten live births will no longer be needed to guarantee a desired family size of five or six *surviving* children. Second, incredible investments in education are likely to be having an effect on the size of the family desired by Arab couples. Combined with rising household incomes, at least in the oil-rich OAPEC countries, education may well be the most powerful force stimulating the demand for family planning services.

My concern has been to focus on the relationship between improvements in female education and changing fertility. By calibrating this relationship and tying the results to a schedule of educational

191

attainment among 'tomorrow's' female reproductive cohort, I have attempted to quantify the likely demand for future family limitation. According to my results, Arab couples will seek to avert some 13 million births over the next twenty years. The implied policy directive is really one of timing, in which Arab governments anticipate the consequences of the educational programs they have chosen to embark upon. Thus, the accent is on 'problem avoidance' by employing a preventive approach. Important features of the preventive approach are that future couples should be forewarned of the ramifications of rapid socio-economic development on their future family size, and that governments should supply family planning services to the extent that family size desires and the welfare of married couples are not compromised.

Closely related to the subject of population is the status of women. My concern with 'upgrading the other half' pertains largely to matters of employment. I begin by dispelling some of the myths about women's opportunities in Arab economies. These pertain to shallow interpretations of the Qur'an and Islamic custom, to fragmentary empirical impressions concerning their work, and to erroneous impressions concerning their preference for formal employment over 'wife' or 'child rearing' roles.

The policy directives that I have proposed incorporate a search for selective interventions. On the one hand, they fully acknowledge that some barriers to boosting the quantity and quality of female skills that exist or are in demand, are simply not amenable to change overnight. On the other hand, they attempt to join forces with social and economic changes which are dismantling barriers as part and parcel of current national development planning. Specifically, three areas of change are identified as fertile grounds for policy action. First, there is the need for women to work in cases where their husbands or fathers are unemployed. Second, there are the indirect effects of male emigration on the demand for women in business and factories. Third, ratification of international conventions is also assessed as a means of singling out countries where the fight for women's emancipation is making very real progress.

Few topics are more central to the question of human resource development than educational planning. As might be expected, Arab education is no exception. Most national development plans have accorded educational investments a high priority and the entire system has undergone remarkable improvement as a result. Yet, it is also true that its capacity to accommodate demands for qualified manpower remains totally inadequate. This condition will surely persist over the next decade or so because deficiencies in the quantity, quality and distribution of education must await sufficient numbers of graduates who have passed through a vastly expanded primary and secondary school system; the systematic expansion of vocational schools or institutes of higher training (technical or university); a substantial improvement in the quality of teacher training; and the correction of extreme inequalities in the distribution of educational investments between urban and rural areas. In addition, little has been done to ensure that the emigration of highly qualified workers to more developed countries will not continue to undermine efforts to integrate educational output with future manpower needs.

In view of the above, there can be little doubt that interim measures are urgently needed to accommodate shortages of key skills in virtually every economic sector, in virtually every country, in rural and in urban areas alike. Accordingly, I have suggested a number of policy directives which include (i) drawing on the skills, education and know-how of currently employed expatriates by persuading them to conduct on-site training courses, (ii) enticing skilled Arab emigrants to return to their home countries to conduct university, technical or extension courses, and (iii) bonding recent graduates for service in underprivileged areas.

In my view, viable alternatives to this approach are virtually non-existent. Moreover, were educational policy-makers to orient entirely to the demand for applied skills, other important functions of formal education would be neglected in the process. These pertain to the preservation and extension of the Arabic culture *per se*. Accordingly, the policy directives that I have proposed aim to accommodate pressing demands for more highly skilled Arab manpower without unduly neglecting the cultural content of Arab education in the process.

Looking ahead

If my inquiry conveys a sense of urgency, it is for one simple reason. Many Arab economies are just setting out on the long path to becoming modern industrialized nations. Faulty planning or neglect now will allow infant problems to become more fully entrenched as the Arab growth machine rolls on. A preoccupation with growth-related investments must be balanced with equal attention to development-related human resource issues. Otherwise, the vicious circle that plagues most Arab countries — including dual economies, concentration of investments in modern enclaves, neglect of agriculture, rural exodus, urban blight, etc. — is likely to take firmer root in the region.

193

To my mind, Arab planners are only beginning to appreciate the extent to which population, employment and manpower problems affect, and in turn are affected by, the vicious circle of underdevelopment. In some countries, this recognition has promoted substantial increases in planned government expenditures for research and the development of manpower (e.g. Saudi Arabia). In other countries, it has been visible in isolated attempts to mobilize human resource potential using rather dramatic measures. As we have seen in previous chapters, examples include imaginative literacy campaigns (Somalia, Sudan), strict enforcement of on-site training for Arab employees (Bahrain), innovative policies to reduce the brain drain (Iraq, Syria), aggressive land redistribution programs (Algeria, Libya), and farsighted measures to develop and utilize female skills for employment (Jordan). While such examples are imbued with worthy intentions, innovative ideas and some prospects for success, it is also true that efforts to synthesize such prospects in the guise of general strategies have a long way to go.

By consolidating information on gaps or deficiencies in the development and utilization of Arab manpower, I have attempted to take the process of mobilizing human resource potential one step further. By spelling out policy directives, I have sought to sketch preliminary farmeworks for strategies that may be of relevance to groups of countries or to the region as a whole. Needless to say, policy directives of the type proposed here will require a great deal of filling out in the future. On the one hand, this will necessitate greater attention to differences in resource endowments between countries and to inter-relations between various dimensions of human resources (e.g. male migration, female employment). Improved access to a broader database will certainly aid in this endeavor over time. On the other hand, it will require a realistic discussion of problems and modalities of implementation — a task that could easily fill a subsequent volume.

In addition to the above, it is important to acknowledge that I have no illusions concerning the fact that real progress in the Arab development effort will require that governments exercise a far greater commitment to tackle inequalities in the distribution of human resources in relation to non-human resources. Differences in per capita incomes between rural and urban areas or between countries are great; access to education, or opportunities for productive employment, are extremely unequal between classes and between men and women; and public funds continue to be allocated to economic sectors in amounts that are clearly in disproportion to the populations they represent. Efforts to correct such inequalities will not only require a rethinking of domestic policy as has been suggested throughout this book. They will require a commitment to regional economic integration and cooperation of much greater significance than has existed in the past.

Unfortunately, many observers surmise that prospects for improved integration and cooperation are not good. Waterbury (1978), for example, forecasts that poverty among the oil-poor countries might be used to advantage by aid-giving OAPEC countries in their quest for regional power and influence. He also suggests that the unequal distribution of oil wealth will serve as an obstacle to cohesion and that this will combine with other forces of divisiveness that have traditionally set Middle Eastern states at odds with one another. Birks and Sinclair (1980b) view the gap between rich and poor countries as a forum within which existing manpower crises will promote political or economic instability, and possibly conflict. Tuma (1980) argues that the wealthier Arab countries have no intention of modifying the *status quo* in favor of the poorer countries and that, as a result, their aid has been rather small or tied to specific projects. His is a particularly scathing indictment on the failure of the Arab brotherhood to tackle inequalities in living levels. Not unsimilar forebodings have been made with respect to 'oil enclaves' in the Gulf countries by Niblock (1980), and with respect to economic problems of a politically isolated Egypt by Hamed (1981).

If the prognoses above turn out to be applicable, then the Arab dream of economic self-sufficiency might well be reduced to empty rhetoric for some time to come. Hopes of ironing out economic and social differences between the oil-rich and oil-poor countries would be diminished, aims of reaching self-sufficiency in food production through an Arab common market would probably be stalled, and efforts to reduce dependency on foreign know-how through inter-regional manpower planning would have little chance of success. Needless to say, failure to integrate and cooperate would also taint the potential success of the policy directives suggested in this book.

To my mind, governments in the region face no greater challenge than to counter such prognoses. And with over 65 per cent of the world's proven oil reserves, representing some US $11,440 billion or some US $249 billion in yearly production,[1] the Arab oil exporting countries have inherited the opportunity of doing just that. Imagine, for example, the gains to the dream of Arab self-sufficiency were the oil-rich countries to alleviate the burden of external debt among the oil-poor countries. External debt has become so massive that it now represents over 40 per cent of the combined gross national product (GNP) of 126 million Arabs. In current dollars it has grown from some US $4,560 million in 1974 to over US $48,000 million in 1980 (Table 7.1, column 1). In constant dollars, it has grown fivefold in the brief span of six years.

From the standpoint of political economy, it is of no small importance that the oil-rich countries have the power to virtually eliminate the dehabilitating effects of this financial burden. If we include Algeria among the oil-rich, these countries have access to some US $93,000 million in net foreign assets alone. Saudi Arabia, of course, dominates with holdings of some US $65,000 million. The important point concerning these assets is that they constitute a surplus which could be used to ameliorate Arab debt without significantly detracting from the pursuit of prosperity. That is, many of the oil-rich countries are presently saturated with national development funds and have access to proven oil reserves for future development investments. While any proposal that net foreign assets might be used for debt relief is likely to be interpreted as wishful thinking, it is also true that Arab dreams of economic self-sufficiency will never materialize if a large majority of the Arab population remains in financial bondage.

Admittedly, governments of the oil-rich countries have sought to help the oil-poor countries to meet their financial obligations through a number of bi- and multi-lateral funding and lending agencies. They have established five national funding agencies, four regional agencies, and have recently launched the 'First Decade of Arab Development'. These efforts have resulted in concessional 'Official Development Assistance' (ODA) to poorer countries of approximately US $5 billion per year between 1973 and 1980.[2] Relative to the performance of OECD countries, Arab donors can be proud of the fact that their aid far exceeds the United Nations target of 1 per cent of GNP. Moreover, the aid performance of most Arab donors – ranging from 4.99 per cent of their combined GNP in 1975 to 2.34 per cent in 1980 – has been qualitatively different from that of most OECD countries. Arab donors have given larger shares of ODA in the form of grants, and they have refrained from using ODA to promote sales of domestic exports or to generate return flows. In other terms, a large share of Arab ODA has not been tied.

Upon closer inspection, however, we observe that the promise of Arab aid is being undermined by forces of political economy on the one hand, and neglect on the other. With respect to political economy, it is the 'confrontation states' of Syria, Jordan and Lebanon that have

Table 7.1 *External debt among the poorer Arab countries, 1970–80*

	1980 debt (US $ millions) (1)	Ratio of 1980 debt to 1970 debt (2)	Debt service payments as % of total value of exports of goods and services		1980 debt per capita (5)	1980 debt per capita as % of 1980 per capita GNP (6)
			1980 (3)	Ratio of 1980/1973 (4)		
Algeria	15,990	16.3	25.6	2.1	836	52.9
Egypt	13,050	6.9	15.8	0.4	279	60.7
Jordan	1,266	8.8	5.3	1.1	338	39.8
Lebanon	194	1.4	na	na	30	1.7
Mauritania	713	16.9	32.4	3.6	305	111.7
Morocco	7,097	8.8	21.8	2.6	319	43.1
Somalia	693	5.2	1.1	0.3	108	92.6
Sudan	3,097	5.7	33.0	2.8	103	35.4
Syria	2,493	9.8	16.5	2.2	273	25.5
Tunisia	2,955	5.8	11.8	1.1	491	43.8
Yemen AR	619	46.6	1.8	na	80	11.8
Yemen PDR	536	441.0	2.8	28.0	245	49.0
TOTALS OR AVERAGE	48,703	12.9	na	na	331	42.6

Source: World Bank, 1981, *World Debt Tables* and *World Development Report*.
Note   na data not available.

been most favored in recent allocations of ODA. In 1980, these 'middle income' countries received more than 70 per cent of all Arab ODA earmarked for Arab countries, though they represented less than 9 per cent of the total Arab population. Over 95 per cent of this aid was in the form of grants. In contrast, six of the poorest Arab countries received only 18 per cent of Arab ODA though they represented 44 per cent of the total Arab population. Of this, only 57 per cent was in the form of grants. As for Egypt, less than 1 per cent of Arab aid was earmarked for this politically isolated, stagnating economy, which contains more than one-quarter of the entire Arab brotherhood.

That the Arab community has agreed to launch its 'First Decade of Arab Development' for the benefit of the five poorest countries must also be applauded with reservation. Towards reducing inequalities between richest and poorest countries, the 1980 Arab Summit sought US $15,000 million for the 'rapid development' of the five poorest countries, of Mauritania, Somalia, the Sudan, and the two Yemens. However, only US $5,000 million was secured and this amount is to be disbursed evenly over a ten-year period. To appreciate the marginal effects that yearly disbursements of US $500 million are likely to have on interregional inequality and development in these countries, consider the following. Between 1976 and 1981, the five countries spent approximately $1,398 million per year on their national develop-ment plans. This translates into approximately $49 per capita per year versus $1,361 per capita per year among the eight oil-rich countries. With an additional US $500 million per year, expenditures among the five poorest countries would rise to only $66 per capita per year. Put differently, the ratios of per capita expenditures of the oil-rich countries versus the five poorest countries would fall from a pre-development decade level of 27.6 to a post-decade level of 20.5. Chances are that the First Decade of Arab Development will mirror the distributional performance of the First United Nations Development Decade (1950–60). That performance can be summed up in one word: failure.

To my mind, the most puzzling feature of Arab aid is that it has been so neglectful of agriculture. Agricultural projects received only 12.4 per cent of the total cumulative lending of the eight major Arab funds up to mid-1981 (Table 7.2, column 3). This means that neglect of agriculture in the national development plans is not being recognized and corrected for in bi- and multi-national lending policy. Up to 1981, agricultural projects in the twelve oil-poor countries were earmarked for only US $816 million, or approximately $89 per agricultural worker

Table 7.2 *Sectoral distribution of cumulative Arab development financing by major Arab funds up to mid-1981*

Funding agency	Date of effective lending/operation (1)	To Arab and Non-Arab recipient countries					To Arab recipients only		
		Total amount of loans $ US mil. (2)	% Distribution				Total amount of loans ($ US mil.) (7)	% Distribution	
			Agriculture (3)	Transport, telecomm., power (4)	Mining, industry (5)	Other (6)		Agriculture (8)	Other (9)
Abu Dhabi Fund	1974	883.7	6.9	57.4	32.1	3.6	717.3	6.7	93.3
Arab Bank (Africa)	1975	353.6	25.5	46.9	21.4	6.2	—	—	—
Arab Fund	1974	1,268.4	11.7	58.5	13.0	16.8	1,268.4	11.7	88.3
Islamic Bank	1975	1,801.0	9.3	53.0	21.8	15.6	903.0	8.1	91.9
Kuwait Fund	1962	2,706.9	17.1	60.1	17.4	5.4	1,594.1	19.8	80.2
OPEC Fund	1976	1,070.3	5.9	33.7	7.6	47.2	178.9	7.1	92.3
Saudi Fund	1975	3,175.0	13.4	63.2	10.9	12.5	1,449.8	13.3	86.7
Iraqi Fund	1978	436.5	6.5	68.4	23.4	1.7	217.6	13.0	87.0
TOTALS OR %		11,695.4	12.4	56.9	16.4	14.3	6,329.1	12.9	87.1

Source: Arab Fund for Economic and Social Development, 'Development Financing Operations of Arab Regional and National Institutes to Developing Countries Up to 30/6/81' (Kuwait: Mimeo).

(Table 7.2, columns 7–8). This compares with approximately US $5,513 million for the non-agricultural sector, or approximately $737 per non-agricultural worker. If we add the entire operating budget of the Arab Authority for Agricultural Investment and Development (US $517 million in 1977), lending allocations per agricultural worker remain barely one-fifth of those per non-agricultural worker.

Clearly, a resorting of sectoral priorities and aid allocations to the poorest Arab countries is in order. Aside from vagaries concerning the need for integrated rural development, etc., the Arab community will be faced with the spectre of an additional 113 million Arabs that will have to be fed in the oil-poor countries within the next twenty years.

Of course, the cause of economic integration and self-sufficiency would also make headway were the Arab governments to commit themselves to a regional approach to, say, the trade and production of food and agricultural products, or the exchange and monitoring of manpower. In the former case, a key ingredient to such an approach would be a system of free and complementary trade. To date, however, most governments have pursued agreements in this respect with lethargy. To illustrate, Kuwait entered agreements in 1973 with Bahrain, Qatar and the UAE to permit the free movement of capital, labor and produce. Yet, when total Kuwaiti imports grew fourfold between 1970 and 1978, its imports from the Arab Gulf countries actually fell from approximately 43 per cent to about 30 per cent (Niblock: 1980). Equally unimpressive is the performance of the Arab Common Market. In 1978, for example, the share of intra-ACM trade in the total trade of the original four members (Egypt, Iraq, Jordan, Syria), was only 2.2 per cent of total exports and 2.1 per cent of total imports. For sake of comparison, member states of the European Economic Community increased their trade with each other 15 per cent within five years of inception (i.e. from 35 per cent to 50 per cent).

With respect to improving information on manpower requirements, it is also difficult to understand why Arab governments have not, as yet, managed to coordinate the development of a central, interregional monitoring agency. Almost all governments recognize the need for such an agency. Yet, few concrete steps have been taken since the International Labour Office terminated its 'International Migration Project' which studied labor movements in the region between 1975 to 1979. In this respect, a recent request by the Secretary General of the Arab Labour Organization for the participation of the ILO in a new Arab regional project to improve on manpower planning and labor market information certainly merits encouragement.[3]

Of course, the job of arresting interregional inequalities in standards of living, trade patterns or manpower deficiencies will not be an easy one, especially in view of the non-complementarity of the Arab economies. For this reason, it would seem appropriate to point to the fact that the governments in the region may be in a position to draw on an important ideological advantage. That is, there is a growing currency in the idea that Islam offers a realistic alternative to inequality and the economic exploitation of one group by another. Hopefully, a strengthened Islamic consciousness, wherein Moslems are enjoined by the Qur'an to oppose social and economic injustice in its various forms, will aid Arab policy-makers in their efforts to cooperate in the difficult task of ameliorating such conditions in the future.

Notes

Chapter 1   Policy concerns, or why this study matters

1 These countries are Bahrain, Iraq, Kuwait, Libya, Oman, Qatar, Saudi Arabia and the United Arab Emirates. Hereafter, I shall refer to this group as the OAPEC countries as they comprise member states of the Organization for Arab Petroleum Exporting Countries.

2 I use the term 'economic integration' in its broadest sense. It includes a common market in which economic and non-economic risks of capital mobilization would be minimized with the absence of nationalization or warfare. It would benefit importing and exporting countries because investments that are of doubtful promise in any specific nation or region could become highly promising in larger markets.

3 See Waterbury (1978), Niblock (1980), Tuma (1980), Weinbaum (1980), Hamed (1981).

4 Iran has returned to fundamentalism with such revolutionary fervor that current development planning is a dead issue. The economy of Lebanon has been demolished by civil war. Egypt has been enmeshed on the frontier of the Arab–Israeli conflict to the extent that actual development planning has been a shadow of its potential. The late President Sadat claimed that funds devoted to maintaining the conflict (about US $60,000 million) would have been sufficient to bring Egypt to the threshold of economic self-sufficiency. The economies of Syria and Jordan have suffered in their conflict with Israel. Syria incurs a monthly bill of US $75 million for its presence in Lebanon. The Saharan war brought poverty-stricken Mauritania to the brink of economic disaster. And the story goes on with respect to Morocco and Algeria in their fight for the Sahara, conflict between Somalia and Ethiopia, Iran and Iraq, Sudan and Libya, etc.

5 For example, labor's contribution to production has been estimated at anywhere between 75 per cent in the early stages of US industrialization to 54 per cent in recent Australian manufacturing (Douglas: 1976). In early US agriculture, the contribution of labor to production has been estimated at about 40 per cent between 1900 and 1945, compared with about 30 per cent for land. Labor's share only began to take second place to physical capital (e.g. real estate, machinery and equipment) during the last decade as US farmers increasingly consolidated their land and turned to labor saving technology (Penson and Lins: 1980). A not unsimilar picture emerges with respect to agriculture in less developed countries. For example, studies of production elasticity among farms in several Asian countries have estimated labor's contribution to productivity to be between 25 and 40 per cent. In most of these studies, labor's contribution was observed to be second only to land (Lau and Yotopoulos: 1979).

6 See Becker (1964), Shaw (1974a), Lockheed *et al.* (1980).

7 This work has been pioneered by Theodore Schultz and Gary Becker at the University of Chicago. See Schultz (1980a, 1980b).

8 This is of major concern to the Arab Labour Organization which is searching for ways of attracting Arabs to replace workers from such countries as the Philippines and South Korea.

9 Were countries to be distinguished as 'capital-rich' versus 'capital-poor', with capital broadly defined to include the stock of both human and physical capital, then it might be appropriate to place, say, Lebanon or Egypt in the 'rich' category.

10 Information on proven oil reserves and projected exports has been obtained from the OPEC Secretariat (see Fesharaki: 1980). In order meaningfully to compare the figures between countries, I have standardized them by population size, thus producing per capita estimates.

11 Throughout the text, Yemen Arab Republic will be referred to as North Yemen; it will be referred to as Yemen AR in the tables. The People's Democratic Republic of Yemen will be referred to as South Yemen in the text and as Yemen PDR in the tables.

12 This conclusion is based on unpublished figures for 1975, obtained from the International Labour Office's Migration for Employment Project.

13 Since many national development plans pertain to five-year periods ending in December of 1980 (or January of 1981), or December of 1985 (or January of 1986), I discuss expenditures of all development plans in the time frame of 1976 to 1981, or 1981 to 1986.

14 See Bunton (1978), MEED (1981).

15 This is a special United Nations classification for purposes of iden-

tifying countries which merit top priority in the allocation of official development assistance.

16 In their review of population and employment data for countries of the region, Birks and Sinclair (1980b) calculate the 1975 crude labor force participation rate at 23.7 per cent for six 'capital-rich' Arab countries, 25.9 per cent for three 'pseudo-capital-rich' countries, and 29.6 per cent for six 'capital-poor' countries.

17 See Tuma (1980) for a superb review.

18 For example, El-Mallakh (1978), a development economist, foresees an era of relatively smooth economic growth assisted by an abundance of available resources, regional cooperation and especially close relations among Iran, Egypt and Saudi Arabia. Such assumptions are often made because they are conducive to the development of economy-wide interactive models, complete with computer simulation, projection and optimal problem solving capacity.

Chapter 2   Harnessing construction and labor migration

1 OAPEC: Organization for Arab Petroleum Exporting Countries.

2 See Bunton (1978), Cassell (1981), MEED (1981), as well as allocations for construction and housing in the 1981–6 round of national development plans.

3 These expatriates were expected to be distributed as follows: 17,000 to Bahrain, 87,000 to Kuwait, 172,000 to Libya, 449,000 to Saudi Arabia, and 147,000 to the United Arab Emirates, Qatar and Oman.

4 Over the 1975 to 1985 period, unskilled labor requirements are expected to grow from about 430,000 to about 550,000; semi-skilled office and manual labor from about 471,000 to 870,000; skilled office and manual labor from about 426,000 to 1,111,000; and, professional and technical labor from about 334,000 to 1,084,000.

5 The project was initiated by the International Labour Office between 1975 and 1979, and was carried out at the University of Durham under the direction of Stacey Birks and Clive Sinclair. By consolidating and cross-checking data from a wide variety of sources and countries, the project has produced a one-of-a-kind database that has yet to be duplicated or significantly updated.

6 See World Bank (1979b), Serageldin and Socknat (1980).

7 Admittedly, individual figures have been hotly contested. To my mind, however, the International Labour Office has made a considerably greater effort systematically to monitor migration flows

in the region than have its harshest critics. These efforts are described by Birks and Sinclair (1980a). Greatest contention centers around the figure of 290,000 emigrants for North Yemen. The Yemeni government claims the figure stood at about 1 million in 1980.

8 Several studies convey the impression that remittances have fed a money economy and that emigration has worked to reduce domestic production. Fergany (1980) argues that if emigration and remittances were cut off, North Yemen would remain among the least developed countries in the world but with a distorted economic structure and a damaging consumption pattern that would not have evolved in the absence of migration.

9 This even applies to new college graduates. In Jordan, Egypt and Syria, underemployment rates of between 10 and 50 per cent among college graduates were not uncommon up to two years after graduation (ECWA: 1978a). The problem persists in Egypt today because the government has pursued an educational policy which has produced far more university graduates than the economy can absorb. It has also guaranteed civil service employment to those who cannot find employment within three years. In 1979, 13,000 were expected to be absorbed into an already oversized government service. Queueing behind these were an additional 40,000 who had been unemployed for one to two years.

10 According to various estimates some US $30,000 million are either on the sidelines or in the works under the direction of ten Arab development funds.

11 Over the same period, grain prices rose by only 30 per cent (Clarke: 1977b).

12 Such problems also affect the OAPEC countries. Expatriates returning home spur imports of luxury goods through their purchases because such goods are often not available in their home country. A tour through the local airports bears this out. Hoards of returning workers can be seen in possession of portable television sets, stereos and cassette-radios.

13 A similar point has been raised with respect to remittances in Jordan (Mazur: 1979).

14 See Clarke (1977a), Amersfoort (1978), Findlay (1978).

15 See Azzam (1980), Serageldin and Socknat (1980).

16 Of course, the work camp approach can also be defended as a means of reducing pressure on urban housing and getting oil workers and their refineries away from the towns.

17 The 1981 to 1986 development plans of Algeria, Morocco and Saudi Arabia aim to slow down rural–urban migration through development and construction in rural municipalities.

18 In a study of three rural villages in North Yemen, Swanson (1979b) argues that there is a clear desire on the part of migrant workers to translate at least part of their remittance-fed wealth into productive enterprise. He also points out that the desire to translate wealth into capital, coupled with a dearth of investment opportunities, has intervened in the relation between wages and land so that land prices have become inflated.

19 See Robinson (1963), Howenstine (1968), Vernez (1976).

20 Examples include Columbia, Mexico, Pakistan, India, Republic of Korea; see Grimes (1976), Strassman (1979).

21 See Araud *et al.* (1973).

22 See Strassman (1979).

23 See UNIDO (1969), Shah *et al.* (1974).

24 Examples include Singapore, Japan, Columbia and the OPEC countries.

25 See Choucri (1977).

26 See Appendix 3.4, and Shaw (1978b).

27 Accurate prediction depends on whether the income effect outweighs the substitution effect which, in turn, is contingent on whether leisure is a normal good − defined as a good − the consumption of which rises with income.

28 Other variables included in the OECD study were differentials in per capita GNP, average wages and salaries adjusted for purchasing power, unemployment, tourist flows as an 'information surrogate', distance and dummy's capturing effects of migration policies, commonality of language, etc. The elasticity attached to differential rates of residential construction (DS) was 1.8. Other statistically significant variables included whether countries shared a common language (dummy with elasticity of 2.6), tourist flows between countries (elasticity of 0.27). Distance was not significant. Combined, these variables produced at R^2 of 0.51.

29 The labor importers, countries 'j', include those in Table 2.1 plus Jordan (a small importer) and Iraq (which has about 40,000 Egyptian and 5,000 Jordanian workers).

30 RC^{us} was measured as annual building permits in the USA, lagged one year. Original data were expressed as a percentage of the trend (see Thomas: 1973, Table 108). RG^{uk} was measured as gross residential building in the UK, lagged. Original data were expressed as a percentage of the trend (see Thomas, Table 107). Migration data were also obtained from Thomas, Table 92, and were expressed as a percentage of the trend.

31 In all studies reported here, every effort has been made to measure building activity at the beginning of the migration period so as to (i) minimize simultaneous equations bias, and (ii) accommodate

the likely time period for construction to affect income and employment opportunities, and migrants perceptions of these opportunities. Further, supply of residential construction is likely to lag by two to three years behind short-term demand. Its short-term behavior appears to be influenced more by availability of mortgage funds, interest rates, federal housing grants, vacancies, changes in inventory under construction, incomes and relative prices that exist previous to time of migration than during time of migration.

32 Also included in the inter-urban study were measures of differential unemployment, manufacturing wages, distance (D) and size of labor force of the sending area (LF_i), Besides CL, the variables D and LF_i were statistically significant with elasticities of −1.12 and 0.35, respectively. As in all studies reported here, significance levels were set at 0.05 or better.

Chapter 3   Energizing traditional agriculture

1 See Chapter 4. Moreover, the Arab Fund for Economic and Social Development (Kuwait) estimates that to accommodate food demand by 1985, production would have to increase over 1975 levels by 125 per cent for wheat, 330 per cent for sugar, 150 per cent for meats, 185 per cent for milk, and 180 per cent for vegetable oils.

2 The disruption of trade arrangements has been most severe between countries in the region in view of (i) domestic political upheavals among one or more trading partners, (ii) ideological differences between nations (e.g. involving Egypt), or (iii) outright war. Moreover, in policy circles much is made of the possibility that non-Arab trading partners could instigate a food embargo to protest against rising oil prices (see Weinbaum: 1980).

3 See Chapter 2 and migration studies on Tunisia (Hay: 1980), Iraq (Al-Jomard: 1979; Costello: 1975), Oman (Oman: 1978), Algeria (Algeria: 1977; Rahmani *et al.*: 1979), Sudan (El-Awad: 1974; Oberai: 1977), Egypt (Nagi: 1974); and Shaw (1978c, 1979c).

4 See Weinbaum (1980), Cuddihy (1981).

5 The Jordan Valley has had limited land distribution as a result of the East Ghor Main Canal development. It is my understanding that more is being contemplated for the future.

6 This observation agrees with the consensus that most of the reforms were not sufficiently aggressive (Warriner: 1973; Springborg: 1977; Richards: 1980).

7   For the sake of comparison, land redistribution programs in Japan, South Korea and Taiwan involved 78, 71 and 66 per cent of the tenanted land, respectively.

8   Richards (1980) claims that the reforms in Egypt not only excluded the poorest peasants, but failed to mobilize them because they were to be a 'passive partner' to the regime (particularly under Nasser).

9   See Griffen (1975), Bouman (1977).

10   See United Nations (1976), Radwan (1977), Kielstra (1978), Tuma (1980).

11   Though agricultural data on North Yemen are incomplete, it is known that the provinces of Ibb and Ta'izz, with 27 per cent of the rural population, have severe problems of land concentration. Between 50 and 60 per cent of the farms are of less than one hectare with access to only 10 to 17 per cent of the total cultivable land base. Further, landlords appear to be exploiting share-croppers who carry out all the work in cultivation and irrigation but receive only one-third of the crop harvested. This is hardly sufficient to meet food requirements and works to restrict the share-cropper's investment in fertilizer, insecticides, etc.

12   Bringing new land into cultivation through reclamation, regulation of water, draining, regulation of grazing rights, etc., has been attempted in the process of developing dry-land farming, new irrigation schemes, settling nomads or relocating communities suffering from drought (espcially in the Maghreb countries). It necessitates the design of supporting social structures, tenure, and marketing services so that the new settlements become an integral part of the national economy.

13   See FAO (1971), Higgs (1978).

14   Though the late President Sadan of Egypt had announced plans to reclaim an essential 315,000 hectares in the New Valley, we must ask: where would the government of Egypt find the estimated cost of $3,000–6,000 per hectare?

15   A recent review of Egypt's land reclamation effort by Voll (1980) concludes that (i) although the investment in the New Lands has averaged from 42 to 60 per cent of the total public investment in agriculture, their contribution to the total agricultural production is less than 1 per cent; (ii) nor has the program been able to provide an adequate livelihood for many of Egypt's rural poor. Through 1978, land in reclaimed areas has been distributed to only 56,000 of Egypt's estimated 1,531,000 landless families. Voll submits that a surer route to food security would appear to be increased investment in Old Lands, where much smaller investments have led to greater returns.

16 Of course, were planners given greater access to oil revenues it might be possible to strike a balance between the modernization of traditional agriculture and the control and utilization of new lands through reclamation and resettlement. This could foster the rehabilitation of liquid assets while simultaneously contributing to food security, and allowing greater opportunity for equity participation by the oil-rich countries.
17 See Griffen (1975), Naciri (1978).
18 See Shaw (1978b), Adams and Howell (1979).
19 This compares with approximately 667,000 farm operator/household heads and 618,000 family workers in the private sector.
20 To some extent, this can be explained by the fact that 82 per cent of the mechanized farm operators reported a non-farm job as their major occupation. This implies absenteeism and urban residence, meaning that the same kinds of pre-reform problems with farm profits exist in a post-reform situation. A similar claim has been made by the National Bank of Egypt which correlates absentee ownership with rental of 46 per cent of the cultivable land (NBE: 1978a).
21 The truth is that most governments, and certainly those of Syria, Egypt, Libya and the Sudan, are being tugged between agribusiness and state farms, tenancy and freehold. Depending on land and water limitations, large-scale mechanization may be the only viable alternative in some regions. This applies particularly to the tiny agricultural sectors of several OAPEC countries where self-sufficiency in vegetables and proteins is desirable, extensive funds are available and plans for large-scale mechanization, costly water schemes and controlled state production are feasible. In other regions, some combination of large-scale mechanization and supervised tenancy or freehold will be most desirable. Use of cooperatives to control production, marketing and pricing has the advantage of rationalizing production without denying the importance of ownership for increasing motivation and retaining labor on the land.
22 Rates of growth of agricultural product were only 33 to 50 per cent of the targeted rates in seven of the largest producers; they were less than 10 per cent in another two. As well as insufficient funding, failure to attain targets is probably attributable to lack of adequate information and skilled manpower, as well as the strong possibility that the targets themselves were unrealistic.
23 Oman presents the most notable exception with an allocation of about 8 per cent versus 1 per cent during the 1976 to 1981 period.
24 This point would seem to be most relevant to Jordan, Saudi Arabia, Syria, Algeria and Libya.

25 Low implementation rates are often attributable to poor administrative capacity in the aid receiving country, lack of qualified manpower to implement projects, or the approval of projects which are out of keeping with the country's needs and abilities.

26 The Arab Authority for Agricultural Investment and Development has a budget of about US $450 million. The International Fund for Agricultural Development in Rome has received about US $435 million for the OAPEC countries. This compares with a combined capital of the three largest bilateral funds (noted above) of about US $7,100 million, and is three times larger than that of the three largest multilateral aid agencies.

27 Tunisian high-yielding varieties also outperformed Mexican high-yielding varieties and were preferred on palatability grounds.

28 See Grabowski (1979), Stryker (1979).

29 In another context, small-scale Mexican ejidos have done as well as big farms in producing from high-yielding varieties (Burke: 1979).

30 A problem with the adoption of high-yielding variety wheat in the Sudan was that local adaptation by researchers was insufficient to render the high-yielding variety wheat as disease resistant as local varieties (Cuddihy: 1981).

31 Of course, improved marketing systems are essential in the production, transport and sale of vegetables.

32 Less than 10 per cent of the cultivated area in Egypt is devoted to fruits and vegetables.

33 The water withdrawal rate from the Jefara is estimated to be about 600 million cubic meters per year. The recharge rate – the Jefara's average annual rainfall is 200 million millimeters – is about 100 to 140 million cubic meters a year. In the past, the country's planners, guided mainly by a desire to increase agricultural production, have not wanted to recognize the problem. One of the few government restrictions to conserve water in the Jafara was the 1976 restriction on the planting of crops which use water heavily, such as tomatoes, citrus fruits and water melons. However, the effect on water conservation appears to have been negligible.

34 The World Bank estimates that more efficient use of water and greater availability of labor could add 10,000 hectares to the 37,000 now in cultivation.

35 According to the International Labour Organization, improvement in existing water management and switching from flood to controlled irrigation could generate in the order of 220,000 new jobs (ILO: 1977a).

36 Admittedly, in some countries, some types of cooperatives may be seen as too democratic, or possibly socialist, by autocratic royal families.

210

37 To date, these results and planned expansions are most applicable to large-scale operations in Saudi Arabia.
38 Oman is one country where the augmentation of employment and incomes through fisheries is considered to be potentially massive.
39 In Somalia, lack of maintenance personnel and of spare parts for existing processing factories led to complete or part-time closure of all factories between 1977 and 1978. Production dropped by 20 per cent as a result.
40 In Egypt, only half of the 31,000 tractors available to cooperative members were operating in 1975 due to lack of maintenance personnel and spare parts. In the Sudan, lack of maintenance personnel has left irrigation channels (serving the massive Gezira scheme) choked with weed and silt, because pumps need repairing or replacing, and telephones – essential to coodinate sluices and pumps – no longer work.
41 Each of these villages is expected to house between 100 and 600 families. The average will be about 200.
42 See Bénachenhou (1978), Hummadi (1978).
43 It is also true, however, that farmers have illegally shifted from food and export crops, or have chosen to pay a fine in order to produce more lucrative crops.
44 This claim applies particularly to a 'politically isolated' Egypt with its lack of capital, loss of skilled manpower to the Gulf, high underemployment of unskilled workers, food shortages, etc.
45 For example, Egypt's accord with Israel resulted in relocation of the Arab Council for Economic Unity to Jordan, a freeze on operations of the Arab Organization for Industrialization, and withdrawal of OAPEC aid; Syria's continued presence in Lebanon has raised questions about political intentions and has motivated the Gulf countries to cut back on their aid.
46 Workers in agriculture, and to a lesser extent in the Arab culture as a whole, have been depicted as having a 'disdain for manual-type work', where farming is considered 'demanding and unrewarding', and employment in agriculture is viewed as a sign of socio-economic failure (Knauerhause: 1976; Birks and Sinclair: 1978c; Kielstra: 1978). These kinds of impressions weigh heavily in the defense of large-scale mechanization, where principles of capital-intensive production have been touted as a remedy to the lethargy of the masses.
47 Durra-fallow has, as its principal grain, sorghum.
48 The remaining 10 per cent derive their major source of income from government transfers or retirement pensions.
49 A decline for urban families from 0.34 to 0.29 in Canada between

1960 and 1970, and no decline in the USA between 1949 and 1969 (i.e. remaining at 0.36).

50 The role of off-farm work in rectifying income inequality has also been observed in Morocco (Andriamananjara: 1976), in Malawi (Chipeta: 1976), in Algeria (Bénachenhou: 1978), in Brazil (Lopes: 1978), and in Nepal (Ashby: 1980).

Chapter 4   Appropriate population policy

1 An attempt has been made by Shaw (1976b) to rationalize these views in terms of socio-economic characteristics.

2 The conventional wisdom that population growth necessarily constrains growth in less developed countries has been questioned in a number of provocative studies by Simon (1975) and Simon and Pilarski (1979).

3 Exhaustive statistical analysis, including regression, path and interactive effects, attributed only 10 to 20 per cent of the decline in birth rates to program effort versus 60 to 65 per cent to improvements in the socio-economic setting. A similar analysis by Anker (1978), which is difficult to fault methodologically, credits family planning with almost no independent effect on fertility.

4 The only exception here might be Libya which restricts access to contraception by law.

5 See Easterlin (1975, 1980) and Mauldin and Berelson (1978).

6 Kirk (1971, p. 147), for example, correlated various national socio-economic characteristics with birth rates in fifteen Islamic countries and found that 'in the Islamic world measures of education clearly stand out as variables most related to natality levels'. Subsequent studies have reached similar conclusions including Audroing (1975), Azzam (1979b), Allman (1978, 1980), Cleland and Rodriguez (1980) and my multivariate analysis of Tunisian fertility summarized in Appendix 4.1.

7 See Cleland and Rodriguez (1980) and Jain (1981). Possible exceptions or inconsistencies in the relationship over the short term are discussed later.

8 See Davis and Blake (1956), Shaw (1974c) and Tabbarah (1976), and studies on Egypt by Abou-Gamrah (1980), on Libya by Ehtewish (1980), on Kuwait by Nagi (1980) and on Turkey by Tanfer (1981).

9 In Syria, illiterate females married at an average age of 17.8 years, compared with 24.5 years for those completing secondary school (1970 census). In Damascus (1976), the figures were 19.3 years and 23.6 years, respectively. In Jordan, between 1960 and 1971,

illiterate Moslem females married at an average age of 18.4 years compared with 22.2 years for those with a university degree. In Lebanon (1972), females marrying between the ages of 17 and 19 years had 4.8 children on average, versus 3.8 for those married between the ages of 22 and 24 years. In Algeria (1971), females marrying between the ages of 17 and 19 years had, on average, 7.5 children by the time they were between the ages of 30 and 39 years, compared with 5.7 children for those marrying between the ages of 20 to 24 years. In the Mauldin and Berelson (1978) study of ninety-four less developed countries, delayed age at first marriage was more highly correlated with drops in crude birth rates than was per capita gross national product or the proportion of the population living in cities.

10 It is known that higher education also tends to secure more absorbing or satisfying employment. In Tunisia, for example, job satisfaction among women influences their desire to have smaller families (Suzman *et al.*: 1976).

11 Furthermore, as education becomes more prevalent, there is considerable evidence to suggest that educated parents anticipate the greater costs attached to having children who must be fed, clothed and transported during their six to sixteen years at school. In this sense, the child's contributory role to the household economy, as, say, unpaid family worker on the family farm, begins to shift toward one of sole dependency (e.g. in metropolitan centers).

12 Jain (1981) also concludes that education can be construed as an agent of change in its own right.

13 This effect is clearly visible in a study of fertility among Egyptian women by Khalifa (1973, 1976), among Kuwaiti couples by Moustafa (1980), and among Turkish women by Tanfer (1981).

14 This is evident from results of the World Fertility Survey covering some twenty countries (Cleland and Rodriguez: 1980).

15 In an excellent review, Cochrane (1979) points out that improved education sometimes raises fertility. This often happens among the illiterate who first experience education, and who live in high infant mortality contexts. In such cases, education tends to have a positive effect on the health of the mother (thus reducing subfecundity), and works to reduce infant and childhood mortality through improved child-care.

16 Admittedly, under-reporting of past fertility is typically more problematic in rural than in urban areas. This means that rural values may appear to be lower than they really are. Also, definitions of rural versus urban areas tend to vary between censuses or surveys in different countries.

17 Schultz's (1972) multivariate analysis of fertility and child depen-

dency in Egypt (1960) also evaluates the effects of employment in agriculture. Contrary to expectation, greater proportions of the labor force in agriculture were negatively associated with fertility. This may be attributable to (i) the highly questionable quality of his 1960 Egyptian census data base, (ii) fewer surviving children in rural than urban areas due to higher sub-fecundity and infant mortality, or (iii) reductions in the average number of live births per reproductive couple due to emigration of females in the most reproductive ages to urban areas.

18 The concept 'opportunity cost' is used by economists to allude to the value of wage earning opportunities in another pursuit that are forgone by devoting all time to one pursuit.

19 While female employment might well produce a greater effect on fertility were it possible to control for the quality of employment (e.g. wage rates), absence of data relegates this hypothesis to speculation.

20 Tunisia presents an exception to this rule. The age of marriage rose between 1956 and 1966 before large numbers of women were enrolled in, or graduated from, secondary school. Delays in marriage at this time were probably linked with unsettling socio-economic developments following independence.

21 This is a major problem with Schultz's (1972) widely cited study of Egyptian fertility. While his study is useful in so far as it singles out a few consistent correlates of fertility, he does not provide guidelines for projecting changes in fertility over time, or how policy-makers might realistically influence fertility. His case is further weakened by the results for Jordan which are generally inconsistent. Finally, his main policy conclusion, that 'we might influence family size desires', is advanced without any realistic discussion of how this might be done over the short or long term.

22 The average number of live births to the entire cohort is based on a summary of the fertility performance of young or beginning wives and older wives alike. Thus, these average figures will be noticeably lower than the average completed family size of, say, married women aged 49 years who have largely completed their reproductive cycle. Use of averages will also help compensate for the under-reporting of cumulative fertility which is typically more serious among the older cohorts of women.

23 Education's positive effect on fertility in such contexts tends to operate through improved health which works to reduce female sub-fecundity, and death among newly born infants.

24 Of course, the regression coefficients in row G of Table A.4.3 of Appendix 4.3 also permit the estimating equation to be expanded to include more finite breakdowns for educational levels (E). The

extent to which this is worthwhile will depend on availability of detailed female enrollment data.

25 By the time today's female cohort finishes its education, it will have aged 19 years. Thus, by the time its members join tomorrow's cohort aged 15 to 49 years, all previous members will not have been displaced. The latter will be largely illiterate and have been included as members of column 1, Table 4.5.

26 This is a standard estimating technique for gauging male or female mortality and survivorship when country data are incomplete or unreliable. The United Nations Model Life Tables are derived specific to a wide range of country types. Only one or two demographic statistics on the country of interest are needed to locate its appropriate Model Life Table. In using infant mortality for entry, I assume that Arab countries with outrageously high infant mortality will experience a 50 per cent reduction within at least ten years.

27 Numerous surveys reveal that rates of celibacy among Arab women are very small (in the order of 2 to 4 per cent). As there is no reason to expect these rates to increase significantly in the near future, I exclude this consideration from my calculations.

28 It is interesting to note that Khalifa's (1973) study of fertility using 1970 data on 569 households in Cairo produces results similar to those reported here. He regresses a fertility measure against a more elaborate 'socio-economic index' to produce a regression coefficient of -0.21. This result is identical to that reported in my Appendix Table A.4.3, rows C through G.

29 In more technical terms, using 1960 census data, the elasticity for 10 fertility/education observations was -0.44 ($r^2 = 0.95$). This compares with -0.46 ($r^2 = 0.92$) for 13 fertility/education observations for the period 1970 to 1976. A pooling of the 23 observations produced an elasticity of -0.43 ($r^2 = 0.94$). These elasticities agree with those presented in Appendix 4.3, Table A.4.3, column 5.

30 In 1971 in Baghdad, Iraq, Ghali and Gadalla (1973) established that the mean of 4.2 pregnancies among 1,095 mothers was reduced to 3.3 surviving children due to loss by foetal deaths (0.4 children on average), still births (0.1), infant deaths (0.3) and childhood deaths (0.1). In 1972, in Sana City, North Yemen, Allman (1978) established that an average of 3.3 children ever born to mothers between the ages of 25 to 29 years would be reduced to 2.4, or by 27 per cent, due to infant and childhood mortality.

31 This is not to say, however, that Arab couples would be totally helpless were Arab governments to deny accessibility to modern or organized family planning techniques. Coitus interruptus is always 'accessible' though questions of reliability prevail.

32 Data in Table 4.6, column 3, are extremely crude. For example, the proportion of married couples using some form of efficient contraception is reported to be between 25 and 30 per cent for Jordan. According to Jordan's 1976 Fertility Survey, 26 per cent of the exposed women reported current use of an efficient method, whereas an additional 12 per cent reported some use of an official method. For urban areas, the percentage currently using contraception was 48 per cent versus 12 per cent for women in rural areas.

33 This point is evident in studies revealing low participation and high rates of discontinuation in a family planning service delivery system in Egypt. See Gadalla *et al.* (1980) and Hassouna (1980).

34 Between 1973 and 1978, the proportion of married women who had used some form of modern contraception doubled to about 15 per cent.

35 See UNESCO (1978b).

36 See Tabbarah (1976) for an excellent account of population education in the face of changing health and economic conditions.

37 In Morocco, between 1968 and 1971, women adopting the IUD and the pill already had 5.3 and 5.0 children, respectively. Corresponding figures for Tunisia in 1970 were 4.7 and 4.4 children, respectively.

38 United Nations Fund for Population Activities (UNFPA), International Planned Parenthood Federation (IPPF), United States Agency for International Development (USAID).

39 International Labour Organization (ILO), Food and Agricultural Organization (FAO), World Health Organization (WHO).

40 This program is under the direction of Kailas Doctor, International Labour Office, Geneva.

41 In Jordan (1972), women with primary education had, on average, 7.3 live births but desired 6.0. See also studies on Egypt by Khalifa (1973, 1976).

Chapter 5 Upgrading women's employment

1 To illustrate this point, over 50 per cent of the university students in Bahrain are women. In Iraq, 30 per cent of the doctors and pharmacists, 33 per cent of all civil servants, and 26 per cent of those working in technical industry are women. In Qatar, long associated with Islam's strict Wahhabi movement, the first two nationals to get Ph.D.s were women.

2 Invariably, these have failed to appreciate the overwhelming importance of the family and traditional sources of women's power gained through devotion to the family.

3 See Badawi (1972), Al-Qazzaz (1978).

4   See ECWA (1978b), Elwan (1978), El-Saadawi (1979), Soffran (1981).
5   The veil also gained support by distinguishing between 'the mothers of believers' (i.e. the Prophet's wives) and other women. Further, in the Abbasid period, use of the veil was diffused by free women wanting to be distinguished from slaves invading the market place at that time.
6   Today, 'women's modesty', meaning seclusion and veiling, has but one function. It serves the male honor. Men are dependent on women's purity because Arabic family honor relies strongly on the sexual virtue of the female (Strehm: 1976; Youssef: 1978). By 'family honor' we mean the knowledge or assurance that the married male's lineage and offspring have not been tampered with by an outsider. Accordingly, 'woman's modesty' is manifest in severe restrictions to ensure that her behavior, dress and inter-actions with others are sufficiently 'modest' as not to tempt the impulses of others, and for her not to be exposed, unguarded or tempted. Conveniently, men appear to have been absolved of any responsibility for falling into temptation. Does this not imply a return to pre-Islamic days when women were burdened with the blame for original sin? This nemesis is a hangover, or rather an embarrassment, which the Arabic culture is seeking to come to terms with today.
7   Inadequacies in the measurement and definition of formal labor force are elaborated in Boserup (1978), Standing (1978) and Keddie (1979).
8   A crude activity rate is a measure of women's employment and is derived as the ratio of the number of economically active women divided by the total number of women in the population.
9   Admittedly, even this rate is open to question for it averages data across censuses as though definitions of working women were the same in all cases. They are not, and this introduces an error of unknown magnitude.
10 Other examples include the Sudan and Mauritania. In the Sudan in 1973, refined female activity rates, which include women of labor force ages only in the denominator, were as high as 22 per cent in some urban provinces. This compares with an urban national average of 10 per cent. In some rural provinces they were as high as 56 per cent compared with a rural national average of 27 per cent. In Mauritania women occupy about 30 per cent of all jobs in the traditional sector, including 20 per cent of those engaged in cattle raising. High female participation rates in rural areas have been observed in many other countries as well where women play an important role in traditional agriculture.

11 It is also true, however, that women employed in services were in less prestigious occupations than were men.
12 In 1976, females constituted 74.8 per cent of the nurses in Bahrain, 63.9 per cent in Jordan and 69 per cent in Kuwait. They constituted 44.6 per cent of the teachers in the United Arab Emirates (1977), 47.6 per cent in Jordan (1976), 53.6 per cent in Kuwait (1975), 52.9 per cent in Lebanon (1974), 43.8 per cent in Qatar (1975) and 45.4 per cent in Bahrain (1975). If we classify Arab women according to professional group, we find a relatively large share in the 'professional, technical and related group'. This group accounts for 54.6 per cent of employed females in Bahrain (1971), 22.4 per cent in Egypt (1975), 40.2 per cent in Kuwait (1974), 28.8 per cent in Libya (1973), and 24.1 per cent in Syria.
13 In 1975–6, 4,500 female Egyptian teachers emigrated to Qatar, Bahrain, Oman, UAE and Kuwait.
14 In response to the United Nations World Plan of Action for the Decade of Women (1975–85), the governments of Jordan, Egypt, Iraq and the Sudan recently established special national departments for women's affairs.
15 See Mernissi (1979) in an article in the *Middle East* magazine.
16 Further, since male children were considered necessary for economic survival, the wife's fertility has been highly valued for centuries. Through her fertility, the control of the household, and the cultivation of the farm family land, she gained considerable bargaining power (Maher: 1978; Youssef: 1978).
17 See Beck (1978), Chatty (1978), Fischer (1978).
18 It is also true that the nature of work in a family business tends to rule out the effects that marital status or dependent children usually have on female participation.
19 See Bowen and Finegan (1969), Standing (1978).
20 In relatively rich countries, such conditions would tend to promote what economists call a 'discouraged worker effect'. That is, a drop in the real wage rate 'package' (wages, benefits, etc.) results in (i) an increase in the cost of market work relative to non-market work and the value of leisure, and (ii) a drop in female labor force participation. In relatively poor countries, however, poorest families with limited assets will have no choice but to send their secondary workers to the market place. Here, need is more important than price considerations and the 'added worker effect' may prevail.
21 Marei's (1979) study of female emancipation in Egypt, Lebanon, Tunisia, Kuwait and Saudi Arabia reveals that the sequence of reforms started with the education of a relatively small number of women, which then led to reforms in the economic and political arena.

22 Among primary aged females, the proportion enrolled in primary school has grown from about 30–50 per cent in 1960 to about 75–90 per cent in 1975 in ten Arab countries, from about 20 to 45 per cent in two countries, from about 5 to 40 per cent in three countries and from 3 to 10 per cent in two countries. Over the same period, enrollments among secondary aged females in the ten countries first mentioned have also doubled from about 20 to 40 per cent, and from about 0 to 20 per cent in the remaining Arab countries.

23 However, the data are hardly above question, labor emigration is just significant at the 0.10 level, and the overall predictive capacity of the estimated equation is low at $R^2 = 0.30$.

24 Jordan serves as an excellent example here; see Anani (1978), Peters (1978).

25 See WCARRD, General (1978).

26 This applies to ten Arab countries representing 75 per cent of the total Arab labor force.

27 This is not to deny that demand for family planning will increase in the future. Dramatic increases in schooling alone are likely to reduce both desired family size and cumulative live births when today's female pupils reach reproductive ages by, say, 1995. See Chapter 4 for elaboration.

Chapter 6 Manpower and educational shortages

1 Structural unemployment arises when the unemployed cannot be matched with vacancies because they do not possess the right skills or live in the right places. Frictional or 'search' unemployment arises because it takes time and resources for workers to get jobs. Frictional unemployment differs from structural unemployment in that it is essentially a short-term condition (see Appendix 1.2).

2 Attempts to ameliorate capital shortages in the oil-poor countries via grants-in-aid from the oil-rich countries are often bogged down by problems of implementation stemming from severe shortages of human capital.

3 In addition to the figures in Table 6.1, the Social and Economic Transformation Plan of Libya estimated expatriate labor needs at 172,000 for the period 1975 to 1980, and the United Nations Economic Commission for Western Asia estimated expatriate labor needs at 147,000 for the United Arab Emirates, Qatar and Oman between 1975 and 1980.

4 Admittedly, projected deficiencies in some of the oil-poor countries may be overstated. That is, national development plans estimate

their manpower needs in terms of rather optimistic target improvements in economic growth and gross national product.

5 'Arabization' is a nationalistic process aimed at welding national unity and national identity. While its implementation has been difficult for school administrators and teachers, it continues to be pursued aggressively in many countries. To illustrate this point, the process got off to a slow start in Morocco. By 1976, however, upper secondary school courses in history, geography and philosophy were being taught by Moroccan teachers in Arabic. By the mid-1980s, policy-makers expect that the goal of complete 'Arabization' of the primary cycle could be realized.

6 Of course, the urgency to improve Arab education is only partially dictated by manpower requirements. Education is perceived as a fundamental human right in most countries. Formal schooling is viewed as a catalyst as well as a product of socio-economic development. Furthermore, investments in schooling are increasingly being enlisted to influence the distribution of income and employment opportunities among the poor.

7 Needless to say, illiteracy also prevents a large proportion of the populace from understanding modernizing trends and events that are coloring the very fabric of Arab society.

8 One of the most outstanding developments in Arab education over the last decade concerns the monumental effort to upgrade female enrollments. Although still dwarfed by developed country (DC) performance, Arab female enrollments are approaching less developed country (LDC) performance in general (see Table 6.4, columns 4–5). Moreover, Arab representation of females in the higher institutes is generally equivalent to LDC performance, and female enrollments in some countries compete with DC performance (e.g. in Bahrain, Kuwait, Qatar and Jordan).

9 In Tables 6.4, 6.5, 6.6 and 6.11 countries are dichotomized as either 'oil-rich' or 'oil-poor' as I wish to convey access to liquid, disposable assets that can be invested in capital stock. Were countries distinguished as 'capital rich/poor', with capital broadly defined to include the stock of both human and physical capital, we might place Lebanon or Egypt in the 'rich' category. See Chapter 1, and the section on methodology for more details on the oil-rich versus oil-poor dichotomy.

10 Far greater financial commitments in the oil-rich countries have been necessary merely to initiate primary school infrastructure.

11 Admittedly, mounting criticism has ruled out the use of these ratios as a standard index of educational quality.

12 In the higher institutes the gap between the oil-rich and oil-poor countries, or even developed countries in general, is considerably

narrower because stringent attempts are being made to ensure quality education.

13 See Tunisia (1977) in the Government Statistical References.

14 These figures agree with a recent UNESCO (1978a) study which observed that some 50 per cent of the primary teachers were underqualified in Lebanon, and some 65 per cent of all teachers were underqualified in Jordan. The problem is particularly acute among teachers in technical institutes.

15 See Khalaf (1977), Al-Kufaishi (1977), Al-Hashil (1977), Al-Shami (1977), Zalatimo (1977).

16 In the past, the government guaranteed civil service employment for university students who failed to secure permanent employment within three years of graduation. While there were an estimated 13,000 queuing for government jobs in 1978, it remains to be seen whether the practice will be discontinued as recommended in the latest Egyptian development plan.

17 Distributional problems and 'urban bias' in development expenditures are elaborated in Shaw (1981).

18 ECWA (1978a) crudely estimates the Arab brain drain from the Middle East at 4,000 professionals annually.

19 The drop-off in the emigration of natural scientists is due to changing immigration preferences which have resulted from freezes on research and development expenditures and curtailment of the space program since the Nixon administration (1968). This led to higher unemployment among scientists in the USA.

20 This loss is partly attributable to the non-return of Arab students who have taken up university or technical training abroad.

21 This has happened with respect to the operation of fish processing plants in Somalia, and the installation of mechanized irrigation systems in Morocco.

22 Sudan pursued an aggressive literacy and adult education program by making it compulsory for government units and private firms to provide opportunities for teaching illiterates and establishing adequate centers of study on the working premises. Somalia pursued a seven month 'Rural Development Campaign' during which 1,250,000 were schooled in Somali script. The program was carried out by 125,000 school students who were sent to reside in rural areas. Students refusing to participate were penalized.

23 Learning-while-doing or instruction via demonstration also helps compensate for limited education or illiteracy among the trainees.

24 Admittedly, the effectiveness of this kind of program can only be hampered by the continued isolation of construction workcamps containing no Arab representation.

25 Specific training can be thought of mainly as an investment by the

firm rather than by the individual. If the worker quits at the end of the training period, the firm's investment would be wasted. Similarly, if the employee bore all the costs and received all the returns, he would suffer a capital loss were he to be fired on completion of the training. Thus, the willingness of workers or firms to pay for specific training should be judged in terms of the likelihood of labor turnover (e.g. people being laid off or quitting).

26 The need for technical or applied manuals written in the Arabic language cannot be overemphasized. Not only is per capita book production in the Arab world less than 10 per cent of production among developed countries in general, but the proportion of titles going to applied sciences seldom exceeds between 5 and 10 per cent (compared with 40 per cent in the USSR and 20 per cent in Switzerland). In recognition of this problem, the Royal Scientific Society of Jordan translated seventy-three trade manuals into Arabic (a five-year project), and initiated the preparation of technical volumes on eight specializations (carpentry, car repair, welding, blacksmiths' work, general electrical repairs, plumbing, heating, as radio and television maintenance). To date, six of the technical volumes have been printed and distributed.

27 At least one empirical study demonstrates that economic returns to informal education are superior to those to formal education (on Tunisia, by Simmons: 1976).

28 According to figures published in the current plan, only a further 9,000 qualified foreigners will be allowed into the country, bringing the total to some 1,069,000 by 1985.

29 This is an extremely crude estimate. It utilizes the UNCTAD (1978) benchmark of US $220,400 as the average imputed capital value of a highly qualified emigrant.

30 Recently published, though somewhat outdated, figures for Qatar suggest that some 670 students were studying abroad in 1975, 600 from Oman (1977), 1,000 from Syria (1975), 2,000–3,000 from Lebanon (1975), 2,260 from the United Arab Emirates (1977), and 4,300 from the Sudan (1976).

31 This point is demonstrated in a study of emigration from the Sudan by Ali (1977).

32 Zahlan (1978) dichotomizes the 'rich' who are the greatest beneficiaries of higher education into 'efficiency seekers' versus 'truth seekers'. He argues that the 'efficiency seekers' are almost exclusively guided by the desire to maximize their personal social and economic welfare. In contrast, the 'truth seekers' tend to place the needs of their community and fellow men first (e.g. the rural doctor who works long hours for one half of the salary he could earn in the city). In a scathing indictment of the *status quo*, he

concludes (p. 45): 'one may safely say that, to-date, there are no truth seekers to speak of in the Arab world'. If Zahlan is right, and there are plenty of examples to back him up, then the onus falls on government to undertake aggressive policies to correct concentrations of educational investments and skills in self-serving and self-perpetuating modern enclaves.

33 As an alternative to bonding, internships or apprenticeships could be incorporated as part of course curriculum. Thus, completion of a degree or applied diploma would require, say, two to three years of experience in places where the country is most in need. This approach would not only help put nationals in touch with the real problems of their country but would tend to reduce the superficiality of higher education which is gearing more and more to the needs of Western societies.

34 Several countries are attempting to decentralize educational investments by locating new technical or university facilities in areas other than the largest or capital cities. For example, in Iraq, seven technical schools were founded between 1976 and 1978, each removed from Baghdad.

35 For example, the government of Egypt requires that graduates of medical schools serve a term in rural areas in return for financial assistance.

36 In 1975, there were approximately 35,000 of these personnel working abroad. Some 40 per cent had a B.A. degree, 26 per cent had received technical education, and 18 per cent had completed secondary school.

37 This explication draws on the work of Addison and Siebert (1979).

Chapter 7 Summary and conclusion

1 These figures are based on proven reserves as of 1979 among the Arab oil exporters. They total some 336.6 billion barrels at a price of about US $34 for a barrel of crude. Daily production in 1979 was estimated at about 21 million barrels per day versus daily consumption of about 1.4 million barrels (see Fesharaki: 1980).

2 A large share of this aid was disbursed by bilateral and multilateral agencies that were financed primarily by OPEC; a large share of the aid went to Arab countries *per se*, and over 50 per cent of the aid was concessional (see OPEC Secretariat: 1981a).

3 As a first step in the Arab Labour Organization's effort, an office is to be set up in Tangier with responsibility for monitoring and locating jobs in the Gulf countries for Moroccans who are unable to find work in their own country.

Bibliography

Abadan-Unat, N., 1978, 'The Modernization of Turkish Women', *Middle East Journal*, Vol. 32, pp. 291–306.

Abdel-Fadil, M., 1975, *Development, Income Distribution and Social Change in Rural Egypt, 1952–70*, Cambridge University Press.

Abdou-Issa, M. S., 1980, 'Modernization and the Fertility Transition: Egypt, 1975', Denver: Paper Presented at the 1980 Meeting of the Population Association of America, April, Mimeo.

Abdul-Wahab, H. M. S., 1978, 'Technical Education: New Paths to Higher Education in Iraq', *Orient* (Hamburg), March, pp. 70–97.

Abou-Gamrah, H., 1980, 'Fertility and Childhood Mortality by Mother's and Father's Education in Cairo, 1976', *Population Bulletin of ECWA* (Beirut: United Nations), Vol. 19, pp. 81–92.

Abu-Aianah, F., 1978, 'Primate Cities in the Arab World', Amman: Paper Presented to the Seminar on Population and Development in the ECWA Region, United Nations Economic Commission for Western Asia, December, Mimeo.

Abu-Ayyash, A., 1980, 'Urban Development and Planning Strategies in Kuwait', *International Journal of Urban and Regional Research*, Vol. 4, pp. 439–72.

Abu-Jaber, K., 1978, 'Development and Its Effect on Jordan's Society', *Orient* (Hamburg), March, pp. 99–110.

Abu-Jaber, K., S. Abdel-Ati and F. Ghoraibeh, 1977, 'Conditions of Some Working Women in Jordan', Amman: Paper Presented at the Economic Commission for Western Asia Seminar on Population, Employment and Development, Mimeo.

Abu-Laban, B., and S. M. Abu-Laban, 1976, 'Education and Development in the Arab World', *Journal of Developing Areas*, Vol. 10, pp. 285–304.

Adams, M. E., and J. Howell, 1979, 'Developing the Traditional Sector in the Sudan', *Economic Development and Cultural Change*, Vol. 27, pp. 505–18.

Addison, J. T., and W. S. Siebert, 1979, *The Market for Labor: An Analytical Treatment*, Santa Monica, Califo: Goodyear Publishing Co.

Affan, K., and L. Olsson, 1978, 'Impact of Rural Development Programmes on Employment and Income Distribution in Sudan', Geneva: International Labour Office World Employment Programme Working Paper, Mimeo, Restricted.

Agraz, O. M. A., and A. M. Ahmed, 1978, 'Regional Assessment of Human Settlement Policies in the Arab Countries', *Habitat International*, Vol. 3, pp. 333–63.

Ahmed, A. H., 1980, 'Recent Performance of Rural Financial Markets in the Sudan', Unpublished Ph.D. Dissertation, Ohio State University.

Al-Abdulkader, A. A., 1978, 'A Survey of the Contribution of Higher Education to the Development of Human Resources in the Kingdom of Saudi Arabia', Unpublished Ph.D. Dissertation, University of Kansas.

Al-Bashir, F. S., 1977, *A Structural Econometric Model of the Saudi Arabian Economy: 1960–70*, New York: John Wiley & Sons.

Al-Hamad, A. Y., 1978, 'The Employment and Income Distribution: Objectives in the Kuwait Fund Development Assistance', *World Development*, Vol. 6, pp. 127–9.

Al-Hamer, I., 1978, 'The Population of Bahrain: A Summary of Past Trends and Future Prospects', Amman: Paper Presented to the Seminar on Population and Development in the ECWA Region, United Nations Economic Commission for Western Asia, December, Mimeo.

Al-Hashil, A., 1977, 'The Formulation of Goals in the Educational Planning Process of Iraq', Unpublished Ph.D. Dissertation, University of Pittsburg.

Al-Jomard, A., 1979, 'Internal Migration in Iraq', in A. Kelidar (ed.), *The Integration of Modern Iraq*, New York: St Martin's Press, pp. 111–21.

Al-Kassab, K. I., n.d., 'Labour Force Planning and Employment Policies in Iraq: 1976–1980', Baghdad: Ministry of Planning, Mimeo.

Al-Kufaishi, H., 1977, 'Education as a Vehicle for National Development in Iraq', Unpublished Ph.D. Dissertation, University of Southern California.

Al-Qazzaz, A., 1978, 'Current Status of Research on Women in the Arab World', *Middle Eastern Studies*, Vol. 13, pp. 372–80.

Al-Rahim, S., 1978, 'Educational Development and Human Resource Planning in Iraq: An Analysis of Trends During the Republican Period', Unpublished Ph.D. Dissertation, University of Texas.

Al-Shami, H., 1979, 'The Impact of Cotton on Economic Development of Egypt', Unpublished Ph.D. Dissertation, University of Wisconsin.

Al-Shami, I. A., 1977, 'Tradition and Technology in the Developmental Education of Saudi Arabia and Egypt', Unpublished Ph.D. Dissertation, University of Michigan.

Al-Thakib, F. T., 1975, 'Women in Contemporary Society', in Cultural and Social Committee for Women (ed.), *Studies on the Conditions of Women and the Arab Gulf*, Kuwait: Fahd Marzouk Press.

Al-Wattari, A. A., 1979, 'Manpower Uses and Requirements in OAPEC States', *Syrie et monde arabe*, Vol. 26, pp. 22–31.

Algeria, 1977, *Annuaire statistique de l'Algérie, 1976*, Algier: Direction des Statistiques et de la Compatibilité Nationale.

Ali, A. B. G., 1977, 'A Note on the Brain-Drain in the Sudan', *Sudan Journal of Economic and Social Studies*, Vol. 2, pp. 14–20.

Ali, A. B. G., 1978, 'Productivity in Sudanese Traditional Agriculture: The Case of the Northern Province', in K. Affran *et al.*, 'Impact of Rural Development Programmes on Employment and Income Distribution in Sudan', Geneva: International Labour Office World Employment Programme Working Paper, Mimeo, Restricted.

Aliboni, R., 1979, *Arab Industrialization and Economic Integration*, New York: St Martin's Press.

Allan, J. A. (ed.), 1973, *Libya: Agriculture and Economic Development*, London: Frank Cass.

Allman, J. (ed.), 1978, *Women's Status and Fertility in the Muslim World*, New York: Praeger.

Allman, J., 1980, 'The Demographic Transition in the Middle East and North Africa', *International Journal of Middle East Studies*, Vol. 12, pp. 277–301.

Allman, J., and A. G. Hill, 1978, 'Fertility, Mortality, Migration and Family Planning in the Yemen Arab Republic', *Population Studies*, Vol. 32, pp. 159–72.

Almeyra, G. M., 1979, 'How Real was Algeria's Agrarian Revolution?', *Ceres*, Vol. 12, pp. 31–5.

Amersfoort, J. M. M., 1978, 'Migrant Workers, Circular Migration and Development', *Lydsckrift Economische en Sociale Geografie*, Vol. 69, pp. 17–22.

Amuzegar, J., 1979, 'Ideology and Economic Growth in the Middle East', *Middle East Journal*, Vol. 28, pp. 1–9.

Anani, J. A., 1978, 'The Labour Situation in Jordan', Kuwait: Paper Presented at the Regional Seminar on Population, Employment and International Migration to the Gulf Countries, Arab Planning Institute, December, Mimeo.

Anderson, D., and M. W. Leiserson, 1980, 'Rural Nonfarm Employment in Developing Countries', *Economic Development and Cultural Change*, Vol. 28, pp. 227–48.

Andriamananjara, R., 1976, 'Labour Mobilization: The Moroccan

Experience', in W. Van Ryckeghem (ed.), *Employment Problems and Process in Developing Countries*, University of Rotterdam Press.

Anker, R., 1978, 'An Analysis of Fertility Differentials in Developing Countries', *Review of Economics and Statistics*, Vol. 60, pp. 58–69.

Arab League, 1975, 'The Agreement, Declarations, Charters and Resolutions Related to the Position of Women', Cairo: Arab League Secretariat, Mimeo, in Arabic.

Arab Planning Institute, 1975, 'Seminar on Human Resources Development in the Arabian Gulf States', Bahrain, Mimeo.

Araud, G., V. Urquidi, G. Boon and P. Strassman, 1973, *Studies on Employment in the Mexican Housing Industry*, Paris: Organization for Economic Cooperation and Development.

Ashby, J. A., 1980, 'Small Farms in Transition: Changes in Agriculture, Schooling and Employment in the Hills of Nepal', unpublished Ph.D. Dissertation, Cornell University.

Askari, H., and J. T. Cummings, 1976, *Middle East Economies in the 1970's*, New York: Praeger.

Askari, H., and J. T. Cummings, 1977, 'The Future of Economic Integration Within the Arab World', *International Journal of Middle East Studies*, Vol. 8, pp. 289–315.

Askari, H., and J. T. Cummings, 1978, 'Food Shortages in the Middle East', *Middle Eastern Studies*, Vol. 14, pp. 326–51.

Askari, H., J. T. Cummings and B. Harik, 1977, 'Land Reform in the Middle East', *International Journal of Middle East Studies*, Vol. 8, pp. 437–51.

Athar, A. N., and M. A. Anees, 1979, 'The Development of Higher Education and Scientific Research in the Arab World', *Journal of South Asian and Middle Eastern Studies*, Vol. 11, pp. 92–100.

Audroing, J. F., 1975, 'Recherche des correlations entre des variables démographiques, sociologiques et économiques dans les pays arabes', *Population*, Vol. 30, pp. 61–79.

Awad, M., 1970, 'Living Condition of Nomadic, Semi-Nomadic and Settled Tribal Groups', in A. M. Lutifiyya and C. W. Churchill (eds), *Readings in Arab Middle Eastern Societies and Cultures*, Paris: Mouton, pp. 135–48.

Azzam, H. T. 1978, 'Labour Migration in the Arab Region: A Structural Analysis', Kuwait: Paper Presented at the Seminar on Population, Employment and International Migration to the Gulf Countries, Arab Planning Institute, December, Mimeo.

Azzam, H. T., 1979a, 'The Participation of Arab Women in the Labour Force: Development Factors and Policies', Geneva: International Labour Organization, World Employment Programme Research Working Paper, Mimeo, Limited Distribution.

Azzam, H. T., 1979b, 'Analysis of Fertility and Labour Force Differen-

227

Bibliography

tials in the Arab World', *Population Bulletin of the United Nations Economic Commission for Western Asia*, No. 16, pp. 39–50.

Azzam, H. T., 1980, 'Labour Market Structure in Saudi Arabia', Beirut: International Labour Organization, Regional Program for the Middle East, Working Paper No. 1, Mimeo, Limited Distribution.

Bachman, K., and L. Paulino, 1979, *Rapid Food Production Growth in Selected Developing Countries: A Comparative Analysis of Underlying Trends, 1961–76*, Washington, D.C.: International Food Policy Research Institute.

Badawi, G. A., 1972, 'Polygamy in Islam', *Al-Illihad*, Vol. 9, pp. 19–23.

Beck, L., 1978, 'Women among Qashqa'i Nomadic Pastoralists in Iran', in L. Beck and N. Keddie (eds), *Women in the Muslim World*, Cambridge: Harvard University Press.

Beck, L., and N. Keddie (eds), 1978, *Women in the Muslim World*, Cambridge: Harvard University Press.

Becker, G.S., 1964, *Human Capital*, New York: Columbia University Press.

Bénachenhou, A., 1978, 'Politiques rurales et migration en Algérie', Geneva: International Labour Office World Employment Program Working Paper, Mimeo, Restricted.

Berkoff, D. J. W., and M. E. Adams, 1979, 'Review Article: Which Way Sudan Agriculture', *Economic Development and Cultural Change*, Vol. 28, pp. 195–8.

Berouti, L. J., 1976, 'Employment Promotion Problems in Arab Countries', *International Labour Review*, Vol. 114, pp. 169–85.

Biehle, J. T., 1978, 'Inflation: Construction Cost Escalation in Saudi Arabia', *Middle East Economic Digest*, June, pp. 15–16.

Birks, J. S., and C. A. Sinclair, 1978a, 'The Sultanate of Oman: Economic Development, The Domestic Labour Market and International Migration', Geneva: International Labour Office World Employment Program Working Paper, Mimeo, Restricted.

Birks, J. S., and C. A. Sinclair, 1978b, 'Human Capital on the Nile: Development and Emigration in the Arab Republic of Egypt and the Democratic Republic of the Sudan', Geneva: International Labour Office, Working Paper, Mimeo, Restricted.

Birks, J. S., and C. A. Sinclair, 1978c, 'Economic and Social Implications of Current Development in the Arab Gulf: The Oriental Connection', Exeter: Paper Presented to the Inaugural Conference of the Centre for Arab Gulf Studies, University of Exeter, July, Mimeo.

Birks, J. S., and C. A. Sinclair, 1978d, 'Country Case Study: The Kingdom of Jordan', Durham: International Migration Project at the University of Durham, Mimeo, Restricted.

Birks, J. S., and C. A. Sinclair, 1980a, *International Migration and*

Development in the Arab Region, Geneva: International Labour Office.

Birks, J. S., and C. A. Sinclair, 1980b, *Arab Manpower: The Crisis of Development*, London: Croom Helm.

Birks, J. S., C. A. Sinclair and J. A. Socknat, 1981, 'Aspects of Labour Migration from North Yemen', *Middle Eastern Studies*, Vol. 17, pp. 49–63.

Boserup, E., 1978, 'Employment of Women in Developing Countries', in L. Tabah (ed.), *Population Growth and Economic Development in the Third World*, London: International Union for the Scientific Study of Population.

Bouman, F. J. A., 1977, 'Land Tenure and Agricultural Development in Le Kef, Tunisia', *Middle East Journal*, Vol. 31, pp. 63–80.

Bowen, W., and T. A. Finegan, 1969, *The Economics of Labor Force Participation*, New Jersey: Princeton University Press.

Braibanti, R., and F. A. Al-Farsy, 1977, 'Saudi Arabia: A Developmental Perspective', *Journal of South Asian and Middle Eastern Studies*, Vol. 1, pp. 3–42.

Bunton, J., 1978, 'Survey: Emphasis will Change but the Construction Boom will Continue', *Middle East Economic Digest*, June, pp. 3–6.

Burke, R. V., 1979, 'Green Revolution Technologies and Farm Class in Mexico', *Economic Development and Cultural Change*, Vol. 28, pp. 135–54.

Bybee, D. A., 1978, 'Muslim Peasant Women of the Middle East: Their Sources and Uses of Power', Unpublished Ph.D. Dissertation, Indiana University.

Cassell, M., 1981, 'Construction: Doing Business After the Boom', *Middle East Review*, London: World Information, pp. 52–7.

CEAO, 1974, 'Le Status legal de la femme musulmane dans plusieurs pays du Moyen-Orient', Commission Economique pour l'Asie Occidentale, E/CONF/60/Sym.IV/17.

Chamie, J., 1981, *Religion and Fertility: Arab Christian–Muslim Fertility Differentials*, New York: Cambridge University Press.

Chamie, M., 1977, 'Sexuality and Birth Control Decisions Among Lebanese Couples', *Signs: Journal of Women in Culture and Society*, Vol. 3, pp. 294–312.

Chamie, M., 1979, 'Employment, Underemployment, Unemployment, and Unacknowledged Employment: A Case Study of Lebanese Women', Beirut: Institute of Women's Studies in the Arab World, Mimeo.

Chatty, D., 1978, 'Changing Sex Roles in Bedouin Society in Syria and Lebanon', in L. Beck and N. Keddie (eds), *Women in the Muslim World*, Cambridge: Harvard University Press.

Chinn, D. L., 1979, 'Rural Poverty and the Structure of Farm Household Income in Developing Countries: Evidence from Taiwan', *Economic Development and Cultural Change*, Vol. 27, pp. 283–302.

Chipeta, C., 1976, 'Family Farm Organization and Commercialization of Agriculture', Unpublished Ph.D. Dissertation, Washington University.

Choucri, N., 1977, 'A New Migration in the Middle East', *International Migration Review*, Vol. 11, pp. 421–43.

Choucri, N., 1978, 'Migration and Employment in the Construction Sector: Critical Factors in Egyptian Development', Boston: Massachusetts Institute of Technology, Technological Planning Program, Mimeo.

Clarke, J., 1977a, 'Jordan: A Labor Receiver, a Labor Supplier', Washington: Paper Prepared for AID/Near East Bureau Seminar on Labor Migration in the Middle East, Agency for International Development, September, Mimeo.

Clarke, J., 1977b, 'Yemen: A Profile', Paper Prepared for the AID Near East Bureau Seminar on Labour Migration in the Middle East, Washington: Agency for International Development, Mimeo.

Cleland, J. G., and G. Rodriguez, 1980, 'How Women's Work and Education Affects Family Size', *People* London: IPPF, Vol. 8, pp. 17–18.

Cleron, J. P., 1978, *Saudi Arabia 2000*, London: Croom Helm.

Cochrane, S. H., 1979, *Fertility and Education: What Do We Really Know?*, Baltimore, Md.: Johns Hopkins University Press for the World Bank.

Cohen, J. M., and D. B. Lewis, 1979, 'Capital Surplus, Labor-Short Economies: Yemen as a Challenge to Rural Development Strategies', *American Journal of Agricultural Economics*, Vol. 61, pp. 523–8.

Cooper, C. A., and S. S. Alexander, 1972, *Economic Development and Population Growth in the Middle East*, New York: American Elsevier Publishing Co.

Cosar, F. M., 1978, 'Women in Turkish Society', in L. Beck and N. Keddie (eds), *Women in the Muslim World*, Cambridge: Harvard University Press.

Costello, V. F., 1975, *Urbanization in the Middle East*, Cambridge University Press.

Coulson, N., and D. Henchcliffe, 1978, 'Women and Law Reform in Contemporary Islam', in L. Beck and N. Keddie (eds), *Women in the Muslim World*, Cambridge: Harvard University Press.

Crotty, M., 1979, *Cattle, Economics and Development*, London: Commonwealth Agricultural Bureau.

Cuddihy, W., 1981, 'Agricultural Price Management in Egypt', *Development Digest*, Vol. 19, pp. 37–45.

Currie, L., 1976, *Taming the Megalopolis: A Design for Urban Growth*, London: Pergamon Press in Co-operation with the United Nations.

Dahhan, O., 1981, 'An Examination of the Literature on Jordanian Women', Beirut: International Labour Organization, Population and Labour Policies, Regional Programme for the Middle East, Working Paper No. 8, Mimeo, Limited Distribution.

Daves, T. E., and H. Van Wersch, 1976, 'Results of Agricultural Planning in Tunisia 1962–1971', in R. A. Stone and J. Simmons (eds), *Change in Tunisia: Studies in the Social Sciences*, Albany: State University of New York Press.

Davis, K., and J. Blake, 1956, 'Social Structure and Fertility: An Analytic Framework', *Economic Development and Cultural Change*, Vol. 4, pp. 211–35.

Davis, S. S., 1978, 'Women, Men and Moroccan Economic Development', Ann Arbor, Mich.: Paper Presented at the 12th Annual Meeting of the Middle East Studies Association, November, Mimeo.

Dawood, H., 1978, 'Integration of Women in Rural Development in the Near East Region', Cairo: Food and Agricultural Organization Regional Office for the Near East, Paper No. 4, Mimeo, Limited Distribution.

Debeausais, M., 1976, 'Employment and Education in Arab Countries: The Data and Their Interpretation', in ILO, *Manpower and Employment in Arab Countries: Some Critical Issues*, Geneva: International Labour Office.

de Janvry, A., 1981, 'The Role of Land Reform in Economic Development: Policies and Politics', *American Journal of Agricultural Economics*, Vol. 62, pp. 384–92.

Demit, S., 1976, *'The Kuwait Fund and the Political Economy of Arab Regional Development*, New York: Praeger.

Dib, G., 1978, 'Migration and Naturalization Laws in the Arab Republic of Egypt, the Hashemite Kingdom of Jordan, Kuwait, Lebanon, the Syrian Arab Republic and the United Arab Emirates', Amman: Paper Presented to the Seminar on Population and Development in the ECWA Region, United Nations Commission for Western Asia, E/ECWA/POP/WG.12/BP.5, Mimeo.

Dickie, P.M., and D.B. Nowsi, 'Dual Markets: The Case of the Syrian Arab Republic', *International Monetary Fund Staff Papers*, Vol. 22, pp. 456–68.

Dorr, S. R., 1981, *Scholars' Guide to Washington, D.C., for Middle Eastern Studies*, Washington DC: Smithsonian Institute.

Douglas, P. H., 1976, 'The Cobb Douglas Production Function Once Again: Its History, Its Testing and Some New Empirical Values', *Journal of Political Economy*, Vol. 84, p. 913.

Durrani, L. L., 1976, 'Employment of Women and Social Change', in R. A. Stone and J. Simmons (eds), *Change in Tunisia: Studies in the Social Sciences*, Albany: State University of New York Press.

Easterlin, R. A., 1975, 'An Economic Framework for Fertility Analysis', *Studies in Family Planning*, Vol. 6, pp. 54–63.

Easterlin, R. A., 1980, 'Fertility and Development', *Population Bulletin of the United Nations Economic Commission for Western Asia* (Beirut), No. 18, pp. 5–40.

The Economist, 1980, 'Rim of Prosperity: The Gulf: A Survey', *The Economist*, 13 December, pp. 3–82.

ECWA, 1974, 'A Preliminary Report on the Status and the Participation of Women in Development in Selected Countries of the ECWA Region', Beirut: United Nations Economic Commission for Western Asia, ECWA/HR/L.2, Mimeo.

ECWA, 1978a, 'The Brain Drain Problem in the ECWA Countries', Beirut: United Nations Economic Commission for Western Asia, E/ECWA/57/Add.2, Mimeo.

ECWA, 1978b, 'Regional Plan of Action for the Integration of Women in Development for the ECWA Region', Beirut: United Nations Economic Commission for Western Asia, E/ECWA/SDHS/CONF. 218, Mimeo.

ECWA, 1978c, 'Evaluation of Home Based Employment Programmes for Lebanese Rural Women', Beirut: United Nations Economic Commission for Western Asia, Social Development and Human Settlement Division, Mimeo.

ECWA, 1978d, 'Estimates and Projections of Population, Vital Rates, and Economic Activity for Members of the Economic Commission for Western Asia', Beirut: United Nations Economic Commission for Western Asia, Mimeo, Limited Distribution.

ECWA, 1978e, *Demographic and Related Socio-Economic Data Sheets for Countries of the Economic Commission for Western Asia*, Beirut: United Nations Economic Commission for Western Asia.

ECWA, 1979, 'The Role of Public Sector in Promoting the Economic Development in Countries of Western Asia: A Brief Report', Beirut: United Nations Commission for Western Asia, Development Division Report 79–2364, Mimeo.

ECWA, 1980a, *The Population Situation in the ECWA Region*, Volumes on Lebanon, UAE, Qatar, Kuwait, Yemen PDR, Syria, Iraq, Saudi Arabia, Egypt; Beirut: United Nations Economic Commission for Western Asia.

ECWA, 1980b, *Bibliography of Population Literature in the Arab World*, Beirut: United Nations Economic Commission for Western Asia.

Egypt, 1977, *Five Year Plan: 1978–1982, Vols I–XII*, Cairo: Ministry of Planning.

Egypt: WCARRD, 1978, 'Country Review Paper of Egypt', Rome:

World Conference of Agrarian Reform and Rural Development, Food and Agricultural Organization, Mimeo, Restricted.

Ehtewish, O. S., 1980, 'Fertility Differentials in the Socialist People's Libyan Arab Jamahiriya', Unpublished Ph.D. Dissertation, Mississippi State University.

El-Agraa, O. M. A., and A. M. Ahmad, 1978, 'Regional Assessment of Human Settlements Policies in Arab Countries', *Habitat International*, Vol. 3/4, pp. 353–64.

El-Asad, S., and A. Khalifa, 1977, 'Fertility Estimates and Differentials in Jordan, 1972–76', *Population Bulletin of ECWA* (Beirut: United Nations), No. 12, pp. 20–6.

El-Awad M., 1974, 'The Factors Influencing Migration to the "Three Towns" of the Sudan', *Sudan Journal of Economic and Social Studies*, Vol. 1, pp. 20–2.

El-Awadi, A. H., 1978, 'Analysis of Some of the Social Problems in Relation to the Labour Force in Kuwait', Kuwait: Paper Presented to the Regional Seminar on Population, Employment and International Migration to the Gulf Countries, Arab Planning Institute; December, Mimeo.

El-Fathaly, O. I., and M. Palmer, 1980, *Political Development and Social Change in Libya*, Lexington, Mass.: D.C. Heath.

El-Huni, A. M., 1978, 'Determinants of Female Labour Force Participation: The Case of Libya', Unpublished Ph.D. Dissertation, Oklahoma State University.

El-Mallakh, R., 1978, 'Prospects for Economic Growth and Regional Co-operation', in J. Waterbury and R. El-Mallakh, *The Middle East in the Coming Decade*, New York: McGraw-Hill.

El-Mallakh, R., 1979, *Qatar: The Development of an Oil Economy*, New York: St Martin's Press.

El-Mallakh, R., and M. Kadhim, 1976, 'Arab Institutionalized Development Aid: An Evaluation', *Middle East Journal*, Vol. 30, pp. 471–83.

El-Saadawi, N., 1979, *The Hidden Face of Eve: Women in the Arab World*, London: Zed Press.

Elwan, S., 1978, 'The Status of Women in the Arab World', *Arab Review*, Vol. 8, pp. 3–6.

Esposito, J. L., 1976, 'The Changing Role of Muslim Women', *Islam and the Modern Age*, Vol. 7, pp. 29–56.

Evans, M. K., 1969, *Macroeconomic Activity: Theory, Forecasting, Control*, New York: Harper & Row.

Evans, P. B., and M. Timberlake, 1980, 'Dependence, Inequality and the Growth of the Tertiary: A Comparative Analysis of Less Developed Countries', *American Sociological Review*, Vol. 45, pp. 531–52.

Faksh, M. A., 1980, 'The Consequences of the Introduction and Spread of Modern Education: Education and National Integration in Egypt', *Middle East Journal*, Vol. 34, pp. 42–55.

FAO, 1971, *An Operational Manual for Resettlement*, Rome: Food and Agricultural Organization.

FAO, 1975, 'Seminar on the Role of Women in Integrated Rural Development with Emphasis on Population Problems', Rome: Food and Agricultural Organization.

FAO, 1976, 'Perspective Study on Agricultural Development in the Sahelian Countries: 1975–90', Vols 1–3, Rome: Food and Agricultural Organization.

FAO, 1979, *Review and Analysis of Agrarian Reform and Rural Development in the Developing Countries since the Mid-1960's*, Rome: World Conference on Agrarian Reform and Rural Development, Food and Agricultural Organization.

Fathaly, O. I., and F. S. Abusedra, 1980, 'The Impact of Socio-Political Change on Economic Development in Libya', *Middle Eastern Studies*, Vol. 16, pp. 225–35.

Fergany, N., 1972, 'Arab Women and National Development: A Demographic Background', Cairo: Paper Presented at the Conference on Arab Women and National Development.

Fergany, N., 1980, 'The Affluent Years are Over — Emigration and Development in the Yemen Arab Republic', Geneva: International Labour Office, World Employment Working Paper, WEP 2–26/WP50, Mimeo, Restricted.

Fesharaki, F., 1980, 'Current Reserves and Production and Likely Exports in the 1980's', *OPEC Review*, Vol. 4, pp. 27–49.

Field, P., 1979, 'OPEC Aid-Expansion of Lending Programmes Since 1973', *Middle East Annual Review*, pp. 141–7.

Findlay, A., 1978, 'Country Case Study: Tunisia', International Migration Project at University of Durham, Mimeo, Restricted.

Fischer, M. J., 1978, 'On Changing the Concept and Position of Persian Women', in L. Beck and N. Keddie (eds), *Women in the Muslim World*, Cambridge: Harvard University Press.

Freedman, R., and B. Berelson, 1976, 'The Record of Family Planning Programs', *Studies in Family Planning*, Vol. 7, No. 1.

Gabbay, R., 1978, *Communism and Agrarian Reform in Iraq*, London: Croom Helm.

Gadalla, S., N. Nosseir and D. F. Gillespie, 1980, 'Household Distribution of Contraceptives in Rural Egypt', *Studies in Family Planning*, Vol. 11, pp. 105–13.

Gafsi, S., and T. Roe, 1979, 'Adoption of Unlike High-yielding Wheat Varieties in Tunisia', *Economic Development and Cultural Change*, Vol. 28, pp. 119–34.

Ghali, F., and F. Gadalla, 1973, 'Fertility Characteristics and Family Planning Knowledge and Practice in Baghdad, Iraq', *Studies in Family Planning*, Vol. 4, No. 6, pp. 143–9.

Ghamdi, M. A., 1977, 'A Study of Selected Factors Related to Student Dropouts in the Secondary Schools of Saudi Arabia', Unpublished Ph.D. Dissertation, University of Michigan.

Gorham, P., 1977, 'The Challenge of Manpower Deployment in the Middle East', Beirut: Economic Commission for Western Asia, Mimeo.

Grabowski, R., 1979, 'The Implications of an Induced Innovation Model', *Economic Development and Cultural Change*, Vol. 27, pp. 723–34.

Graziani, J., 1974/5, 'The Momentum of the Feminist Movement in the Arab World', *Middle East Review*, Vol. 2, pp. 26–33.

Griffen, K. B., 1975, 'Income Inequality and Land Distribution in Morocco', *Blangladesh Economic Studies*, Vol. 3, pp. 319–48.

Griffen, K. B., and A. K. Ghose, 1979, 'Growth and Impoverishment in the Rural Areas of Asia', *World Development*, Vol. 7, pp. 361–83.

Grimes, O. F., Jr, 1976, *Housing for Low-Income Urban Families: Economics and Policy in the Developing World*, Baltimore, Md.: John Hopkins University Press for the World Bank.

Guha, S., 1970, 'The Contribution of Non-Farm Activities to Rural Employment Promotion', *International Labour Review*, Vol. 109, pp. 235–49.

Haddad, H. S., and B. K. Nijim (eds), 1978, *The Arab World: A Handbook*, Illinois: Medina Press.

Haffar, A. R., 1975, 'Economic Development in Islam in Western Scholarship', *Islam and the Modern Age*, Vol. 6, pp. 5–22.

Halliday, F., 1977, 'Migration and the Labour Force in the Oil Producing States of the Middle East', *Development and Change*, Vol. 8, pp. 263–92.

Hamed, O., 1981, 'Egypt's Open Door Economic Policy: An Attempt at Economic Integration in the Middle East', *International Journal of Middle East Studies*, Vol. 13, pp. 1–9.

Hammouda, A. H., 1980, 'Jordanian Emigration: An Analysis of Migration Data', *International Migration Review*, Vol. 14, pp. 357–83.

Hassan, M. F., 1979, 'Agricultural Development in a Petroleum-based Economy: Qatar', *Economic Development and Cultural Change*, Vol. 27, pp. 145–69.

Hassouna, M. T., 1980, 'Assessment of Family Planning Service Delivery in Egypt', *Studies in Family Planning*, Vol. 11, pp. 159–66.

Hay, M. J., 1980, 'A Structural Equations Model of Migration in Tunisia', *Economic Development and Cultural Change*, Vol. 28, pp. 345–58.

Helmy, A., 1978, 'The Role of Arab Women in the Labor Force', West Berlin: Paper Presented to the Conference on Vocational Training, Mimeo.

Hemmasi, M., n.d., *Migration in Iran: A Quantitative Approach*, Pahlair University, Publication No. 8.

Higgs, J., 1978, 'Land Settlement in Africa and the Near East: Some Recent Experience', *Land Reform, Land Settlement and Co-operatives*, Rome: Food and Agricultural Organization, pp. 1–29.

Hill, A. G., 1975, 'The Demography of the Kuwaiti Population of Kuwait', *Demography*, Vol. 12, pp. 537–48.

Ho, S. P., 1979, 'Decentralized Industrialization and Rural Development: Evidence from Taiwan', *Economic Development and Cultural Change*, Vol. 28, pp. 77–96.

Holt, J., and V. Belbelian, 1979, 'Water Resources − Potential and Problems in Development', *Middle East Annual Review*, pp. 99–109.

Howenstine, E. J., 1968, 'The Role of Housing Policy in Economic Growth and Stabilisation', in OECD, *The Role of Trade Unions in Housing*, Paris: Organization for Economic Cooperation and Development.

Huffman, W. E., 1980, 'Farm and Off-Farm Work Decisions: The Role of Human Capital', *Review of Economics and Statistics*, Vol. 62, pp. 14–23.

Hummadi, I. A., 1978, 'Economic Growth and Structural Changes in the Iraqi Economy with Emphasis on Agriculture', Unpublished Ph.D. Dissertation, University of Colorado.

Huzayyin, S. A. (ed.), 1973, *Urbanization and Migration in Some Arab and African Countries*, Cairo: Cairo Demographic Center, Monograph Series, No. 4.

Huzayyin, S. A., and T. E. Smith (eds), 1974, *Demographic Aspects of Socio-Economic Development in Some Arab and African Countries*, Cairo: Cairo Demographic Center, Monograph Series, No. 5.

Ibrahim, S. E., 1975, 'Over-Urbanization and Under-Urbanism: The Case of the Arab World', *International Journal of Middle Eastern Studies*, Vol. 6, pp. 29–45.

Ibrahim-al-Kassab, K., 1978, 'Labour Force Planning and Employment Policies in Iraq: 1976–80', Amman: United Nations Economic Commission for Western Asia Seminar, ECWA/POP/WG.12.

Iglitzin, L. B., and R. Ross (eds), 1976, *Women in the World: A Comparative Study*, Santa Barbara, Calif.: Clio Books.

ILO, 1976a, *Growth, Employment and Equity: A Comprehensive Strategy for the Sudan*, Geneva: International Labour Office.

ILO, 1976b, *Manpower and Employment in Arab Countries: Some Critical Issues*, Geneva: International Labour Office.

ILO, 1977a, *Economic Transformation in a Socialist Framework: An*

Employment and Basic Needs Oriented Development Strategy for Somalia, Geneva: International Labour Office.

ILO, 1977b, *Labour-Force: 1950–2000, Vols 1–3*, Geneva: International Labour Office.

IPPF, 1973, 'Unmet Needs in Family Planning: Appendices', London: International Planned Parenthood Federation, Paper Presented to the International Conference of Planning for the Future, October, Mimeo.

IPPF, n.d., 'Law and Planned Parenthood: A Comparative Legal Survey in Selected Countries in the Middle East and North Africa', Beirut: International Planned Parenthood Federation, Mimeo.

Iraq, 1973, 'Population Growth and Development in Iraq', Baghdad: Ministry of Planning, Paper Prepared for the 1974 United Nations Population Inquiry, Mimeo.

Issa, S. M., 1979, 'The Distribution of Income in Iraq, 1971', in A. Kelidar (ed.), *The Integration of Modern Iraq*, New York: St Martin's Press.

Jain, A. K., 1981, 'The Effect of Female Education on Fertility: A Simple Explanation', *Demography*, Vol. 18, pp. 577–96.

Jomo, K. S., 1977, 'Islam and Weber: Rodinson on the Implications of Religion for Capitalist Development', *Developing Economies*, Vol. 15, pp. 240–53.

Jordan, 1979, *Jordan Fertility Survey, 1976*, Vols I and II Amman: Department of Statistics.

Kaikati, J. G., 1980, 'The Economy of Sudan: A Potential Breadbasket of the Arab World?', *International Journal of Middle East Studies*, Vol. 11, pp. 99–123.

Keddie, N. R., 1979, 'Problems in the Study of Middle Eastern Women', *International Journal of Middle East Studies*, Vol. 10, pp. 225–40.

Keilany, Z., 1980, 'Land Reform in Syria', *Middle Eastern Studies*, Vol. 16, pp. 209–24.

Kelidar, A. (ed.), 1979, *Integration of Modern Iraq*, New York: St Martin's Press.

Kerdus, S., 1979, 'The Literacy Programme in Libya', *Teachers of the World*, Vol. 2, pp. 11–13.

Khalaf, R. A., 1977, 'Vocational Agriculture in Jordan: A Formative Evaluation of the Secondary Schools Curriculum', Unpublished D.Ed. Dissertation, University of North Carolina.

Khalfallah, R. A., 1979, 'Migration, Labor Supply and Regional Development in Libya', Unpublished Ph.D. Dissertation, University of Oklahoma.

Khalifa, A. M., 1973, 'A Proposed Explanation of the Fertility Gap Differentials by Socio-Economic Status and Modernity: The Case of Egypt', *Population Studies*, Vol. 27, pp. 431–42.

237

Khalifa, A. M., 1976, 'The Influence of Wife's Education on Fertility in Rural Egypt', *Journal of Biosocial Science*, Vol. 8, pp. 53–9.

Khani, A., 1978, 'Apres quinze ans de développement économique en Syrie', *Syrie et Monde Arabe*, Vol. 25, No. 23, pp. 1–8.

Khouja, M. W., and P. G. Sadler, 1979, *The Economy of Kuwait: Development and Role in International Finance*, London: Macmillan.

Kidd, C. V., and J. L. Thurston, 1977, 'Higher Education and Development in the Sudan', Khartoum: Institute of Higher Education, Mimeo.

Kielstra, N., 1978, 'The Place of the Agrarian Revolution in the Algerian Approach to Socialism', *Social Scientist*, Vol. 7, pp. 69–89.

Kirk, D., 1971, 'A New Demographic Transition?', in National Academy of Sciences (ed.), *Rapid Population Growth*, Baltimore, Md.: Johns Hopkins University Press, pp. 123–47.

Knapskog, K., 1977, 'Industrial Growth in Agricultural Environment; Agriculture and Oil Industry: An Example from the District of Roma', Rome: Norges Sardbruksokonomische Institute, No. F–258–77.

Knauerhause, R., 1975, *The Saudi Arabian Economy*, New York: Praeger.

Knauerhause, R., 1976, 'Social Factors and Labour Market Structure in Saudi Arabia', New Haven, Conn.: Yale Economic Growth Center Discussion Paper No. 247, Mimeo.

Koenigsberger, O., 1975, 'The Absorption of Newcomers in the Cities of Developing Countries', New York: United Nations Document A/CONF.70/RPC/BP/22.

Kohli, K. L., 1977, 'Regional Variations of Fertility in Iraq and Factors Affecting It', *Journal of Biosocial Science*, Vol. 9, pp. 175–81.

Kuwait: WCARRD, 1978, 'Country Review Paper of State of Kuwait', Rome: World Conference of Agrarian Reform and Rural Development, Food and Agricultural Organization, Mimeo, Restricted.

Lapham, R. J., 1972, 'Population Policies in the Maghrib', *Middle East Journal*, Vol. 26, pp. 1–10.

Larmuth, J., 1979, 'Desert: A Man-made Disaster', *Middle East Economic Digest*, May, p. 10.

Larsen, T. B., 1979, 'Population Revolution: Running to Stand Still', *Middle East*, July, pp. 57–60.

Larson, D. K., 1976, 'Impact of Off-Farm Income on Farm Family Income Levels', *Agricultural Finance Review*, Vol. 36, pp. 7–11.

Lau, L. F., and P. A. Yotopoulos, 1979, 'Resource Use in Agriculture: Applications of the Profit Function to Selected Countries', *Food Research Institute Studies*, Vol. 17, No. 1.

Laurent, C., and G. L. Campi, 1978, 'Part-time Farming in French

Agriculture: Developments between 1963–70', in OECD, *Part-time Farming in OECD Countries*, Paris: Organization for Economic Cooperation and Development.

Lawless, R. I., 1980, *The Changing Middle Eastern City*, London: Croom Helm.

Lebanon: WCARRD, 1978, 'Country Review Paper of Lebanon', Rome: World Conference on Agrarian Reform and Rural Development, Food and Agricultural Organization, Restricted, Mimeo.

Lecomte, J., and A. Marcoux, 1976, 'Contraception and Fertility in Morocco and Tunisia', *Studies in Family Planning*, Vol. 7, pp. 182–8.

Lees, F. A., and H. C. Brooks, 1977, *The Economic and Political Development of the Sudan*, London: Macmillan.

Lipton, M., 1977, *Why Poor People Stay Poor: Urban Bias in World Development*, London: Temple Smith.

Lockheed, M. E., D. T. Jamison and L. J. Lau, 1980, 'Farmer Education and Farm Efficiency: A Survey', *Economic Development and Cultural Change*, Vol. 29, pp. 37–76.

Lopes, L. G. V., 1978, 'Time Allocation of Low Income Rural Brazilian Households: A Multiple Jobholding Model', *Dissertation Abstracts International*, Vol. 38, p. 6235.

Maher, V., 1978, 'Women and Social Change in Morocco', in L. Beck and N. Keddie (eds), *Women in the Muslim World*, Cambridge: Harvard University Press.

Mahmoud, L. D., 1978, 'A Proposed Program for the Improvement of Teacher Education in Bahrain', Unpublished Ph.D. Dissertation, University of Texas.

Marei, W. A., 1979, 'Female Emancipation and Changing Political Leadership: A Study of Five Arab Countries', Unpublished Ph.D. Dissertation, Rutgers University.

Mauldin, W. P., and B. Berelson, 1978, 'Conditions of Fertility Decline in Developing Countries: 1965–75', *Studies in Family Planning*, Vol. 9, No. 5.

Mauritania: CMRADR, 1978, 'Rapport national de Mauritanie', Rome: Conférence Mondiale sur la Réforme Agraire et le Développement Rural, Food and Agricultural Organization, Mimeo, Limited Distribution.

Mazur, M. P., 1979, *Economic Growth and Development in Jordan*, Boulder, Colo.: Westview Press.

McLachlan, K., 1979, 'Iraq: Problems of Regional Development', in A. Kelidar (ed.), *Integration of Modern Iraq*, New York: St Martin's Press.

MEED, 1978, 'Egypt: Special Report on Manpower', *Middle East Economic Digest*, May.

239

Bibliography

MEED, 1979, 'Focus on Iraq', *Middle East Economic Digest*, February, pp. 110–12.

MEED, 1981, 'Construction and Contracting: Special Report', *Middle East Economic Digest*, March.

Mellor, J. W., 1966, *The Economics of Agricultural Development*, Ithaca, N.Y.: Cornell University Press.

Mernissi, F., 1975, 'Obstacles to Family Planning Practice in Urban Morocco', *Studies in Family Planning*, Vol. 6, pp. 418–25.

Mernissi, F., 1978, 'Historical Insights for New Population Strategies: Women in Pre-Colonial Morocco, Changes and Continuities', Paris: United Nations Educational, Scientific and Cultural Organization, Division of Applied Social Sciences, Mimeo.

Mernissi, F., 1979, 'But We Have Overcome', *Middle East*, June, pp. 59–60.

Mertaugh, M. T., 1976, 'The Causes and Effects of Rural–Urban Migration in Morocco, 1960–70', Unpublished Manuscript, Mimeo.

Middle East and North Africa, 1979/80, London: Europa Publications Ltd.

Middle East Annual Review, 1980, Essex: World Information.

Miller, D. R., 1976, 'International Migration of Turkish Workers: A Special Case in the Public Policy of Income Distribution and Employment', Geneva: International Labour Office, World Employment Working Paper, WEP 2–23/WP41, Mimeo, Limited Distribution.

Minces, J., 1978, 'Women in Algeria', in L. Beck and N. Keddie (eds), *Women in the Muslim World*, Cambridge: Harvard University Press.

Monardes, A. T., 1978, 'An Economic Analysis of Employment in Small Farm Agriculture: The Central Valley of Chile', Unpublished Ph.D. Dissertation, Cornell University.

Morocco: CMRADR: 1979, 'Réforme agraire et développement rural dans le royaume du Maroc', Rome: Conférence Mondiale sur la Réforme Agraire et le Développement Rural, Food and Agricultural Organization, Mimeo, Restricted.

Moustafa, S. A. A., 1980, 'Measures of Kuwaiti Wives' and Husbands' Attitudes on Fertility', Unpublished Ph.D. Dissertation, University of Oklahoma.

Naciri, M., 1978, 'Inégalités dans les milieux ruraux au Maroc', *Bulletin Économique et Social du Maroc* (Rabat), No. 136/7, pp. 193–200.

Nagi, M. H., 1974, 'Internal Migration and Structural Changes in Egypt', *Middle East Journal*, Vol. 28, pp. 261–82.

Nagi, M. H., 1980, 'Excessive Fertility in Kuwait: Patterns and Implications', Denver, Colo.: Paper Presented at the 1980 Meeting of the Population Association of America, April, Mimeo.

Nakhleh, E. A., 1977, 'Labor Markets and Citizenship in Bahrain and Qatar', *Middle East Journal*, Vol. 31, pp. 143–56.

Nath, K., 1978, 'Education and Employment among Kuwaiti Women', in L. Beck and N. Keddie (eds), *Women in the Muslim World*, Cambridge: Harvard University Press.

NBE, 1978a, 'The Agricultural Sector Developments: 1970–77', *Economic Bulletin* (Cairo: National Bank of Egypt), Vol. 31, pp. 336–56.

NBE, 1978b, 'The Arab Food Gap, 1967–76', *Economic Bulletin* (Cairo: National Bank of Egypt), Vol. 31, pp. 235–51.

Nelson, H. D. (ed.), 1978, *Morocco: A Country Study*, Washington DC: American University Press.

Nelson, H. D. (ed.), 1979a, *Algeria: A Country Study*, Washington DC: American University Press.

Nelson, H. D. (ed.), 1979b, *Libya: A Country Study*, Washington DC: American University Press.

Nelson, J. A., 1978, 'Guarantees: A Banker's View of Financial Risks', *Middle East Economic Digest*, June, p. 23.

Niblock, T. (ed.), 1980, *Social and Economic Development in the Arab Gulf*, London: Croom Helm.

Nyang, S. S., 1976, 'The Islamic State and Economic Development: A Theoretical Analysis', *Islamic Culture: An English Quarterly*, Vol. L, pp. 1–23.

Oberai, A. S., 1977, 'Migration, Unemployment and the Urban Labour Market: A Case Study of the Sudan', *International Labour Review*, Vol. 115, pp. 211–23.

Oman, 1978, 'Development Plans Realistic Aims', *Syrie et Monde Arabe*, Vol. 25, pp. 9–13.

OPEC Secretariat, 1981a, *OPEC Papers*, Vienna: Organization of Petroleum Exporting Countries.

OPEC Secretariat, 1981b, *OPEC Bulletin*, Vienna: Organization of Petroleum Exporting Countries.

Oweiss, I. M., 1977, 'Strategies for Arab Economic Development', *Journal of Energy and Development*, Vol. 3, pp. 103–14.

Pakizegi, B., 1978, 'Legal and Social Positions of Iranian Women', in L. Beck and N. Keddie (eds), *Women in the Muslim World*, Cambridge: Harvard University Press.

Penrose, E., and E. F. Penrose, 1978, *Iraq: International Relations and National Development*, Boulder, Colo.: Westview Press.

Penson, J. B., Jr, and D. A. Lins, 1980, *Agricultural Finance*, New Jersey: Prentice-Hall.

People, 1980, 'Key Findings Highlight Diversity', *People* (London: IPPF), Vol. 8, pp. 5–7.

Peters, L. E., 1978, 'The Status of Women in Four Middle East Communities', in L. Beck and N. Keddie (eds), *Women in the Muslim World*, Cambridge: Harvard University Press, pp. 311–50.

Phan-Thuy, N., 1979, 'Promotion de l'emploi au Maroc par la pleine utilisation de la capacité industrielle', Geneva: International Labour Office, World Employment Programme Working Paper, Mimeo, Restricted.

Prothro, E. T., and L. N. Diab, 1978, 'Evolution of the Muslim Family in the Arab East', Amman: United Nations Economic Commission for Western Asia, Mimeo, Limited Distribution.

Purvis, M. J., 1976, 'The Adoption of High-Yielding Wheat', in R. A. Stone and J. Simmons (eds), *Change in Tunisia: Studies in the Social Sciences*, Albany: State University of New York Press.

Radwan, S., 1977, 'The Impact of Agrarian Reform on Rural Egypt: 1952–75', Geneva: International Labour Office, World Employment Programme Working Paper, Mimeo, Restricted.

Ràhmani, B., P. G. Hare and D. Ghosh, 1979, 'An Economic Analysis of Migration from Algeria to France', University of Stirling: Discussion Paper No. 76, Mimeo.

République Tunisienne, 1977, *Cinquième plan de développement 1977–81*, Tunis: Ministère du Plan.

Richards, A., 1980, 'The Agricultural Crisis in Egypt', *Journal of Development Studies*, Vol. 16, pp. 303–21.

Richards, P. J., 1979, 'Housing and Employment', *International Labour Review*, Vol. 118, pp. 13–26.

Richardson, H. W., 1978, 'Growth Centers, Rural Development and National Urban Policy: A Defense', *International Regional Science Review*, Vol. 3, pp. 133–52.

Rivkin, M. D., 1976, *Land Use and the Intermediate Size City in Developing Countries: With Case Studies of Turkey, Brazil and Malaysia*, New York: Praeger.

Rizk, H., 1977, 'Trends in Fertility and Family Planning in Jordan', *Studies in Family Planning*, Vol. 8, pp. 91–100.

Roberts, H., 1979, *An Urban Profile of the Middle East*, London: Croom Helm.

Robinson, H., 1963, 'Inter-American Housing Financial Sources and Policies', in *Capital Formation for Housing in Latin America*, Washington: Pan-American Union.

Rodinson, M., 1974, *Islam and Capitalism*, New York: Pantheon Books.

Ross, L. A., 1977, 'Yemen Migration — Blessing and Dilemma', Washington, DC: Prepared for US AID Seminar on Near East Labor Flows, September, Mimeo.

Ryohei, K. L., 1978, 'Off-Farm Employment and Farm Adjustments: Micro-Economic Study of the Part-Time Farm Family in the United

States and Japan', Unpublished Ph.D. Dissertation, University of Wisconsin.

Sack, R., 1976, 'An Attitudinal Portrait of the Modern Worker', in R. A. Stone and J. Simmons (eds), *Change in Tunisia: Studies in the Social Sciences*, Albany: State University of New York Press.

Salacuse, J. U., 1978, 'The Arab Authority for Agricultural Investment and Development: A New Model for Capital Transfer in the Middle East', *Journal of World Trade Law*, Vol. 12, pp. 56–66.

Salmi, J., 1978, 'La Politique de développement ou le développement de l'inéqualité', *Bulletin Économique et Social du Maroc* (Rabat), No. 136/7.

Sari, D., 1979, 'Tendances générales de l'évolution de la population agglomérée en Algérie (1966–77)', *L'Afrique et l'Asie Modernes*, August, pp. 62–9.

Saudi Arabia: WCARRD, 1979, 'Country Review Paper of Saudi Arabia', Rome: World Conference of Agrarian Reform and Rural Development, Food and Agricultural Organization, Mimeo, Restricted, in Arabic.

Sayigh, Y. A., 1978a, 'A Critical Assessment of Arab Economic Development, 1945–77', Amman: Paper Presented to the Seminar on Population and Development in the ECWA Region, United Nations Economic Commission for Western Asia, Mimeo.

Sayigh, Y. A., 1978b, *The Economies of the Arab World: Development Since 1945*, London: Croom Helm.

Sayigh, Y. A., 1978c, *The Determinants of Arab Economic Development*, London: Croom Helm.

Schultz, T. P., 1972, 'Fertility Patterns and Their Determinants in the Arab Middle East', in C. A. Cooper *et al.* (eds), *Economic Development and Population Growth in the Middle East*, New York: American Elsevier Publishing Co.

Schultz, T. W., 1980a, 'Nobel Lecture: The Economics of Being Poor', *Journal of Political Economy*, Vol. 88, pp. 639–51.

Schultz, T. W., 1980b, 'Effects of the International Donor Community on Farm People', *American Journal of Agricultural Economics*, Vol. 62, pp. 873–8.

Sebai, Z. A., 1974, 'Knowledge, Attitudes and Practice of Family Planning: Profile of a Bedouin Community in Saudi Arabia', *Journal of BioSocial Science*, Vol. 6, pp. 453–60.

Sedghi, H., 1976, 'Women in Iran', in L. B. Iglitzin and R. Ross (eds), *Women in the World: A Comparative Study*, Santa Barbara, Calif.: Clio Books.

Serageldin, I., and J. Socknat, 1980, 'Migration and Manpower Needs in the Middle East and North Africa, 1975–85', *Finance and Development*, Vol. 17, pp. 32–6.

Bibliography

Shah, P., *et al.*, 1974, *Prefabricated Construction in Industrially Developed Countries*, Montreal: Proceedings of the Third International Symposium on Lower Cost Housing Problems, May, Mimeo.

Shaw, R. P., 1974a, 'Costs and Returns of Education in Five Agricultural Areas of Eastern Brazil: Comment', *American Journal of Agricultural Economics*, Vol. 56, pp. 655–6.

Shaw, R. P., 1974b, 'Modelling Metropolitan Population Growth and Change: The IPPS Simulator', *International Journal of Socio-Economic Planning Sciences*, Vol. 8, pp. 169–80.

Shaw, R. P., 1974c, 'A Conceptual Model of Rural–Urban Transition and Reproductive Behavior', *Rural Sociology*, Vol. 39, pp. 70–91.

Shaw, R. P., 1975, *Migration Theory and Fact*, Philadelphia: Regional Science Research Institute.

Shaw, R. P., 1976a, 'Feasibility of National Population Growth Targets in LDC's', *International Journal of Socio-Economic Planning Sciences*, Vol. 10, pp. 17–26.

Shaw, R. P., 1976b, 'Government Perceptions of Population Growth', *Population Studies*, Vol. 30, pp. 77–86.

Shaw, R. P., 1976c, *Land Tenure and the Rural Exodus in Chile, Columbia, Costa Rica and Peru*, Gainesville: University of Florida Press.

Shaw, R. P., 1978a, 'Modifying Metropolitan Migration', *Economic Development and Cultural Change*, Vol. 26, pp. 677–92.

Shaw, R. P., 1978b, 'Population, Labour Force and Rural Employment Strategy for the Five Least Developed Arab Countries', Kuwait: Arab Fund for Economic and Social Development, Mimeo.

Shaw, R. P., 1978c, 'Migration interne dans le Maghreb: Aspects distributionnels et directives de planification sectorielle', Tunis: Une Contribution du B.I.T. au Séminaire du Maghreb sur la Population et le Développement du CEDOR, Juin, Mimeo.

Shaw, R. P., 1979a, 'Canadian Farm and Non-Farm Family Incomes', *American Journal of Agricultural Economics*, Vol. 61, pp. 676–82.

Shaw, R. P., 1979b, *Canada's Farm Population: An Analysis of Incomes and Related Characteristics*, Ottawa: Queen's Printer.

Shaw, R. P., 1979c, 'Migration and Employment in the Arab World: Construction as a Key Policy Variable', *International Labour Review*, Vol. 118, pp. 589–605.

Shaw, R. P., 1979d, 'Shifts in Parity, Poverty and Sources of Farm Family Income in North America', *Economic Development and Cultural Change*, Vol. 27, pp. 645–52.

Shaw, R. P., 1980a, 'Bending the Urban Flow: A Construction–Migration Strategy', *International Labour Review*, Vol. 119, pp. 467–80.

Shaw, R. P., 1980b, 'Education, Multiple Jobholding and Agricultural Development', Unpublished Manuscript, Mimeo.

Shaw, R. P., 1981, 'Is the Arab World Overpopulated? A Look at the Five Poorest Arab Countries', in ECWA (ed.), *Population and Development in the Middle East*, Beirut: United Nations Economic Commission for Western Asia, In Press.

Sheehan, G., 1978, 'Labour Force Participation Rates in Khartoum', in G. Standing and G. Sheehan (eds), *Labour Force Participation in Low-Income Countries*, Geneva: International Labour Office, pp. 165–75.

Sherbiny, N. A. (ed.), 1981, *Manpower Planning in the Oil Countries*, Connecticut: JAI Press Inc.

Sherbiny, N. A., and M. Y. Zaki, 1974, 'Programming for Agricultural Development: The Case for Egypt', *American Journal of Agricultural Economics*, Vol. 56, pp. 114–21.

Sherbiny, N. A., and M. Y. Zaki, 1975, 'Interregional Comparative Advantage Models in Developing Agriculture', *Journal of Development Studies*, Vol. 12, pp. 3–17.

Shihata, I. F. I., and R. Mabro, 1979, 'The OPEC Aid Record', *World Development*, Vol. 7, pp. 161–71.

Shiloh, A., 1974/5, 'Egypt: Demography, Ecology and the Lumpenproletariat', *Middle East Review*, Vol. 2, pp. 34–42.

Shorter, F. C., 1979, 'Croissance et inégalitiés au recensement de Damas', *Population*, Vol. 34, pp. 1067–86.

Siddigi, M. N., 1972, *Some Aspects of the Islamic Economy*, Delphi: Markazi Maktaba Islami.

Simmons, J., 1976, 'The Determinants of Earnings: Towards an Improved Model', in R. A. Stone and J. Simmons (eds), *Change in Tunisia: Studies in the Social Sciences*, Albany: State University of New York Press.

Simon, J. L., 1975, 'The Positive Effect of Population Growth on Agricultural Savings in Irrigation Systems', *Review of Economics and Statistics*, Vol. 57, pp. 71–9.

Simon, J. L., and A. M. Pilarski, 1979, 'The Effect of Population Growth Upon the Quality of Education Children Receive', *Review of Economics and Statistics*, Vol. 61, pp. 572–84.

Sinha, J. N., and M. J. Murad, 1980, 'Population Redistribution, Employment and Development in Syria', Beirut: International Labour Organization, Regional Program, Population and Labour Policies Working Paper No. 6, Mimeo.

Smock, A., and N. Youssef, 1977, 'Egypt: From Seclusion to Limited Participation', in J. Grele (ed.), *Women: Roles and Status in Eight Countries*, New York: John Wiley & Sons.

Soejono, I., 1977, 'Growth and Distributional Changes of Paddy Farm Incomes in Central Java, 1968–74', Unpublished Ph.D. Dissertation, Iowa State University.

Bibliography

Soffran, L. U., 1981, *The Women of the U.A.E.*, London: Croom Helm.

Springborg, R., 1977, 'New Patterns of Agrarian Reform in the Middle East and North Africa', *Middle East Journal*, Vol. 3, pp. 126–42.

Standing, G., 1978, *Labour Participation and Development*, Geneva: International Labour Office.

Stone, R. A. (ed.), 1977, *OPEC and the Middle East: The Impact of Oil on Societal Development*, New York: Praeger.

Stone, R. A., and J. Simmons (eds), 1976, *Change in Tunisia: Studies in the Social Sciences*, Albany: State University of New York Press.

Strassman, W. P., 1979, *Housing and Building Technology in Developing Countries*, East Lansing: Michigan State University Press.

Strehm, J., 1976, 'Algerian Women: Honor, Survival, and Islamic Socialism', in L. B. Iglitzin and R. Ross (eds), *Women in the World: A Comparative Study*, Santa Barbara, Calif.: Clio Books.

Stryker, R. E., 1979, 'The World Bank and Agricultural Development: Food Production and Rural Poverty', *World Development*, Vol. 7, pp. 325–36.

Stubbs, G. M., 1979, 'Population Policy in the Arab Countries, 1945–78', New York: United Nations Population Division, Mimeo, Restricted.

Sudan: WCARRD, 1978, 'Country Review Paper of Sudan', Rome: World Conference on Agrarian Reform and Rural Development, Food and Agricultural Organization, Mimeo, Restricted.

Suleiman, M. W., 1978, 'Changing Attitudes Toward Women in Egypt: The Role of Fiction in Women's Magazines', *Middle Eastern Studies*, Vol. 14, pp. 352–69.

Suzman, R., K. A. Miller and M. Charrad, 1976, 'Employment Effects on Fertility Control in Tunisia', in *Recent Empirical Findings on Fertility: Korea, Nigeria, Tunisia, Venezuela, Phillipines*; Washington DC: Smithsonian Institute Interdisciplinary Communications Program, Monograph Series No. 7.

Swanson, J. C., 1979a, *Emigration and Economic Development: The Case of the Yemen Arab Republic*, Boulder, Colo.: Westview Press.

Swanson, J. C., 1979b, 'Some Consequences of Emigration for Rural Economic Development in the Yemen Arab Republic', *Middle East Journal*, Vol. 33, pp. 34–45.

Sweet, M. L., and S. G. Walters, 1976, *Mandatory Housing Finance Programs: A Comparative International Analysis*, New York: Praeger.

Tabbarah, R., 1971. 'Toward a Theory of Demographic Transition', *Economic Development and Cultural Change*, Vol. 19, pp. 257–76.

Tabbarah, R., 1976, 'Population Education as a Component of Development Policy', *Studies in Family Planning*, Vol. 7, pp. 197–201.

Tabbarah, R., 1977, 'Population and Development in Lebanon', *Popula-*

tion Bulletin of the United Nations Economic Commission for Western Asia, No. 12, pp. 12–19.

Tabbarah, R., N. A. Mamish and Y. Gemayel, 1978, 'Population Research and Research Gaps in the Arab Countries', Beirut: United Nations Economic Commission for Western Asia, Population Division, Mimeo, Restricted.

Taboli, A. O., 1976, 'An Economic Analysis of Internal Migration in the Libyan Arab Republic', Unpublished Ph.D. Dissertation, Oklahoma State University.

Tanfer, K., 1981, 'The Relationship of Education to Fertility in Turkey', Washington D.C.: Paper Presented to the 1981 Meeting of the Population Association of America, March, Mimeo.

Tapinos, G., 1978, 'Possibilités de transfert d'emploi vers les pays d'émigration en tant qu'alternative aux migrations internationales des travailleurs: la cas français', Geneva: International Labour Office World Employment Working Paper, Mimeo, Restricted.

Taylor, D. C., 1968, 'Research on Agricultural Development in Selected Middle Eastern Countries', New York: Agricultural Development Council, Mimeo.

Tessler, M. A., with J. Rogers and D. Schneider, 1978, 'Women's Emancipation in Tunisia', in L. Beck and N. Keddie (eds), *Women in the Muslim World*, Cambridge: Harvard University Press.

Thomas, B., 1973, *Migration and Economic Growth: A Study of Great Britain and the Atlantic Economy*, Cambridge University Press, 2nd Ed.

Thorne, M., and J. Montague, 1976, 'Family Planning and the Problems of Development', in R. A. Stone and J. Simmons (eds), *Change in Tunisia; Studies in the Social Sciences*, Albany: State University of New York Press.

Tinker, I., 1976, 'Women in Developing Societies: Economic Independence is Not Enough', in J. R. Chapman (ed.), *Economic Independence for Women: The Foundation for Equal Rights*, Beverly Hills, Calif.: Sage Publications.

Tinker, I., M. Bramsen and M. Buvinic (eds), *Women and World Development*, New York: Praeger.

Tuma, E. H., 1970, 'Agrarian Reform and Urbanization in the Middle East', *Middle East Journal*, vol. 24, pp. 163–77.

Tuma, E. H., 1980, 'The Rich and the Poor in the Middle East', *Middle East Journal*, Vol. 34, pp. 413–17.

Tunisia: CMRADR, 1979 'Rapport national de la Tunisie', Rome: Conférence Mondiale sur la Réforme Agraire et le Développement Rural, Food and Agricultural Organization, Mimeo, Limited Distribution.

UAE, 1978, *Annual Statistical Abstract*, United Arab Emirates, Ministry of Planning, Central Statistical Department.

247

UNCTAD: 1978, 'Report of the Group of Governmental Experts in the Reverse Transfer of Technology', Geneva: United Nations, TD/B/C.6/28, Mimeo.

UNDP, 1976, 'A Preliminary Investigation into the Social Situation and Needs of Women in Villages in Bahrain', New York: United Nations Development Program, Mimeo.

UNESCO, 1970, 'Trends in General, Technical, and Vocational Education in the Arab States', Marrakesh: Third Regional Conference of Ministers of Education in the Arab States, United Nations Educational, Scientific and Cultural Organization, Mimeo.

UNESCO, 1973, 'Étude sur les relations existant entre les possibilités d'éducation et les responsabilités d'emploi offertes aux femmes au Leban', Beirut: United Nations Educational, Scientific and Cultural Organization, Mimeo.

UNESCO, 1977a, 'Recent Quantitative Trends and Projections Concerning Enrollment in Education in the Arab Countries', Paris: United Nations Educational, Scientific and Cultural Organization, ED 77/CONF.206/COL.3, Mimeo, Limited Distribution.

UNESCO, 1977b, 'New Prospects in Education for Development in the Arab Countries', Abu Dhabi: Conference of Ministers of Education and those Responsible for Economic Planning in the Arab States, United Nations Educational, Scientific and Cultural Organization, ED 77/CONF.206/COL.4, Mimeo, Limited Distribution.

UNESCO, 1977c, 'The Education of the Arab People of Palestine', Abu Dhabi: Conference of Ministers of Education and those responsible for Economic Planning in the Arab States, United Nations Educational, Scientific and Cultural Organization, ED 77/CONF. 206/COL.8, Mimeo, Limited Distribution.

UNESCO, 1978a, 'Politiques et plans d'éducation dans les Etats Arabes dans les années 70: résumes et synthèse', Paris: United Nations Educational, Scientific and Cultural Organization, C.55, Mimeo.

UNESCO, 1978b, *Population Education: A Contemporary Concern*, Paris: United Nations Educational, Scientific and Cultural Organization.

UNFPA, 1979a, 'Sudan: Report of Mission on Needs Assessment for Population Assistance', New York: United Nations Fund for Population Activities, Report No. 17, Mimeo, Restricted.

UNFPA, 1979b, 'Jordan: Report of Mission on Needs Assessment for Population Assistance', New York: United Nations Fund for Population Activities, Report No. 18, Mimeo, Restricted.

UNICEF, 1972, 'Role of Arab Women in National Development', Cairo: United Nations International Children's Emergency Fund, Mimeo.

Bibliography

UNIDO, 1969, *Construction Industry*, Vienna: United Nations Industrial Development Organization.

United Nations, 1971, *Social Programming of Housing in Urban Areas*, New York: United Nations, No. E.71.IV.10.

United Nations, 1976, *Progress in Land Reform: Sixth Report*, New York: United Nations.

United Nations, 1979, *World Population Trends and Policies*, Vols I and II, New York: United Nations, ST/ESA/SER.A/62/Add 1.

Van Ryckeghem, W. (ed.), 1976, *Employment Problems and Policies in Developing Countries: The Case of Morocco*, Rotterdam University Press.

Vernez, G., 1976, 'A Housing Services Policy for Low-Income Urban Families in Developing Countries', *Ekistics* (Athens), pp. 42–7.

Voll, S. P., 1980, 'Egyptian Land Reclamation Since the Revolution', *Middle East Journal*, Vol. 34, pp. 127–48.

Warriner, D., 1971, 'Employment and Income Aspects of Recent Agrarian Reforms in the Middle East', in ILO, *Agrarian Reform and Employment*, Geneva: International Labour Office, pp. 76–96.

Warriner, D., 1973, 'Results of Land Reform in Asian and Latin American Countries', *Food Research Institute Studies*, Vol. 12, pp. 115–32.

Waterbury, J., 1978, 'The Middle East and the New World Economic Order', in J. Waterbury and R. El-Mallakh, *The Middle East in the Coming Decade*, New York: McGraw-Hill.

Wazzan, S., 1975, 'Evaluation of the Existing Size of Family Holdings in the Newly Reclaimed Area with the Aim to Determine a "Viable" Size', Rome: Report for UNDR/FAO Project on Integrated Development and Settlement of New Lands Irrigated by High Dam Waters in Egypt, Food and Agricultural Organization, Mimeo.

WCARRD: General, 1978, *Review and Analysis of Agrarian Reform and Rural Development in Developing Countries since the Mid-1960's*, Rome: World Conference on Agrarian Reform and Rural Development, Food and Agricultural Organization, Mimeo.

Weinbaum, M. G., 1980, 'Food and Political Stability in the Middle East', *Studies in Comparative International Development*, Vol. 15, pp. 3–27.

White, E. H., 1978, 'Legal Reform as an Indicator of Women's Status in Muslim Nations', in L. Beck and N. Keddie (eds), *Women in the Muslim World*, Cambridge: Harvard University Press.

Winpenny, J. T., 1978, 'Housing and Jobs for the Poor', *Development Research Digest*, No. 1, pp. 25–30.

World Bank, 1976, *World Bank Tables*, Baltimore, Md.: Johns Hopkins University Press.

World Bank, 1979a, *World Development Report*, Baltimore, Md.: Johns

Hopkins University Press.

World Bank, 1979b, 'Interim Report: Assessment of Migration Situation in 1975 and Preliminary Projections of Labour-Importing Country Manpower Requirements to 1985', Washington DC: World Bank, Mimeo, Restricted.

Yahya, H., 1980, 'Human Capital Migration from Labor-Rich to Oil-Rich Arab States, and the Consequences for the Jordanian Economy', Unpublished Ph.D. Dissertation, Oklahoma State.

Yemen PDR: WCARRD, 1978, 'Country Review Paper of People's Democratic Republic of Yemen', Rome: World Conference of Agrarian Reform and Rural Development, Food and Agricultural Organization, Mimeo, Restricted.

Young, H. B., 1976, 'Social Class and Impairment of Growth and Health', in R. A. Stone and J. Simmons (eds), *Change in Tunisia: Studies in the Social Sciences*, Albany: State University of New York Press.

Youssef, N. H., 1972, 'Differential Labor Force Participation of Women in Latin American and Middle Eastern Countries: The Influence of Family Characteristics', *Social Forces*, Vol. 51, pp. 254–72.

Youssef, N. H., 1974, *Women and Work in Developing Societies*, Berkeley: University of California at Berkeley, Monograph Series, No. 15, REPAL.

Youssef, N. H., 1976, 'Women in the Muslim World', in L. B. Iglitzin and R. Ross (eds), *Women in the World: A Comparative Study*, Santa Barbara, Calif.: Clio Books.

Youssef, N. H., 1977, 'Education and Female Modernism in the Muslim World', *Journal of International Affairs*, Vol. 30, pp. 191–209.

Youssef, N. H., 1978, 'The Status and Fertility Patterns of Muslim Women', in L. Beck and N. Keddie (eds), *Women in the Muslim World*, Cambridge: Harvard University Press.

Youssef, N. H., 1979, 'Fertility of Rural Women: Suggestions for New Directions in Research', Geneva: International Labour Office, Mimeo.

Yusef, H., 1965, 'In Defense of the Veil', in B. Rivlin and J. Szyliowic (eds), *In Defense of the Veil*, New York: Random House.

Zahlan, A. B., 1978, 'The Arab Brain Drain', Jordan: Paper Presented to the Seminar on Population and Development in the ECWA Region, United Nations Economic Commission for Western Asia, E/ECWA/POP/WG.12/BP.19, Mimeo.

Zahlan, A. B., 1981, *The Arab Brain Drain*, London: Ithaca Press.

Zalatimo, F. R., 1977, 'The Development of the Education System in the State of Kuwait since 1961', Unpublished Ph.D. Dissertation, Southern Illinois University.

Zikma, N. A., 1976, 'The Status of Women in Islam', *Journal of the*

Islamic Medical Association, Vol. 7, pp. 19–31.

Ziwar-Daftari, M. (ed.), 1980, *Issues and Development: The Arab Gulf States*, London: MD Research and Services, Ltd.

Zurayk, H., 1977, 'The Effect of Education of Women and Urbanization on Actual and Desired Fertility and on Fertility Control in Lebanon', *Population Bulletin of the United Nations Economic Commission for Western Asia*, No. 12, pp. 32–41.

Zurayk, H., 1978, 'The Changing Role of Arab Women', Amman: Paper Presented at Seminar on Population and Development in the Region of West Asia, United Nations Economic Commission for Western Asia, November, Mimeo.

Zurayk, H., 1979, 'A Two Stage Analysis of Determinants of Fertility in Rural South Lebanon', *Population Studies*, Vol. 33, pp. 489–504.

Government statistical references

Algeria

Algeria, 1977, *Annuaire statistique de l'Algérie, 1976*, Direction des Statistiques et de la Compatibilité Nationale.

Algeria, 1977, '1000 villages socialistes en Algérie', *Maghreb Machrek: Monde Arabe*, Juillet/Août/Sept.

Algeria, 1978, 'Données globales sur la population et sa répartition géographique', Direction des Statistiques, Secrétariat d'État au Plan.

Bahrain

Bahrain, 1974, *Statistics of the 1971 Population Census*, Statistical Bureau, Ministry of Finance and National Economy.

Bahrain, 1977, *Social Indicators for Bahrain*, Directorate of Social Affairs, Ministry of Labour and Social Affairs.

Bahrain, 1978, *Statistical Abstract, 1977*, Directorate of Statistics, Ministry of State for Cabinet Affairs.

Bahrain, 1978, 'The Population of Bahrain: A Summary of Past Trends and Future Prospects', Paper Prepared by I. Hamber, Director of Statistics.

Egypt

Egypt, 1978, *Economic Bulletin* (National Bank of Egypt), Vol. 31, Nos 2, 3, 4.

Egypt, 1978, *Statistical Yearbook, 1978*, Central Agency for Public Mobilization and Statistics.

Iraq

Iraq, n.d., *Statistics of Private Building and Repair Permits, 1971*, Central Statistical Organization, Department of Construction Statistics, Ministry of Planning.

Iraq, 1972, *1971–72 Household Budget and Living Conditions Survey*, Central Statistical Organization, Ministry of Planning.

Iraq, 1973, 'Population Growth and Development in Iraq', Baghdad: Ministry of Planning, Paper Prepared for the 1974 United Nations Population Inquiry, Mimeo.

Iraq, 1973, *Results of the 1971 Census of Agriculture*, Central Statistical Organization, Ministry of Planning.

Iraq, 1977, *Bulletin of the Central Bank of Iraq*, No. 1, January/ March, Statistics and Research Department.

Iraq, 1977, *Iraq in Figures*, Central Statistical Organization.

Iraq, 1978, *1977 Statistical Yearbook*, Central Statistical Organization, Ministry of Planning.

Jordan

Jordan, 1972, *National Fertility Survey in Jordan*, Department of Statistics.

Jordan, 1976, *Agricultural Statistical Yearbook and Some Results of the Agricultural Census, 1975*, Department of Statistics.

Jordan, 1976, *The Multi-Purpose Household Survey, Sept./Dec.*, Department of Statistics.

Jordan, 1977, *Central Bank of Jordan: Fourteenth Annual Report*, Department of Research and Statistics.

Jordan, 1977, *Employment Survey, August*, Department of Statistics.

Jordan, 1979, 'Report of Mission on Needs Assessment for Population Assistance', United Nations Fund for Population Activities, Report No. 8.

Kuwait

Kuwait, 1978, *Annual Statistical Abstract*, 15th edn, Central Statistical Office, Ministry of Planning.

Kuwait, 1978, *Economic Report for 1978*, Central Bank of Kuwait.

Kuwait, 1978, *Sixteenth Annual Report*, Kuwait Fund for Arab Economic Development.

Libya

Libya, 1977, *Economic Bulletin*, Central Bank of Libya, Vol. 16, No. 5–6.

Libya, 1977, *Statistical Abstract, 1975*, Census Statistical Department.

Libya, 1977, *Twenty Second Annual Report*, Central Bank of Libya.

Libya, 1977, *Vital Statistics of the Socialist People's Republic of Libyan Arab Jamahiriya*, Census and Statistical Department.

Libya, 1978, *Annual Survey of Large Construction Units, 1976*, Census and Statistics Department, Secretariat of Planning.

Libya, 1978, *Report on the External Trade Statistics, 1977*, Census and Statistics Department, Secretariat of Planning.

Mauritania

Mauritania, 1973, *Annuaire statistique, 1971*, Direction de la Statistique et des Études Économiques.

Mauritania, 1974, 'The Current Economic Situation and Prospects of Mauritania', Washington D.C.: World Bank, Report 243–Mau, Mimeo.

Mauritania, 1978, *Bulletin annuaire*, Banque Centrale de Mauritanie.

Mauritania, 1978, 'Mauritanie: education–problèmes et perspectives', Paris: UNESCO, ED/EDD–EFM/95, Mimeo.

Mauritania, 1979, 'Report of Mission on Needs Assessment for Population Assistance', United Nations Fund for Population Activities, Report No. 17.

Morocco

Morocco, 1977, *Annuaire statistique du Maroc, 1976*, Direction de la Statistique.

Morocco, 1977, 'L'Agriculture morocaine en 1975', *Syrie et Monde Arabe*, Vol. 24, No. 282.

Morocco, 1978, 'La Question agraire au Maroc', *Bulletin Économique et Social du Maroc*, No. 2.

Morocco, 1978, *La Situation économique du Maroc, 1977*, Secrétariat d'État au Plan et au Développement Régional.

Morocco, 1978, *Le Maroc en chiffres, 1977*, Secrétariat d'État du Plan et du Développement Régional.

Morocco, 1979, *Economic Indicators*, Banque Marocaine du Commerce Exterieur, No. 22.

Morocco, 1979, *Rapport annuel exercice, 1977*, Banque Nationale pour le Développement Économique.

Oman

Oman, 1974, *Family Expenditure Pilot Surveys*, Development Council, National Statistical Department.
Oman, 1977, *Statistical Yearbook, 1976*, Development Council, Directorate General of National Statistics.
Oman, 1978, 'Development Plan's Realistic Aims', *Syrie et Monde Arabe*, Vol. 25, No. 293.

Qatar

Qatar, 1977, *Economic Survey of Qatar, 1974–75*, Ministry of Economy and Commerce.

Saudi Arabia

Saudi Arabia, 1977, *Statistical Yearbook, Twelfth and Thirteenth Issue*, Central Department of Statistics, Ministry of Finance and National Economy.
Saudi Arabia, 1978, *Annual Report, 1978*, Saudi Arabian Monetary Agency.
Saudi Arabia, 1978, *The Statistical Indicator*, Ministry of Finance and National Economy.
Saudi Arabia, 1979, 'Education in Saudi Arabia', *Syrie et Monde Arabe*, Vol. 26, No. 304.
Saudi Arabia, 1979, *Statistical Summary*, Research and Statistics Department, Saudi Arabian Monetary Agency.

Somalia

Somalia, 1977, *Public Sector Investment Programme for 1977; Implementation for 1974–77*, State Planning Commission.
Somalia, 1978, *Annual Report and Statement of Accounts*, Central Bank of Somalia.
Somalia, 1978, *Bulletin No. 43*, Research and Statistics Department, Central Bank of Somalia.
Somalia, 1978, *Statistical Abstract, 1977*, Central Statistical Department, State Planning Department.

Sudan

Sudan, 1976, *Economic and Financial Statistics Review*, Vol. 18, No. 2.

Government statistical references

Sudan, 1978, *Eighteenth Annual Report, 1977*, Bank of Sudan.

Sudan, 1979, 'Report of Mission on Needs Assessment for Population Assistance', United Nations Fund for Population Activities, Report No. 9.

Syria

Syria, 1977, *Quarterly Bulletin* (Central Bank of Syria), Vol. 15, No. 4.

Syria, 1977, *The Annual Statistical Bulletin of the Ministry of Social Affairs and Labour*, Ministry of Social Affairs and Labour.

Syria, 1978, *Rapport économique syrien*, L'Office Arabe de Presse et de Documentation.

Syria, 1978, *Statistical Abstract, 1978*, Central Bureau of Statistics.

Syria, 1978, *Thirty-First Statistical Abstract*, Central Bureau of Statistics.

Tunisia

Tunisia, 1975, *Recensement général de la population et des logements*, Institute National de la Statistique, Ministère du Plan.

Tunisia, 1977, 'L'Enseignement en Tunisie – vingt ans après la réforme de 1958', *Maghreb Machrek: Monde Arabe* (Paris), October/December.

Tunisia, 1978, *Annuaire statistique de la Tunisie, nouvelle serie, 1976–77*, Institute National de la Statistique.

United Arab Emirates (UAE)

UAE, 1977, *UAE Oil Statistical Review*, Statistics Department, Ministry of Petroleum and Mineral Resources.

UAE, 1978, *Annual Statistical Abstract*, Central Statistics Department, Ministry of Planning.

UAE, 1978, *UAE Currency Board Bulletin* (Currency Board), Vol. 5, No. 1.

UAE, 1979, 'Economic and Social Development in Abu Dhabi', *Syrie et Monde Arabe*, Vol. 26, No. 304.

Yemen Arab Republic (AR)

Yemen AR, 1975, *Socio-Economic Report, 1970–74*, Central Planning Organization.

Yemen AR, 1976, *Foreign Trade Statistics*, Central Bank of Yemen.

Yemen AR, 1977, *Appraisal of Investment Opportunities in the Indus-*

trial Sector, Main Report, Vol. 1., Central Planning Organization.

Yemen AR, 1977, 'Report of the FAO Programming Mission to Yemen Arab Republic', Food and Agricultural Organization.

Yemen AR, 1977, *Statistical Yearbook, 1976*, Statistics Department, Central Planning Organization.

Yemen AR, 1978, *Seventh Annual Report, 1977/78*, Central Bank of Yemen.

Yemen AR, 1979, *Financial Statistical Bulletin* (Central Bank of Yemen), Vol. 6, No. 3.

Yemen, People's Democratic Republic (PDR)

Yemen PDR, 1976, *Education Statistics, 1975/76*, Central Statistical Office.

Yemen PDR, 1977, *Labour Force Bulletin*, Central Statistical Office.

Subject index

Abu Dhabi Fund for Arab Economic Development, 72, 199

age at marriage: education and, 108; fertility and, 105, 212

agrarian reform, 60–4; absentee landholders and, 64; future possibilities of, 64; subsequent productivity after, 88; success of, 61, 208

agriculture, 57–99; absentee landlords, 68, 209; agrarian reform, 60–4; challenges facing, 57; development strategies, 59–60; feeder roads, 98; food requirements, 57; human capital needs, 80; imports, 57; interregional cooperation and integration, 85–7; landless workers, 58–9; large-scale mechanization, 66–8; major policy interventions, 60–8; national development plan expenditures on, 7–8, 68–72; off-farm employment, 90–5; off-farm employment and construction, 98–9; off-farm employment contribution to farm family income, 93–4; off-farm employment and returns to education, 95–8; physical resource constraints, 88–90; policy directives, 72–8; policy directives and animal husbandry, 78; policy directives and cooperatives, 76–9; policy directives and fisheries, 79–80; policy directives and high yielding varieties, 73–4; policy directives and improving irrigation, 75–6; policy directives and intensifying and diversifying crops, 74–5; policy directives and off-farm employment, 90–5; poor performance of, 7–9; poverty in, 58; rates of realized investments in, 69; reclamation and resettlement schemes, 64–6; reliance on food imports, 7–8; restrictive controls in, 84–5; storage facilities, 98; subsistence farmers, 58; targeted growth rates, 204; trade arrangements in, 57, 200; worker motivation in, 87, 211

aid: external debt and, 196–8; interregional, 69–72; official development assistance, 196

Algeria: fertility by female occupation, 106; fertility predictions, 109; landless agricultural workers, 59; large-scale mechanization in agriculture, 67; migrant remittances, 27; off-farm employment, 81–2, 97, 212; oil-poor classification, 5; wage and price controls in agriculture, 84

Subject index

demand for family limitation,
118; remittances, 27; student/
teacher ratios, 166; women in
the labor force, 134, 153

OECD countries: international
migration and construction in,
49–51
off-farm employment, 80–4,
90–5; construction and, 98–9;
development strategy and,
90–5; neglect of, 80; potential
contribution to family income,
80, 90–5; reasons for en-
couraging, 81–2; returns to
education and, 95–8
oil-rich versus oil-poor dichotomy:
rationale for, 4, 15, 203
Oman: cooperatives, 76; fishery
potential, 79, 211; household
expenditures on food, 8;
irrigation efficiency, 75;
migrants in the labor force,
24; oil-rich classification, 4
Oman statistics: agriculture,
70–1, 89; crude birth rates,
101; education, 164; employment in construction, 39;
land reform, 62–3; national
development plan expenditures,
18–19, 70–1, 165; population,
101; projected demand for
family limitation, 118; women
in the labor force, 134, 153
on-the-job training, 175–8;
certification of, 176–7; general
training and, 176, 184; returns
to, 177, 222; specific training
and, 176–7, 184, 221–2
OPEC Fund for International
Development, 173
OPEC Secretariat, 20–2

policy directives: agriculture and,
72–85; construction and,
36–45; education and, 175–
83; guidelines for formulating,
14–15; off-farm employment
and, 90–5; population and,

117–20; women and, 139–51
political constraints, 2, 15–16,
195, 202, 204, 211
population: contraceptive use
and, 117–18, 216; demand for
family planning, 8–10, 100–5;
distribution problems and,
34–5, 38–41; family planning
infrastructure, 117–20;
fertility predictions and, 104–
15; government perceptions of
problems concerning, 35,
100–2; growth of, 100–1;
population control biases,
8–10, 101–2, 145–6;
pressure, 8, 100; urban concentration of, 34–6
population control bias, 101–2,
145–6
population distribution, 34–6;
government perceptions concerning, 35; migration policies
and, 42, 205
poultry production, 79

Qatar: cropping diversity, 75;
irrigation efficiency, 75;
migrants in the labor force, 24;
oil-rich classification, 4;
women's opportunities for
employment, 134, 147, 153
Qatar statistics: agriculture,
70–1, 89; crude birth rates,
101; education, 164; employment in construction, 39; land
reform, 62–6; national development plan expenditures, 18–
19, 70–1, 165; population,
101; projected demand for
family limitation, 118; student/
teacher ratios, 166; women in
the labor force, 134, 153
Qur'an; 120; development
ideology and, 200–1; women's
emancipation and, 131–3

regression analysis: data for
fertility/education analysis
and, 123–5; female activity

265